Coolie, Come Out and Fight!

There is greatness in all people, find it in yourself, Carim, and in everyone you meet.

Reverend Sigamoney, 1957

Mohamed F (Mac) Carim

Coolie, Come Out and Fight!

A South African memoir
of love, courage and
journeys to a better place

PORCUPINE PRESS

Johannesburg

First published by Porcupine Press in 2013
Porcupine Press
PO Box 2756
Pinegowrie, 2123
South Africa
info@porcupinepress.co.za
www.porcupinepress.co.za

ISBN: 978-1-920609-13-9

Produced by Porcupine Press
Cover and text designed by www.wimrheeder.co.za
Set in 10.5 point on 13.5 point, Minion Pro
Printed by Mega Digital, Cape Town

CONTENTS

ACKNOWLEDGEMENTS

This book would not have happened without the confident intelligence of Johnathene Beyers our niece who, when I talked about returning to school to get a degree, asserted: 'With all the experiences you and Aunty Hajoo have accumulated, around the world you don't need a degree Uncle Mac, you should write a book instead'.

Thanks to family and friends who read excerpts and offered constructive criticism, sound feedback and welcome encouragement; especially to sister Ayesha Haffajee for clarifying or confirming things and sister Farida Mayet for reading, crying and spurring me on.

Much appreciation to friend Dr Yoon Jung Park who jerked me out of lethargy, drove me around to the sites of my childhood, and got me writing again.

Thanks to Ursula and Thilo Thormeyer and Uschi's mother Vera for reading my work, giving me valuable inputs from another perspective and reinforcing me positively with the words, 'Don't change a thing'.

Appreciation also to Rob Nairn and the staff of the Kensington Samye Dzong Buddhist Centre, who allowed me unlimited access to the Shrine Room to meditate and write.

I couldn't have done it without my brother Enver Carim who read every line often refreshing my memory and coaching me every step of the way. I'm ever thankful to you Boet.

My profound gratitude for the positive feedback from distinguished writers Ferial Haffajee, Darryl Accone and David Robbins whose positive feedback, summarised on the back cover, means more to me than they may ever know.

The advice and guidance from Porcupine Press' Gail Robbins and Clare-Rose Julius has been invaluable and they gave of it freely and proactively. Their knowledge, experience and skills are much appreciated.

**This book is for Hajoo,
without whom little would have gone right.**

PRELUDE:
A MAGIC CARPET RIDE

What happened that wondrous Cape Town morning in December 1987 was magical, if not a miracle.

It was just after five in the morning when I left the Ritz Protea Hotel in Sea Point and walked down the hill to Main Street. I could barely contain myself. Here I was, at 52, walking down streets in the city of my birth that I had last visited at the age of six. I was exhilarated – and things just got better.

My wife Hajoo, our friend Suriya Veerappan and I had arrived in Cape Town the day before. The three of us were visiting South Africa from Toronto. Suriya was staying in Lenasia with her family and we were with Hajoo's sister and brother-in-law, Farida and Abdul Mayet, in Johannesburg. I had read about a South African Airways special to Cape Town that included a free car and accommodation in a superior hotel in the suburb of Sea Point. The name 'Sea Point' had stirred up emotions in me that were pleasant but confusing and Hajoo suggested that we make Sea Point our holiday base, and see if we could find out what these feelings were about.

The flight to South Africa's 'Mother City' seemed endless and, as we came in to land, my mind was a riot of excitement, shadowy memories, and impatient curiosity. I was born here in 1936, 'deported' with my parents to the Transvaal in 1938, and came back to visit for the last time in 1942. Now, after nearly a half century, I was back, having worked in 33 countries and visited more than 60, on four continents.

Cape Town was, and still is, one of the most naturally beautiful cities in the world. This fact alone was enough cause for my exhilaration. But mostly, I was eager to check out the memories from my childhood with Hajoo's cousin, Janey Halim, who was meeting us at the airport.

Hajoo, now 50, was concerned she might not recognise her cousin. They had last been together in Johannesburg in 1946. Hajoo had been eight years old then and Janey seven. As it happened recognition wasn't a problem. I scanned the waiting crowd and, though I had never laid eyes on Janey before, I spotted her immediately. The resemblance between these two Halim women was remarkable. We walked straight up to her and Janey welcomed us to the Cape with warmth that touched us deeply.

Janey (left) with Hajoo

On the drive to the hotel, the cousins began catching up on a life time apart, and Suriya and I were enthralled by their animated conversation about people, places and events. After check-in the conversation continued over tea. Later I had a chance to describe to Janey the three specific places that had stuck in my mind most of my life and which I was hoping to see again.

I remembered a large house surrounded by sand that seemed to be sitting on a vast beach but there was no sea – just miles of white sand. Another memory was of a place of steep hills, narrow cobblestone streets and a dark, cool corner shop smelling of spice that sold the most amazing toffee apples and spinning tops.

The most vivid memory, however, was of a glorious day spent on a beach. I remember sitting on a wide, flat, smooth black rock surrounded by white sand and eating the reddest, sweetest watermelon ever. Close by was this huge, shiny black metal pipe glistening from the sun and sea water. It ran out from a retaining wall behind us into the ocean. And when we kids weren't gorging on pickled fish, koeksusters, ginger beer or watermelon, we were running screaming along the pipe and jumping off it into the brine. I remember watching my gorgeous Mom with her dress bunched up around her knees and my Dad with his white slacks rolled up high, exploring the small, shallow tidal pools that were everywhere. They were splashing each other, shrieking with laughter and enjoying this time as much as any of the children.

'How I wish I could see those places again,' I said to Janey

'The place of sand is probably Athlone, where you were born,' Janey responded. 'In the 30s and 40s, it was almost entirely covered in sand. It is part of what we refer to as the Cape Flats. The narrow cobblestone streets are in Bo Kaap, which, in the old days, was known as the Malay Quarter and was the traditional residential area for Cape Town's Muslim community. I'll drive you to those places in the week.'

The location of the particular beach, the black rock and the metal pipe was not so easily identified. 'The entire coast here is made up of black rocky areas partly covered by beach sand. To find your beach will be almost impossible,' she said. 'The large metal pipe is probably a sewage outlet. So you are looking for a public beach that was reserved for non-whites,' she added with a hard edge to her tone, 'No whites-only beach would have had any kind of pipe pumping rubbish into the sea where white people swam.'

It was agreed that Janey would bring her daughters Tasneem and Shahnaaz over to meet us the next afternoon and as she left the hotel I asked for directions to the sea front, little knowing that a miracle was beginning to unfold. 'Turn right outside the front of the hotel, walk down the hill to the t-junction, turn left into Main Road, then right again down any street and you'll end up by the sea.'

Now, here I was, approaching the Sea Point beachfront, while Hajoo and Suriya were probably only just beginning to stir. The sky was a brilliant blue and a light breeze rustled the trees lining the narrow streets as I strode past well-kept apartment buildings many of which had balconies resplendent with summer flowers.

The street I had walked down reminded me of Rue Thomas Edison in Ramlet al Baidah in Beirut, where Hajoo and I and our sons had once lived. Block after block of attractive apartment buildings, close to the sea, and not a single house to be seen.

The smell of the ocean and the sight and sound of waves crashing on rocks or sandy beaches has always had a special effect on me and I was in high spirits as I crossed the four-lane dual carriageway at the bottom of the hill. I skipped over the wide sidewalk and leaned over the retaining rock wall for my first sight of the Cape Atlantic in virtually a lifetime. What I saw blew my mind. There, spread out below me, was 'my' beach, 'my' black rock and 'my' pipe. Was this a miracle or what? Of all the streets I could have chosen, what force was it that guided me randomly to walk down the one street that led directly to my black rock on my beach?

As I made my way down the stone steps onto the sand, I saw that my metal pipe was still glistening in the sun and the wetness, but that it had clearly lost its battle with rust. The black shine of old had browned with age and corrosion had eaten gaping holes into the surface, upon which hysterical six year olds could once safely run and jump into the swells – but now could never again.

With great joy I saw that my black rock was as wide, flat and smooth as I remembered it. As I sat there in a dreamlike trance I was six years old again. The sound of my parents' laughter as they frolicked among the shallow rock pools was real once more. I heard, again, my mother shriek in joyous protest as my father splashed her. I saw again how she bunched her white dress high up above her knees as she skipped out of reach of the water. I could feel the watermelon juice run down my chin and drop in sticky globs on to my sun-warmed stomach. And the slippery run on the pipe followed by the knee-hugging jump into the surf was as breathtaking as ever.

How long this reverie lasted, I cannot say. Like some magical carpet, this flat spread of rock had captivated me again. It carried me back, over five decades, into a kaleidoscope of sweet and bitter memories, each one as vivid as the other, each as demanding of my mind-space. Soon I had lost all sense of time and was being carried, willy-nilly, along my family's volatile road in search of a better life in a better place somewhere.

1
FRUIT, BEADS AND CHANTILLY LACE

Deck Passengers

The year was 1914. The Great War had broken out in Europe and Abdullah Carim Haji Amon Poonjanee left Porbandar, Kathiawar in Gujarat, India with two young children for a vague promise of a better life for his family in South Africa. How, I wondered, was the decision made that my grandfather should strike out with the two boys and leave my grandmother behind to manage on her own with their youngest until he could send for them?

Did the community he left behind know what calibre of man Grandpa was, or how well he would succeed in a land where reports of segregation and discrimination were common? Could they have known that he would gain community respect to the point where all who knew him would address him as Pe – pronounced as in 'pear', the fruit – which signifies 'respected father or grandfather?'

What thoughts went through Pe's head as he and his sons lay curled up together under the stars on the deck of the steamship? Was he confident there was a better place for his family somewhere in South Africa? Did it scare him that there were no life jackets or life-boats allocated to lowly deck passengers in case of emergencies? How did this now single dad manage his one boy's lingering seasickness and the other's persistent diarrhoea? What dreams and hopes and fears did that company of hardy deck passengers share under the blazing sun? They steamed out of Bombay harbour on the 21-day journey across the Arabian Sea and the Indian Ocean, down the African coast from Mogadishu to Mombasa and Dar-es-Salaam and ever southwards to South Africa – where they believed happiness and prosperity awaited them – and where they would often have to fight to get what they wanted and defend what they built?

My uncle, Tar Mohamed Abdul Carim, was six when they reached Cape Town and my dad, Ahmed Abdul Carim, just four. My father's name was immediately corrupted by a colonial immigration officer who entered it into the records phonetically – and so Ahmed became Amod and thus it was spelled for the rest of his life. The clan name Poonjanee was not recorded.

Whatever support system Pe may have had in Cape Town was obviously inadequate. While Tar Mohamed managed to attend school Ahmed, or Amie as my dad was nicknamed, had to be secured by a rope to the fruit cart Pe had begun operating at street corners in the city centre. As Daddy described the scene, 'I was tied around the waist to the cart. The rope was long enough so that I could move around on the pavement and short enough so that I couldn't wander off out of Pe's sight. I cried because I couldn't go to school with my brother, but I started enjoying the street after I began selling beads. People were nice to me and I sold a lot, but I hated the food – always bread or roti with overripe fruit.'

I heard these stories when I was very young and didn't know enough to ask the questions I would ask now. How did Pe, a Muslim from Gujarat, expect to succeed in an African country dominated by British, European, African and Christian cultural norms and values and overshadowed by segregationist laws? How long were they on the street each week? How and where did the child rest during the day? What did they do for toilet facilities, drinking water or the hot masala tea that my grandfather loved so much? Pe worked at two and three jobs after hours and on weekends when the city centre closed down, but I don't remember hearing what work he did and there was no talk of where they slept.

To this day, the image of a tethered five-year-old boy selling beads while his father sells fruit stirs me deeply.

Boom Street – Asiatic Bazaar

Town planning in colonial South Africa was based on race. The town centre and adjacent leafy green residential areas were for whites. Far out of town was the dusty township for blacks. Somewhere between would be the tiny Indian community huddled around its usual Asiatic bazaar with the odd Chinese family of shopkeepers. The Coloured community often didn't have a location of their own and were then strewn in pockets in both the black and Indian locations.

Boom Street was part of Pretoria's Asiatic bazaar – a bustling ghetto main street similar to Indian street bazaars all across the country. It boasted a range of shops and eating-places that serviced the non-white communities. It also attracted a good many whites who simply couldn't resist the vibrancy of the neighbourhood, with its kaleidoscope of colours, cacophony of sounds, multifarious fragrances of spice and especially the bargains it offered.

Here one would rub shoulders with black families calling out animatedly to one another across the street, Indian women in bright multi-coloured saris, coloured couples arm-in-arm and wide-eyed white visitors. People would be shopping for Basmati rice, corriander, turmeric and garam masala, school wear for children, fabrics for curtains and dresses or mango, lemon and mixed achaar, the famous homemade pickles. As they shopped to the sounds of Indian sitars and African concertinas many would be munching on spicy samoosas, bhajias or exotic sweet meats and sampling the excellent cardamom-laced masala tea on offer.

It was in this lively corner of South Africa's capital city, in 1924, just ten years after he started selling fruit on the streets of Cape Town and working at whatever else he could, that Abdullah Carim and his wife Janub settled and opened their first store – a so-called silk bazaar.

The family emporium was known for the quality of its goods and the excellence of its service. People came from far and wide to Pe's shop to buy such exceptional goods as Chantilly lace, Spanish shawls and beaten Indian brassware in addition to the lovely silks, satins and cottons that made up his basic stock in trade. It was said that my grandfather was one of the first retailers to import and sell Persian carpets directly to the public. Legend also has it that Pe, an unlettered man, carried all the details of his numerous transactions in his head.

His entrepreneurial sharpness and success derived not from any formal training, but from an inherent flair for commercial enterprise characteristic of the Poonjanee clan in particular and people from Gujarat in general. He used no professional business management systems, as we know them today. Daddy couldn't remember any written contract that Pe ever entered into, perhaps because he conducted business on the belief that, for a deal to succeed, all parties should truly benefit – otherwise it wasn't a good transaction.

Pe's business growth and expansion was based on opportunities perceived and risks taken off the cuff, not on any sophisticated business plan. The important thing for the Poonjanees was financial liquidity. This was seen as key to driving costs down by making it possible to make rapid buying decisions and conclude quick purchases at the best prices in return for 'cash on the barrel'. To them liquidity was defined as good cash flow and easily converted assets such as gold and jewellery.

I was once told of a great aunt who arrived in South Africa from Kathiawar outwardly a virtual destitute. She disembarked with only two suitcases of clothing representing what the customs officer presumed were her sole possessions. The family was much relieved, after they got her home, when she revealed the form of capital she was carrying from the community back home to invest in South Africa – gold bangles covering her arms from elbow to shoulder.

My grandfather's human resource management policy was straightforward: The oldest children worked full time in the business as soon as they could read, write and count adequately. The younger ones continued being educated so long as they showed merit or were not needed in the business. His financial management system consisted of books of account that were rudimentary; the formal banking system was avoided as far as possible and insurance cover on goods purchased and in transit ended immediately the shipment arrived in store.

These archaic business practices eventually spelled disaster for the family business when a fire raged through the shop and destroyed everything, including a huge amount of cash that should have been in a bank. Nothing was insured and the foundation that my grandfather established for a significant business dynasty was reduced to smoke and ashes.

Abdullah's Neckwear – No. 1 Diagonal Street

After the disaster in Pretoria, the family moved to Johannesburg and quickly reinvented themselves. They occupied two semi-detached houses at 55 Marshal Street, Ferreiratown, which they converted into one four-bedroom home. It was here, in rooms in the yard, that they established their third enterprise, manufacturing ties, scarves and other clothing accessories, using the high-speed cut-make-and trim (CMT) production approach.

Success in the CMT business is sustained by maintaining the lowest cost possible through design simplicity, high volume production and mass distribution. Pe understood this instinctively. With the help of their 11 children and my mother, he and Ma built a successful family business supplying goods, at wholesale, to buyers who came from everywhere.

Then Pe established his landmark shop – Abdullah's Neckwear – at No 1 Diagonal Street, on the corner of Market Street, in Johannesburg's spirited Asiatic bazaar. My dad explained that this shop was the main reason the family CMT business succeeded so well. Getting into the retail end of the supply chain enabled the family to understand the needs of the buying public and enabled the family to anticipate trends and focus production accordingly.

Years later, as a teenager, I would help-out on Saturdays and assist my youngest uncle, Noor Mohamed, known to all as Chotoo, who eventually took over the store. By this time its glory days were over. In its heyday, however, when Pe was in action and segregation had not yet intensified into apartheid, it was the centre of hustle and bustle. Located superbly close to the city centre, in the heart of what was then Johannesburg's largest Asiatic bazaar, it attracted large numbers of retail customers off the street and was also readily accessible to wholesale buyers. As the business grew, its reputation for quality and price spread far and wide.

My dad was both serious and joking, one time, when he told me what to do if ever we were lost or stranded. 'Find the local Asiatic bazaar. Find the oldest Indian shopkeeper and tell him who you are – Mohamed Fazl Amod Abdullah Carim Haji Amon Poonjanee via Kathiawar, via Porbandar, via Bombay, via Abdullah's Neckwear – No 1 Diagonal Street corner of Market Street, Johannesburg. They will know who you are and will feed you and get you back home.'

I remember loud laughter about our mile-long name and all the 'vias'. None of us ever got so badly lost that we needed to rely on our lineage to find our way back, but, over the years, I had the opportunity to test the strength of my identity and the validity of my dad's claim that '... they will know who you are'.

On these occasions, when I talked to older Indian people – complete strangers – the same question would invariably be asked: 'Tu khono poiro che?' 'Whose son are you?' With tongue in cheek, I'd rattle off the whole 25-word identification statement in a single breath. I thought it was funny, but I never once got a laugh. The old folk listened carefully and in every case, they somehow knew who my family was. Some knew of the Poonjanees, or the Carims or Abdullah 'tie-wallah' – the tie-fellow. Remarkably every one knew of Abdullah's Neckwear – No 1 Diagonal Street. Had any of us been lost or stranded, I know for sure these strangers would have got us home.

While Pe and Ma had lost the opportunity in Pretoria to grow a flourishing business dynasty, their immigrant spirit and resourcefulness empowered them to re-establish themselves in Johannesburg and build a relatively good life. Ma was the inside person – the homemaker – attending to the needs of her husband and her 11 children as well as the spouses and offspring of the married ones, and Pe was the leader and business driver.

Carim Family – Back row from left: – Uncle Bob, Daddy and Uncle Hassim, Pe, Uncles Abu, Moosa (Pietie) and Tar Mohamed. Seated from left: Aunties Hanifa, Bhaima, Ma, Aunty Miria and Mummy with brother Enver. Front from left: Zohra, me, Aunty Rabia, Uncle Chotoo

And I know they did not live by bread alone. Pe found joy, for example, in sitting for hours with my brother Abdullah on his lap. He would carefully peel grapes, remove the seeds, stuff the grapes with sweet rice and patiently feed them to Dooli – his nickname – until Ma or my mum would gently remind him that enough was enough.

Ma and Pe also found joy in the family limousine and often went for long drives through the leafy white northern suburbs of Johannesburg where we would stop to stare at the lovely properties we could never own, even if we could afford to buy them. One of my earlier and most pleasant recollections was sitting behind the steering wheel in the car while my uncles washed it. It was a huge black Hollywood-style 1936 luxury car with white-wall tyres, luggage rack on the back, white-wall spares on both front fenders, and white bone or ivory knobs and buttons on a high-gloss wooden dashboard. I remember it well because I made it my business to try and be around whenever the car was being cleaned.

Ma died when I was a teenager. Pe died shortly after Hajoo and I were married in 1957. In four decades the couple from Kathiawar had advanced from informal street vendors and hawkers to respected business owners in the formal sector. Their estate included Bendor, a prime commercial building in central Port Elizabeth that boasted some of South Africa's most prominent chain stores as its tenants.

More importantly, they had left a legacy of daring, risk taking, hard work and perseverance that inspired people who knew them and that seemed to have rubbed off on their children, grandchildren and great grandchildren.

2
STRIKE ONE – THE BETRAYAL

How was a deportation order served in South Africa's Cape Province in 1938? Was there a separate order especially for me, a two-year old, with my name on it? Mum and I were both born in the Cape – could we legally be deported back to the Transvaal with my Indian father?

When Daddy told me the story, I didn't ask the right questions so the answers will never be known.

It seems the whole drama had started five years earlier, in 1933, with marriage plans being made for my father without his knowledge and ended with a devastating betrayal.

The first time Amie took the marriage plans seriously was when Ma asked him to peer into a room where he could secretly see his bride-to-be. As he told it, 'I took a good look and decided to jump the window as soon as possible and move to Cape Town.'

The Alabaster Beauty and the Swarthy Moor

In 1933, Cape Town was Amie's oyster. He was a dapper, dark, and handsome whippersnapper with a great gift of the gab, his father's keen instincts for trading opportunities and a willingness to work hard. He arrived in the Mother City, immediately established a business, married a Cape Town beauty and, in April 1936, I was born, the first of six children. But none of this came without struggle, courage, determination and sharp thinking.

When Amod Abdul Carim and Josephine Medell met it was love at first sight. They both told me so. Mummy was an 18-year-old alabaster-skinned 'Cape-coloured' Catholic living with Italian nuns in a convent when she met and fell in love with this 25-year-old black Indian Moslem salesman. The relationship horrified her family. This was not surprising in a time when a person's strength of character, quality of spirit and brilliance of personality counted for naught if the hue of the pigmentation wasn't right.

Amie was the proverbial 'Moor'; a term used in a derogatory way by some Christian coloureds to describe a person who is swarthy, Muslim and therefore utterly alien. How in heaven's name could this Moor aspire to be part of a genteel fair-skinned coloured family, particularly one that believed they were related to Italian aristocracy?

Mummy and Daddy

Throughout my life people have told me what a great beauty my mother was – as a girl, a young lady and as a mature woman. She was also described as gracious and refined. These attributes may be ascribed, as I heard it, to the training and loving treatment she received from the nuns who held her in special regard because of her mysterious Italian heritage.

As the story went, it was these nuns who told my mother that she was descended from Italian nobility. It seems my maternal grandfather, Joseph Medell, was the illegitimate love child of a daughter of a branch of the House of Orsini in Italy. The birth took place in secret and, with the help of the church, baby Joseph was sent to a convent in South Africa, then placed in a foster home and raised as a son of a coloured fishing family.

When Josephine and Amie decided to get married in 1935 resistance came from every quarter – the family, the church, the coloured community. The opposition was so bad it may even have been threatening. For this reason friends had to help the couple elope, go into hiding and be married in secret. I have sometimes wondered about this: If the Catholic nuns thought so well of Mummy and treated her so lovingly, what force would drive her to elope with Daddy under such frightening circumstances? Would love have been enough?

As a teenager I once asked my mother about excommunication from the Catholic Church because she converted to Islam, took her mother-in-law's Muslim name – Janub – and agreed to raise her children as Muslims. I remember her response well: 'I was told I could be forgiven for marrying a non-Catholic if my children were raised as Catholics, but that I would be excommunicated and burn in hell if I brought you all up as Muslims.'

Mummy seemed angry rather than just upset. She believed no priest or nun could come between her and God simply because we were raised as Muslims. 'I do not need a church or a mosque to communicate with Allah, and it does not matter what religion anyone follows as long as one lives a good life. That is what God wants from us.'

The marriage, between Janub and Amie – the Alabaster Beauty and the swarthy Moor – was born out of great love. It overcame narrow-minded intolerance and bridged enormous cultural diversity. As it turned out, the main threat to this marriage was not religion. It was the debilitating pressure of prejudice and discrimination placed on ordinary people and communities in the South Africa of those times.

Like his father before him, Amie grew his business in Cape Town instinctively as needs arose, without any formal business plan. Soon after he arrived in the Mother City, he began importing ties, head and neck scarves, aprons, skirts and handkerchiefs from the family CMT business in Johannesburg, and hawked them himself on the city streets and door-to-door, directly to the public. It seems he even tried flogging his merchandise to the nuns at the convent, where he first laid eyes on his wife-to-be.

After he and Josephine (now Janub) were married, they started their own CMT factory with two Singer sewing machines and began supplying hawkers and distributors at wholesale. By December 1935 the family business was stabilising, their marriage, supported by good friends in the Malay community, was happy, and my mother was five months pregnant with me. Then, when King George V died on January 21, 1936 and South Africa went into mourning, a huge opportunity presented itself.

Most everyone wanted a black tie, scarf, arm band or hat band and every family of British descent expected their domestic staff to wear black skirts, aprons and head scarves as a sign of respect – so long as it didn't cost too much.

Demand for inexpensive black clothing and accessories skyrocketed and Amie scrambled to borrow money and increase production capacity to six machines. He had come to Cape Town to make a better life for himself and his family, and was willing to take risks and fight hard to make his place in the sun. He instinctively recognised this as his chance. He rushed around buying up all the low-cost black cloth he could find – job lots, abandoned consignments, factory end runs and all the black remnants available. Janub immediately stopped colour runs and converted all production to black. As fast as Amie could provide the cloth, Janub saw to it that the goods were produced and made ready for shipment.

In 1908, after Henry Ford had streamlined his advanced conveyor-belt production system for the breakthrough Model-T automobile he famously declared: 'You can have any colour Model-T you want so long as it's black.' I enjoy the thought that my parents may actually have said the same to the machinists: 'You can produce any colour you want so long as it's black.'

Thanks to superior quality, prices and service, the business continued to flourish long after the King's mourning period ended. Now it was time to open a retail shop like the one at No.1 Diagonal Street in Johannesburg. This would enable my parents to monitor buying trends and supply clients with the right designs, at the right time, at the right price. Daddy again borrowed heavily and the store was duly opened in the heart of Cape Town, in an excellent business area forbidden to 'non-whites'.

Knowing it was illegal for us to own or occupy premises on Adderley Street, Daddy did what many Indians were obliged to do in those days. He found a white person – a nominee or proxy – to front for us as the enterprise's legal face. The required permits and approvals, the bank accounts, the rental and other agreements and the stock were all recorded in the proxy's name. The proxy appeared, to all intents and purposes, as the 'owner', while my parents presented themselves to the public as employees.

I never understood how this proxy arrangement actually worked. In any event, the mechanism put in place to secure the ownership-interests of my parents failed. The trusted proxy or nominee betrayed them and had Daddy deported back to the Transvaal; together with his wife and me, his two-year old son.

It seems, when he jumped the window and escaped to Cape Town, it never occured to Amie to get the police permission required by all Indians before they could travel from one province to another. So, when he entered the Cape Province, he was an illegal and when we were deported, Mum and Dad lost the entire business lock, stock and barrel.

The fire that raged through the family Silk Bazaar in Boom Street years earlier and reduced to ashes the dreams of my grandparents was an accident with no predetermined malicious intent. The destruction of the business foundation that Amie and Janub established in Cape Town, however, was no accident. It was the kind of larceny that was taking place all over the country. This was aided by a government in support of white chambers of commerce whose members felt threatened by evidence of superior Indian business acumen, enterprise and fortitude.

3
THE TROYEVILLE
FRUIT MARKET

Ma's Enchanting Backyard

When South Africa entered the Second World War in September 1939, Amie and Janub were battling to recover from the disastrous loss of their business in Cape Town. These were uncertain times – and not just because of the war. No one could foresee what far-reaching consequences the betrayal and deportation would have on our family – not just economically, but also on our mental, spiritual and emotional lives.

We had returned to Jo'burg the previous year and, for a while, we were a family of three wandering gypsies making camp wherever we could afford the rent. In rapid succession, we stayed in a tiny bright single room in Ma and Pe's back yard, then in a dark, dank room and kitchen in a wet slimy courtyard in a building on Market Street. I remember, it was in this horrible place that we ate only spoiled reject cheese with bread and tea and little else for weeks on end, even though third grade steak was only six pence a pound and rice a penny ha'penny.

Then we moved into an unremarkable two-roomed place in Wolhuter Street in Malay Camp, and after that into a proper house on Anderson Street, one plot east of Ferreira Street in Ferreirastown, once occupied, it was said, by Mahatma Gandhi. This house had two bedrooms, a separate dining room and kitchen and it actually had a toilet in the yard we were not obliged to share.

All these places were within walking distance of the Carim family's growing cut-make-and-trim factory on Marshall Street. Mummy, pregnant with brother Enver, worked as a machinist here, with her three sisters-in-law; my foois – aunts – Bhaima, Hanifa and Miria, and she brought me along with her to work each day.

Daddy held down three jobs. He was a full-time driver-salesman for Parisian Bakery, a part time salesman for Pe and sold yeast for the

Anchor Brand yeast factory. My father left too early each morning for us to say goodbye, so I was always excited to see him when he came to collect Mum and me from Ma's house each evening.

Ma's back yard was a magical place that provided safety, adventure and learning for me and my cousin Zohra, Uncle Tar Mohamed's daughter, who was two years older than me. In this haven was the buzzing CMT factory, the sunny room where we once stayed, a flower garden ablaze with colour, and an aromatic herb garden overflowing with coriander or cilantro, mint, curry leaves and red and green chilli bushes. The yard was pre-school and kindergarten, and Zohra, me and the family's pet baboon, Baby, were the only pupils.

Ma did not teach the three Rs. Instead, she kept us occupied in ways that developed in us a work ethic and social skills. She taught us to be obedient, helpful and useful, and I was often asked to pick the herbs for the day's cooking. Even the baboon tried everyday to be of service. After we bathed each morning it was fun watching Baby picking through Zohra's hair in the morning sunshine. I laughed when she smacked my cousin lightly on the head when Zohra moved and interrupted the baboon's concentration. Ma told me Baby was looking for tiny non-existent 'animals' to remove and was grooming us as she would her own babies.

I enjoyed playing games on the factory floor and Ma had quickly turned my play into productive work. The game was to see how much material cuttings and cotton waste I could stuff into bags. Although I am now past 76, I still remember the whirr of the sewing machines and the smell of machine oil in the small factory. I can still conjure up images of my mum and aunts huddled over the sewing machines turning out ties, aprons and scarves by the thousands. I also remember tracing, with my fingers, along the cast-iron Singer logo on the filigree foot pedal of the machines, between working to fill the bags and keeping the floor clear of production waste.

Being allowed to sit behind the wheel pretending to drive Pe's Hollywood limousine each time the car was being washed, was, for me, a great joy, and doing the lakhri – the stick-dance, with my foois during family celebrations was a delight. As the women danced and sang, I particularly enjoyed being taken aside and having intricate orange-coloured mehndi designs affectionately painted on the palms of my hands and on my feet by women I didn't know, but who seemed to love me.

If, from all these wonderful adventures, you asked me to choose my best times, it would definitely be when I helped Zohra make the celebrated green dhana – coriander – chutney.

Just outside the kitchen door leading into the yard was this amazing stone – a slab of thick granite like a large flat pillow, with an indentation in the middle the size and depth of a soup plate. After first washing our hands thoroughly and then the black stone, Zohra would half fill the hollow with an exotic mixture that Ma had prepared – sliced green chillies, slivers of garlic, some jiroo – cumin – and lots of dhanya leaves. After Zohra added a squeeze of lemon juice we would take turns crushing the mixture using a mango-shaped granite stone that fit exactly into the indentation. We started by pounding the mixture with the stone and when it was crushed we began rolling the stone and grinding the mixture until it was a smooth fine paste. From time to time Ma would come out, have a taste, tell us how good it was and suggest a little more salt or lemon juice. She always reminded me not to touch my face or neck or my 'birdie' with my chutney and chilli stained hands, saying, 'You touch, you burn.'

Never, in all my years, in all the countries I've visited, have I seen or handled a pestle and mortar so uniquely designed and so cool to the touch. From this enchanting earth stone radiated a mysterious energy that seemed to join forces with Zohra and produce chutney that delighted those for whom it was so lovingly prepared.

These were happy years for me. Ma and Pe's home was never more than a walk from wherever we were staying in Malay Camp or Ferreiratown, and it was the constant in my life. Mummy was close by in the back yard factory, but ever present, and I knew Daddy would be home every evening.

Then suddenly all this changed.

Opportunity reared its ugly head one day, and Mummy and Daddy thought they absolutely had to take another risk at another business. So we moved once again, far away from Ma this time, to a dreadful place called Troyeville where, as a boy, I would learn that I could be loved for no reason other than who I was, and be hated for the same reason.

Coolie, Come Out and Fight!

Each Sunday morning, in this new place, Peter, Gavin and Porky[1] would accompany their father to church, dressed in their best, faces gleaming and hair slicked back flat. In church they presumably sang loud praises to their Lord. They would have been taught to 'love thy neighbour as thyself' and to 'do unto others as you would have them do unto you'. Then, after church, these so-called Christian brothers would shamelessly come to the shop looking to bloody the nose of the coolie boy, or split his lip, or colour his eye blue. Their hateful cry was always the same – 'Coolie, come out and fight!' and there were always at least three of them.

They never called me by any of my given names. My grandfather named me Mohamed, my mother registered me, as Faizel, the births office misspelled the name and it appears as Fazl on all official documents, and Ma and Pe nicknamed me Mumdoo. Despite all these names, the one that stuck in the years that we lived in Troyeville was 'coolie.'

This terrible trio terrorised many of the kids in the neighbourhood, white and non-white, and their modus operandi was well known. Fat, snotty-nosed Porky, the youngest, would provoke things by pocketing our marbles or grabbing someone's top or kite or just shove somebody. Soon as anyone reacted defensively, the brothers stepped in. Peter, the eldest, would take on the bigger boys and Gavin fought chaps my size.

Their idea of a fair fight was that they used no sticks, stones or kicking – only Queensbury rules of boxing. The fact that Gavin was seven and I was not yet six, that he was heavier and taller than me, and that he had a longer reach did not seem unfair to them. When they called me out to fight and I looked to Daddy to stop it, his only response was: 'You need to begin now to fight your own battles. Remember what I told you: straight left, straight left and, when you see an opening, come in with a right cross!'

I think I understood then, young as I was, that Daddy wouldn't be there to protect me from life and that I would have to fend for myself.

That straight left and right cross manoeuvre worked for Gavin much better than for me because of his longer reach and because, as we found out later, these three brothers trained at the local boxing club four nights a week.

---

[1] For reasons of privacy and memory lapse some names in this book have been changed.

I couldn't win against Gavin. These bare-fisted fights lasted hours and I usually came home with a swollen lip, a bloody nose or an eye that was turning blue. In the beginning it was awful, then gradually I began giving as well as I got. I learned to duck fast and low, spring forward and hook upwards, when Gavin expected me to weave backwards instead. Nevertheless, he always came out better off.

It was a black boy, the son of a domestic worker in the neighbourhood, who one day dug the pellet out of my bum with a matchstick. Simon Simelane never talked. Even though the coolie boys were sometimes invited to play with the white kids, the kaffir boy never was. He just stood on the sidelines silently looking. He was watching and listening the day Peter called out to me, 'Hey coolie you can come with to the koppies if you let me shoot you in the bum with my new pellet gun – but you must pull down your broeks and bend over.'

The City of Johannesburg lies sprawled over an undulating reef or chain of sunlit hills and cool shady valleys that we call koppies. They radiate the same energy as Ma's enchanted garden. Playing hide and seek, cowboys and crooks or just losing oneself among the shadowy bushes and trees, the rocky outcrops and the shoulder-high wild grass on those hills in Troyeville and Kensington was something I loved more than anything. And so, I pulled my shorts down and bent over without hesitation.

The crack of the BSA airgun distracted me from the actual pain of the pellet as it embedded in my skin and I was startled at how deep the thing went. It was difficult to pry the pellet loose with my fingernails and, in any case, I couldn't see the wound. Simon was watching as I vainly tried to dislodge the shot. He picked up a used matchstick from the pavement, wiped the dirt off on his shirt, stretched the skin around the bleeding hole between the thumb and index finger of his left hand and, very gently, dug loose the copper pellet from my buttock.

To this day, I deeply regret what happened next. I remember trying to staunch the blood with the inside of my short pants, I remember the rowdy white boys already nearly a block away and Peter shouting back at me, 'Hey Coolie you coming or what?' I don't remember if I thanked Simon or not, or what I said to him. But I do remember, with everlasting shame, that I did not stay behind with the sensitive, compassionate black boy who had shown me so much tenderness. Instead, I hastened away, blood running down my leg, to join the horrible white boys who were my relentless tormentors.

The whole time I lived in Troyeville I felt vulnerable and exposed to danger. I only felt really safe in bed, at Gold Street School or when I disappeared into my private hideaway above the storeroom in our back yard. From here I would travel to far-off lands through my adventure books and Classic Comics. My secret place was the space between a makeshift ceiling and the galvanised iron roof. It was no higher than the Joko Tea plywood packing crate, which I used, with other cardboard boxes, as a screen to prevent anyone from seeing me.

I think my parents lived the same way – always at risk, always threatened – and hiding behind a pile of work. They were once more fighting against the current of segregationist laws as they had done when setting up the shop in Adderley Street, Cape Town. This time they didn't use a proxy. They had purchased a small property on the south-west corner of Nourse and Corneilia Street. This brought in rental income from a tiny triplex of houses attached to a fish and chips shop, a fruit and vegetable shop and a shoe repair shop in a whites-only suburb using Mummy's maiden name.

When the three tiny shops were converted into the marginally larger Troyeville Fruit Market, and smartly painted in white and apple green, and the Carim family took up residence in the storerooms in the back, most members of the white community were outraged, and municipal inspectors immediately began their snooping.

As my mother once described it, a typical conversation with an inspector, mostly in Afrikaans, went somewhat like this:

Inspector: Who owns this property and this business?

Mummy: I do.

Inspector: Who is that Indian?

Mummy: My manager.

Inspector: Whose children are these?

At this point Mummy would sidestep the question by offering the inspectors a cool drink or ice cream and packs of cigarettes.

Here was an inconsistency peculiar to South Africa at the time: An Indian man owning and occupying property in a white's only area that is registered in the name of a coloured woman, who has 'white' papers and who admits she is cohabiting with her Indian 'manager' who should not even be living in the area. And then there are these children, ranging in complexion from alabaster to macchiato to swarthy, all calling this 'white' woman 'mother' and who all have strange names like Mumdoo, Enver, Dooli, Adam, Zarina and Shirene.

While I fought my battles with the three Bully Boys and other nasties in the area, Mummy and Daddy were being spiritually, emotionally and physically pounded by their own struggles.

As a driver-salesman for Parisian Bakery Daddy had to be up at four each day, pack his lorry and leave the bakery by 5am and be offloading fresh hot bread at his first customer by 6am. He would be home soon after noon, have lunch and then be off again in his old Chevrolet, delivering yeast to tiny Indian and Chinese-operated shops in a huge area that stretched from Jeppe through Ferreirastown and all the way to Fordsburg, Pageview, Vrededorp, Newclare and Sophiatown.

While Daddy was on the road, Mummy managed the shop and raised four, then five, then six children. With the help of Jeffrey Indaba and other itinerant domestic workers, she got the older ones off to school and cared for the younger ones. She did the buying for the shop, which meant dealing with fast talking salesmen and sharp deliverymen who often tried to get away with short delivering or short changing her. The harassment from inspectors was constant as they searched for technical reasons to rid the neighbourhood of this unwanted family. Although the white buying public generally resented our presence, they were poor people who kept coming back because of the good prices and generous credit they received at the Troyeville Fruit Market.

On weekends, Mummy got some respite from the customers while Daddy and we children helped clean out the shop, restock the shelves and the large counter-fridge, discard the over-ripe fruit and aging vegetables, and Daddy would do his sign writing on the storefront windows.

Our father performed like an artist and it was a treat watching him signwrite. First, he concocted several mixtures of water, Bon Ami window cleaner, cubes of Reckitt's Blue rinse, and crushed coloured blackboard chalk. Then he dipped a soft cloth into the watery paste and, with expansive flourishes of calligraphy and his own brand of poetry, announced to all who would read:

Best quality and best prices here!
No fresher fruit and veg anywhere!
Our prices cannot be beaten!
You'll taste the goodness when the freshness is eaten!
WE LEAD OTHERS FOLLOW!

Emblazoned across the bottom and sides were the specials:

Apples and Pears - four for a tickey
Watermelons - 6d- each
Pumpkins and Cabbages - 4d a half
Carrots - 2d bunch

As the morning sun streamed through the multi-coloured sign writing on the windows, past the gleaming white pillars that held up the galvanised iron roof, it cast a festive mood that enlivened our shop and drove George Papas, the Greek competitor on the opposite corner, crazy. The Jewish butcher and the Chinese grocer on the other two corners actually admired Daddy's artistic handiwork, and how attractive our shop always looked, and told us so. I wonder if Daddy ever made a connection between his flair for window painting, Nick's anger at his inventiveness, and the fact that vandals repeatedly smashed our windows over the years.

On those Sundays when she was not too tired, Mummy created mouth-watering delights for lunch. The smell of cooking wafted from the tiny kitchen from about eleven and the instant she called everyone quickly crowded into the tiny space that served as a kitchen and family room. There was no dining room or dining table – just a work surface in what Mummy called 'the cooking place,' and a few chairs, but plenty of space on the beds in the other 'spaces.'

A popular Sunday favourite was slices of roast leg of lamb simmering in thick, tangy brown gravy. This always came with mint sauce, mashed pumpkin or squash, bright colourful carrots and peas or green beans, with potatoes roasted to a golden brown. There was always at least three pieces extra-crisped especially for me.

Some Sundays it was spicy khurie and kitchree with aloo fry, which, if you don't know, is exotically spiced sour milk or yoghurt poured over turmeric-flavoured yellow rice, mixed with golden sultanas and a good sized serving of diced potatoes sautéed in cumin, coriander and chilli powder.

'People say khurie and kitchree is poor people's food,' Daddy once remarked, 'but I think it's the food of angels.'

While Mummy did her magic in the tiny kitchen, Daddy would be sitting with baby Zarina on his lap, and later baby Shirene as well, regaling us all with stories and songs.

We loved to hear about the American Negro, Joe Louis, the heavy weight champion of the world, who had won the title in 1935 and who people all around the world, especially non-whites in South Africa, proudly called the Brown Bomber. The part we liked best was how 'the mad man Hitler' had announced to the world that no black man could ever beat Max Schmelling, because of the superiority of the Aryan race. Daddy could barely contain himself as he told us how the Brown Bomber smashed 'the Great Aryan' into defeat in just 124 seconds of the first round on the night of June 22, 1938. 'People were still finding their seats and already the fight was over, and the world danced' he would laugh uproariously.

Our father had a good repertoire of songs and we heard them all, one time or another. After Zarina was born he learned a new song especially for her that he sang endlessly: 'Zarina Bibi baat tamari, kaan laga kê sune sune sune – 'Zarina sweet little sister the sound of your words, so beautiful, my ears are compelled to listen, listen, and listen.' After Shirene was born he would have both his daughters on his lap and the mantra would be sung to both of them using their names interchangeably.

The song that touched me more deeply than I could ever know at that age was the 1930 Fain, Kahan and Norman ballad made famous by Maurice Chevalier that Daddy sang to our Mother:

> *If the nightingales could sing like you*
> *They'd sing much sweeter than they do*
> *For you brought a new kind of love to me*

> *If the sandman brought me dreams of you*
> *I'd want to sleep my whole life through*
> *For you brought a new kind of love to me*

I know that I'm the slave, you're the queen
But still you can understand
That underneath it all you're a maid
And I am only a man

I would work and slave the whole day through
If I could hurry home to you
For you brought a new kind of love to me.

Mummy would interrupt her cooking and come listen as he sang his song for her, and even the noisiest of the little ones would quieten down and we would all sit enthralled. Then lunch would be served and as we sat enjoying the marvellous cooking, Daddy would never fail to remind us: 'When you die and go to heaven this is the kind of food you'll get. And if you go to hell you'll have to eat English food.' Then laughter would fill that tiny space that was our home and love and happiness would fill our hearts and the meanness of Troyeville would be pushed back till Monday.

Matombo Bags & the Joe Louis Punch

What helped transform the Troyeville Fruit Market from a mediocre shop into a thriving business was hard work, entrepreneurial savvy and the liquor laws of the time.

It was illegal for any non-white – African, Chinese, Coloured, and Indian – to consume 'European' spirits, wine and beer. They were allowed only a traditional African brew called ntomboti or skokiaan, which was contemptuously referred to, by officials, as 'kaffir beer.' This beer could only be purchased and consumed in huge, overcrowded, badly located beer halls which government owned and controlled and from which they profited immensely.

Many non-whites who wanted a drink ignored this demeaning regulation and frequented the more accessible shebeens – illegal drinking places – that mushroomed everywhere. Many shebeens were grotty places in dismal back yards often serving cheap liquor in tin mugs or fish paste jars and skokiaan in recycled jam tins. Many others were sophisticated establishments, offering a quality choice of spirits, wine and beer as well as the traditional brew, served with food and cool African jazz that made for a classy ambiance. These shebeens also offered safety and security by employing bodyguards and paying for police 'protection.'

Shebeens bought their 'European' liquor from white 'runners,' and often produced their own home brew using traditional methods and ingredients that included brown bread, malt – matombo – yeast and a simple fermentation process. One enterprising backyard brewer added pineapples to the mix, skin and all, which significantly increased its potency. She called it 'Joe Louis Punch' after the mighty Brown Bomber.

It was difficult for illicit backyard brewers to get hold of these ingredients, especially the yeast, which was criminal for blacks to possess. Thanks to Daddy's connections at the bakery, the yeast factory and elsewhere, Mummy was able to provide a one-stop shopping service to these entrepreneurs. She supplied them with all their needs, including the precious yeast and, for added punch, even the pineapples, at good prices.

The Troyeville Fruit Market flourished. Soon the area that was used as a sleeping space for us boys was used to store matombo. On delivery day large hessian bags of malt were stacked tightly together sometimes up to the ceiling, blocking out much of the light. There was now barely enough room to squeeze past from the shop into what remained of our living quarters and, as a consequence, the old shoemaker shop had to be turned into sleeping space for us four boys.

4
THE BLONDE BOMBER &
THE BOARDING SCHOOL

Innocent Love

For as long as we were allowed, Sally van Rensburg was my best friend in Troyeville. We were together as often as she could get away from looking after her ailing mother and younger brother. I can still see her pretty, pale face, blonde hair that was almost white, scrawny, long, thin bony legs and hear her strange English with her strong Afrikaner accent. She was always running errands for her mum, barefoot and in the same washed out white dress with faded blue flowers that was worn so thin it could rip at any time. And she was always hungry. Best of all she liked to box.

To toughen us up Daddy had bought Enver and me a set of new boxing gloves. Since we weren't allowed to join the boxing club at the local white school where Gavin trained, we started our own on the sidewalk by the shop. Our ring was a space enclosed by a length of rope tied waist high to the burglar-proof bars on the windows of the shoemaker shop, pulled taut twice around a pillar on the kerb-side edge of the pavement, then, in a straight line, twice around a second pillar and back to the burglar-proof bars, completing an almost perfect square. Even now, I don't understand why, in boxing, a perfect square is called a 'ring.'

For just a few minutes at a time, Daddy acted as trainer. I can hear him now: 'Straight left, straight left!' 'Protect your chin with your left shoulder.' 'Duck, weave, move, move faster, stay on your toes.' 'Weave sideways, get under his straight left and go for the solar plexus.' We had bottles of water for the fighters; we unpicked the stitching of empty flour bags for towels and used apple boxes as stools. What we did not have were enough fighters. There was just Enver and me and the occasional white boy who wanted a go at boxing, until his parents stopped him from associating with the non-Europeans. Simon lived in a rural township

36

in the Eastern Transvaal somewhere and would suddenly appear on a weekend or during his school holidays and just as suddenly disappear. While he was in Troyeville he boxed with us a few times.

Enver boxed well and in time was a better fighter than me. He eventually fought for Doolah Joseph's Yanks Boxing Club in a regional coloured association and did us all proud. Little brother Dooli would one day become the lightweight champion of the British Army on the Rhine and would fight for his regiment, the Royal Electrical and Mechanical Engineers, in various parts of Europe and the UK. But now, he was still a toddler and, much to our annoyance, Mummy declared he was too small to join our club. Adam too would become an accomplished boxer and win honours in the British navy as a young adult, but he was just a baby now. Finding members for our 'club' was proving to be a real problem

Then, thank Heaven, from nowhere, this Afrikaner girl pipes up, 'I osso wanner borkx!'

The first time she landed a solid right cross it knocked me silly and immediately earned her the name 'The Blonde Bomber'. Even at seven I was conditioned to think that girls were not as tough as boys: 'Boys are made of snakes and snails and puppy dog tails, girls are made of sugar and spice and everything nice'. Nice my eye! Here was this scrawny, barefoot girl punching almost as fast as Gavin and giving as hard as she got. She was too tall for Enver to fight, a little taller than me and with a slightly longer reach. Otherwise, she and I were evenly matched.

Between sparring with Enver, training with Sally and being forced to face Gavin I became a pretty good fighter. It was during these years that I began growing the 'steel caps on my elbows' that all short people need to help them elbow their way through the push and shove of life.

Sally and I boxed as often as we could. But we also spent time making and flying kites, playing marbles and keneckie and going to the koppies when we could. She had found a way for us to be together and still tend to her baby brother and run errands for her mother. We simply combined everything. When she was babysitting Hansie, she brought him along to watch as we boxed. We flew the kite up Eleanor Street as we went together to get their electric heater fixed with Hansie, Enver and Dooli in tow. We played marbles along the way to the chemist to fetch her Mum's medicine. Without anything being said, we understood, even at age seven and nine, that I would never visit her house. I never set eyes on her mother and there was no talk of a father.

I suspect one of the reasons Sally was allowed to be my friend was because of the fruit and vegetables she frequently took home from our shop. Mummy had made it very clear: 'If you don't overdo it and only if the fruit is very ripe, you can give the girl some.' It wasn't much, but occasionally Sally and Hansie would go home with a bunch of softer bananas, a bag of partially bruised apples or perhaps a paw-paw or a watermelon from which a part might have to be cut away. I always gave her the best I could get away with. Mummy, who must have known how desperately I needed a friend, would place a small cabbage or a quarter-pumpkin into one of the brown paper bags before I added the fruit.

The Queen of Mangoes

At lunch, many years later in Barbados, while we enjoyed a tropical mango desert, a UNDP official would tell me about the culture of poverty in the Caribbean, and my mind would fly back to the first time I saw Sally Van Rensburg eat a mango.

There is a way of eating a ripe mango on a hot day that I think Sally and I perfected. The mangoes were first placed in the Good Humour ice cream coldbox in the shop and were really cold by the time we finished three rounds of boxing. Then we sat on the edge of the pavement with our feet in the gutter rolling the heavenly fruit in our hands between open palms and squeezing with our fingers until they were soft, and the mango flesh completely pulverised. Only when you can feel the liquidised flesh through the skin, squishing between your palms, is the mango ready to share its divine juice with you.

I bit a fair sized hole in my mango and slurped large gobbets of cool pulp into my mouth, letting it slide delectably down my throat. Sally preferred to savour her gift from the gods a whole lot longer. She nibbled the tiniest opening in her mango and took the littlest sips of the nectar, which she allowed to play around on her tongue for as long as possible before reluctantly allowing it to disappear down her throat. 'Jissie dis lekker – Jeez, it's good!' she would groan.

When there was nothing more to suck out of my mango, I pulled open the skin and scraped off the last traces of flesh between my teeth. Then I began sucking on the cool moist fibres of the pip until they were utterly juiceless, tasteless and a pale yellow. In the process, according to Sally, I shared far too much of my mango with my chin, nose and cheeks. 'Jislike but you can wace!' she would tell me off, and, with a boxers' flour-bag towel, wipe my face clean with one hand while continuing blissfully to take tiny sips of her mango.

'You wanner borkx more?' she asked. 'Finish your mango' I responded. No, she said, 'I spaar – save – it for after.' We boxed in the morning. Then, with Hansie, a group of waifs and strays from Eleanor Street and my two brothers we walked down Cornelia Street to the koppies. Sally was still sipping sparingly on her everlasting mango. Mine was already finished. We played for a while in that magical place and, only on our way back to the shop, did she finish sucking out the juice and begin scraping clean the skin between her teeth. She took Hansie home and came back later to see if there was to be more boxing or playing. Now, she was working on the mango fibres. Sally finally finished eating that mango just before she went home later that afternoon. By then the fibres had been sucked white as snow, as if they had been washed and bleached in a really strong detergent by a supremely determined mango queen.

The undoing of our friendship was our love for the enchanted koppies and the fear and intolerance that lived in the hearts of members of the Troyeville community. I was eight that last time I went to the koppies with Sally and ended up banished to the Muslim Association Boarding School. She was ten.

Daddy broke the news that Enver and I had been enrolled in the Boarding School by saying 'The police are coming for you!' and scared the living daylights out of me. Then he told Mummy and me what Mr. Schneider his bookmaker friend had told him.

It seems that members of Sally's church were very upset that an Afrikaner girl was so friendly with the coolie boy from the shop. They thought that the unholy relationship had to be stopped, especially the shameless boxing. The matter was reported to the dominie of the church. He spoke to a member of the congregation, a senior policeman, who agreed that this relationship was unacceptable, but said that the police could do nothing to stop it unless there was proof of some wrongdoing. And so someone was assigned to secretly follow us children to the koppies that day and this person reported back that I had kissed Sally van Rensburg.

It was a lie! Sally had introduced into our lives the concept of a platonic relationship – that rare and beautiful friendship between male and female that includes love and sensitivity but no sexy kissing and such stuff – a type of male/female closeness that few people understand and fewer have the privilege to experience.

At seven and eight I enjoyed kissing girls. I also fell in love constantly – first with my grade one teacher, Mrs Adams, then with Loretta Jacobs, Delarosa Thomas and that amazing Tamil/ Coloured/Jewish girl from Denver with the copper-bronze skin. Stanley Yensin, my Chinese classmate from Jeppe, was good at arithmetic. He tried to keep a record of the kisses I got, but lost count.

But I say again: the whole kissing thing with Sally was a lie, made up by cruel people who professed to follow the word of God, but who had lost any connection with the spirit of Allah. They and their dominie feared the impact that a loving relationship between two children across racial and religious lines would have on their shrivelled, narrow-minded brand of Christianity.

Fresh Wild Bhajee, Fresh Bottled Butter and Bitter Marmalade Jam

'You love us,' I wailed, 'why are you sending us away?' I was fighting back and arguing that Sally and I could tell the Dominie we did not kiss on the koppies and he would believe us because we were telling the truth and Christians love the truth. 'Talk to the police and give them some fruit and cigarettes same as you give the inspectors,' I implored. Nothing helped. Within two days Enver and I were driven to a bitter place of unhappiness. There we would stay for what seemed a thousand years and during this time Sally would disappear forever from my life.

Experience has taught me that there is hardly ever just one reason for something important happening. Enver and I were sent away firstly, because we were growing up like weeds in Troyeville. Our parents had little time to supervise us and the boarding school seemed a good solution. With Enver and me gone, better care could be given to Dooli and Adam.

The second reason would have been shrinking living space. Like alien invaders, bags of matombo, now a primary source of family income, had crowded us out of our sleeping quarters, and Mummy and Daddy were expecting their fifth child.

I think the third and most compelling reason our parents rushed us off so quickly was fear. The memory of the loss of their business in Cape Town, and the real possibility that this could repeat itself here must have panicked them. This thing with Sally van Rensburg, the Church and the police would have seemed far more serious than dealing with inspectors who could be bought off cheaply. Race relations had become ugly in South Africa. Now Mummy and Daddy would have feared that behind the scenes some white business group would be colluding with municipal officials and offering money to get rid of us and acquire a good business location.

And so it was that Daddy and Mummy, brothers Dooli and Adam and tiny baby Zarina were squeezing together as best they could in the shrinking space behind the shop while Enver and I were trying to get along in the boarding school when the Second World War ended in May 1945. I remember well, as a cadet, marching in our khakis in a special celebratory parade led by Regimental Commander Matheson and receiving an extra portion of stale bread and horrible marmalade jam to commemorate the occasion.

My school life had started in Gold Street Indian Government Primary School in City and Suburban in Johannesburg in 1943 and I had been very happy there. I loved my ever-pleasant Grade 1 teacher, Mrs Adams. Our principal was the popular community activist Reverend Sigamoney, who showered us all with affection. And I made a best friend on the very first day at school, a certain Dicky Halim, brother of Hajoo, the girl I would marry a lifetime later. Then suddenly Enver and I were removed from Gold Street and shipped off to a dreadful place far from home.

This institution was considered by its admirers as a first-rate learning centre that prepared youngsters for life in the secular and Muslim worlds by providing a structured and disciplined learning environment. Critics of this place described it as little more than a glorified reform school for difficult kids, orphans and juvenile delinquents, controlled by ultra-conservative teachers who used antiquated disciplinary methods bordering on cruelty.

At the time we were there, allegations against school officials of physical and sexual abuse were making the rounds. There were also stories of corrupt administrators embezzling funds by purchasing and supplying the students with substandard food, paying inflated prices and pocketing the money they skimmed.

The best I can say for this place is that it was an extraordinary training ground for developing survival skills. My memories of it include often being hungry, picking out weevils from the rice on our plates at meal times and, while tending the extensive gardens, searching in nearby fields for wild sour bhajee – a kind of spinach – to eat. Some of us boys were always carrying a small bottle containing milk and shaking it endlessly until it changed into a kind of butter we could eat with the stale bread and horrible marmalade jam we all hated.

I particularly remember the fighting. I often came to blows to protect a place in the numerous queues for fruit, for a shower, for a change of clothing – our own good clothes having all been stolen within days of our arrival. I also had to stand up to bigger boys who, when they found out about the goodies Mummy and Daddy brought us on their visits, demanded a share.

Once every week the fruit bell would ring. Hundreds of boys would run madly from all directions into a crush at an assembly point and struggle to receive a pear, an apple or some grapes. They stampeded because they knew there would not be enough to go around. I pushed and shoved and often punched my way to the front of one of the four line-ups to secure the weekly ration of whatever was going for brother Enver and me. At six Enver was the very youngest in the school at the time and was popularly known as Keppies, a name he got because he wore his green regulation school cap at a jaunty angle, with the sun-visor flipped up. Some school monitors liked his great personality and I could often get an extra portion for us by pleading, 'Ek sê, gee bietjie ekstra vir Keppies – I say, give a little extra for Keppies.'

Although I learned to say prayers and read the Koran in Arabic and could say the Gujarati alphabet, I had difficulty with Gujarati and resisted reading words and reciting Koranic verses in Arabic that I didn't understand. And most of the madressa teachers weren't helpful since they didn't speak Arabic and couldn't translate for me or explain.

Nor was I inspired by the narrow focus on the word rather than the spirit of Allah. I have no recollection of any discussion about compassion, tolerance or love and there was no joy or happiness or celebration of God in the atmosphere. I do not recall any of us ever receiving gestures of kindness, friendship or support from the lay or religious teachers such as was showered on us at the Gold Street School.

On the contrary, my most vivid images are of three teenagers being tarred and feathered, in medieval fashion, for some infraction. I can still see the boys with their hands tied in front of them and the house superintendents pouring hot tar over their heads. I can smell the tar running down their chests and arms as they were pushed and prodded through the mob of pupils who were given handfuls of feathers and instructed to throw it on them till they resembled giant feathered insects from another world.

Even though I was only a child, I got the sense that the friendly, happy, compassionate Allah that I trusted and loved and who protected me was not the same God these people were talking about. I learned nothing spiritually here that would help me though my life.

It seems to me Sally too, would have learned very little of spiritual value from the members of her church, whose doctrinaire thinking is accurately reflected in the revealing tale that made the rounds in the 1950s.

As the story went, a policeman is on the beat in suburban Johannesburg. He walks past a whites-only church, looks into the open door and sees a black man on his knees in front of a statue of Jesus. In a rage he storms into the church and at the top of his voice roars, 'Hey, what are you doing on your knees in front of Jesus in a white church?' 'I am scrubbing the floor, baas,' replies the man. 'Oh, alright' says the appeased policeman, 'but God help you if I catch you praying.'

We were saved from the unforgiving Boarding School when Enver and I were home for the school holidays in 1946. My mother had sat crying at the kitchen table watching us ravenously wolf down loads of fresh bread and butter – no marmalade thank you very much. Her decision to remove us from this institution and return us to Gold Street School was made in an angry instant when we showed her the white sores and inflammation in our mouths from eating the wild sour bhajee.

The thought of returning to a school where teaching and learning happened in an environment of love and caring filled me with a happiness that was shot through with a bitterness that came from knowing that Sally van Rensburg, like Simon Simelane, had disappeared from my life forever.

I cannot see Sally's face anymore, but I see clearly the faded blue flowers on her dress and recall the paleness of her skin. It's as if the time we had together, in the hot African sun, was never long enough for her to get some colour on her face and arms before she was again pulled back into the shadows of poverty, ignorance and prejudice.

Sigamoney School

Apart from the time at the Boarding School, I attended the Gold Street Indian Government School – till I was nearly fourteen..

Mrs Adams got me reading my very first day at school. She pointed to the letter 'i' on a poster on the wall and asked us what it was. 'A one with a dot on top,' I answered with no hesitation. I was seven and full of beans and so were all the kids in the class – especially my best school friend Dicky Halim. During the lunch break that first day I gave him one of the two pennies I had for spending and a bite of my apple. Then we shared our lunches with each other and after that, we were inseparable.

In the beginning, school was great. I enjoyed the work and won prizes for coming first or second in class. Then gradually the shine wore off. After I moved up from Mrs Adams' class school work became a bore. By the time I was ready for high school, the only things I enjoyed were Mr Thumbran's singing classes, anthology, the school plays and the year-round football, cricket and boxing.

I remember the excitement that electrified us backstage on the opening night of our musical rendition of Dick Whittington at Selbourne Hall in President Street, Johannesburg. Or the buzz during the train ride back from the Benoni location – ghetto – where we boys had won the soccer prize and a number of boxing trophies, and the girls had taken top honours in soft and netball. Looking at us, you might say we were young, gifted and full of beans and not yet damaged by disappointment.

Reverend Sigamoney was a keen advocate of these extracurricular activities. Dicky, I and most other kids were dedicated participants in the various competitions between the Olympians, Trojans, Corinthians and our own house, the Spartans. It's almost as if we all subconsciously knew that non-white kids in South Africa had more to gain from sports and the performing arts than we would ever gain from the government-controlled academic curriculum.

We learned heroic things about the Great Trek of the Afrikaner nation, about the fact that 'the sun never set on the British Empire' and about the marvels of the Renaissance in Europe. However nothing was taught of the Ghana and Mali Empires, of the great achievements of the Aztecs and the Incas or of the glory of the Mughal and Ming dynasties of the East.

I suspect our principal, the Reverend Father Sigamoney, had concerns about this, and that's why he pushed us in the classroom, drove us on the soccer field and in the boxing ring, and inspired us with many words of encouragement, including these that I never forgot: 'There is greatness in all people. Find it in yourself, Carim, and in everyone you meet.'

This was a poor school in a poor neighbourhood, that's why the daily line up, in winter, for the free vegetable soup was so long. Needy or not, anyone could join the queue and it usually moved so fast that, on icey days, the soup was always still hot by the time I received my portion in a large tin mug.

Over the years, my wife Hajoo and I would talk about this soup. We would remember that the large butter beans and the thick slices of potato, combined with the bright yellow of turmeric and the smell of curry leaves was very much like her Mum's butter bean curry that we both loved so much. We would pity those Muslim kids who did not want the soup because it was made by a Tamil Hindu lady. And we felt sorry for the snobs who missed out because they were too embarrassed to be seen lining up with the poorer kids for free food.

What we pupils did not know was that the question of school feeding was a loaded socio-political issue in the country at the time. Non-white community leaders such as Reverend Sigamoney had to choose between a school feeding programme for hungry children or a bigger allocation of funds for school equipment and supplies. For some this may not have been a critical matter, but there were too many children who began each day on nothing more than a bellyful of water.

The populist knee-jerk reaction was for more learning tools rather than food. 'Education Is the Key to Our Future' seemed to be the slogan, 'Education First'. But there were those who argued that nutrition through a balanced diet was more important. Such leaders insisted that an adequately fed child would learn more effectively despite having to write on a cracked slate, read from a torn textbook, or share a desk that was falling apart, than one who, because of malnutrition, was incapable of concentrating properly and internalising learning no matter how good the equipment was.

But what did we children know about issues of nutrition, budget allocations and the politics of education?

Home with the Halims

When I started school in City and Suburban it was arranged that I would walk with Dicky and his older sister Timie each afternoon to the Halim home in Doornfontein. Mrs Halim would keep an eye on me until my father came to collect me after he finished work.

I know that we each had something to eat and that homework was done but I have no recollection of that. What I do remember well were the breathtaking games we played on Beacon Road with the Halim siblings – Timie, Dicky and Hajoo; Bobby and Ayesha were too grown up, Bashir was still a toddler, Farida a baby and Yusuf was not yet born. We were joined by the other neighbourhood kids – the Koopoos, the Hills and the Adams – all of us bursting with excitement,

A group of us would come together, a broomstick and an old tennis ball would appear, and within minutes sides would be chosen and the most vigorous game of rounders – our street version of baseball – would be on. Or with three empty jam tins and a tennis ball an entire block of children would be exhilarated, for hours, by the game 'drie blikke' – three tins.

This game required, from the 'attacking' team, good co-ordination between eye and arm to throw the ball accurately and knock the stack of tins down. Then they needed great speed and dexterity to rush in, collect the scattered tins, rebuild the stack in split-seconds and, in the process, avoid being tagged by the 'defending' team. The objective of the defending team was to ensure that all attackers were tagged before they were able to rebuild the three-tin stack. To succeed in this, defenders had to be able to throw the ball straight, catch well and run really fast to tag the attackers and so prevent them from reassembling the scattered tins.

Games changed all the time. It could be drie blikke or rounders today. Another day it would be eggy or keneckie or we may decide to play five stones, spin top, shoot marbles, skip rope or play hop-scotch.

What each of these games had in common was the degree of passion and joy with which these kids applied to them, not just here but in streets everywhere. These were the forties. Television had not yet invaded South African neighbourhoods and stolen our minds. It had not yet undermined the innovative and creative ability of street kids to transform a broomstick or three empty jam tins into such magical and inexpensive instruments of fun and games.

Looking out from their cars, people driving through this shortcut from town to the more affluent Eastern suburbs could not be expected to see that these sparkling kids lived in overcrowded conditions and were often hungry. They would not know that most of these children were repeatedly embarrassed because their parents could not pay their school fees, had to share clothing and sometimes were obliged to push cardboard into their school shoes because of the holes in the soles.

Many of these street urchins would marry and while most would not make it past high school, they would serve as launching pads for their own children and grandchildren to rise high. The offspring of the Halim siblings would make important contributions to society, in information and communications technology, medicine and nursing, journalism and the media, teaching, trade diplomacy, corporate management and business ownership. Some would be nationally and internationally recognised for their work.

5
STRIKE TWO –
THE SCREWS TIGHTEN

We moved away from Troyeville into Jajbhai's Building during the July school break in 1949 for two reasons – family fear and Mummy's fatigue.

Even before the National Party came to power in 1948, we were being subjected to a rising tide of malevolence from members of the Troyeville community. Their anger manifested itself through the smashing of our shop windows, physical attacks on my brothers and me and two unsolved hit and run incidents with trucks.

The first bakkie could have killed toddler Zarina who was sitting at the edge of the sidewalk, and possibly brother Dooli as well, who was playing close by, had it not been for Jeffrey who threw Zarina to safety and was seriously injured in the act. In the other 'accident' the truck killed our much loved dog Timmy, and, as brother Enver and I remember: 'How we cried.'

Jeffrey recovered completely from his injuries, the perpetrators were never identified and the insecurity that these so-called accidents produced penetrated deeply into the family psyche.

In rapid succession, between 1948 and 1950, the new government would pass the Population Registration Act that classified people by race; the Group Areas Act that defined where different races may live; the Prohibition of Mixed Marriages Act and the Immorality Act that made it illegal for whites and non-whites to marry or be lovers; and effectively discouraged even innocent friendships between so called Europeans and non-Europeans.

It seemed as if these laws were being passed expressly to get at my parents – the Alabaster Beauty and the Swarthy Moor.

Some time before, a government inspector, frustrated because he could not trip Mummy and Daddy up, had stormed out of the shop, shouting, 'Eendag sal ons julle kry, julle koolies – one day we'll get you, you coolies!'

Now they could. Government was arming petty officials with vast powers over individuals and communities. Soon there would be no wriggle-room left. Mummy could only legally own the property in Troyeville if she could prove she was white. If she was indeed white then living with Daddy she would be in violation of the Mixed Marriages and Immorality Acts. If she were non-white then by owning a property in Troyeville, she would be guilty of an offence under the Group Areas Act.

My parents were smart enough to know that businessmen like George Papas and the proxy that robbed them in Cape Town, aided by vengeful government inspectors, would be scheming in the shadows to get their hands on our property. The probability of losing everything again would have become clear to them, levels of anxiety and fear would have escalated and the psychological effects on their minds would have been terrible.

Humphrey Bogart, Mr K and the Gangsters

Mummy was now almost always tired and Daddy was hardly ever around. He left home for the bakery before we kids were up in the morning, was back for lunch then out again on the yeast round. He helped us in the shop for a while in the late afternoon then, after dinner he would be gone again – heaven knows where to. Then one day I found out.

'Put on your coat and come with me!' One look at my mother's face and I quickly did what she said. Mummy was still very beautiful, but she was not as light or gentle as I remember her at Sea Point, or in Ma's enchanted garden. This wintry evening her face was rock hard as we sat in silence on the two trams to Fordsburg.

Friday nights Daddy did the weekly fruit and veggie buying at the big market in Newtown. From about six pm trucks would begin rolling in from the countryside and he would be there by seven, with the other night-buyers, waiting to select and bid, auction style, for the best produce, load up our 1936 Chevrolet van and be home around ten. It was now Sunday and he was not back yet. Grimly, Mummy had phoned around and tracked him down to Mr K's gambling den on Mint Road in Fordsburg.

This was not the first time I went looking for my father. I remember when we lived in Anderson Street, being sent a few blocks to call him home from the billiard saloon next to the Goldberg Bioscope on Fox Street, on the edge of Malay Camp. Or from the Cosy Cafe close by on the corner of Bekker Street, in Chancellor House, the building where Attorneys Nelson Mandela and Oliver Tambo would one day have their law offices.

This was gangster land. Here, directly opposite the Magistrates' Court, I would sometimes see such prominent underworld personalities as Sharif Khan, Essop Mayet, Sarang, Cassim Delaire, and other lesser known but just as dangerous figures. It was here that the famous shoot out took place, when four gunmen came after the legendary Mr Khan, revolvers blazing. As they told it, 'He dropped to the ground, rolled out the cafe door, onto his knees, shot two of them, and then raced after a truck, grabbed its side-rails and allowed it to drag him to safety.'

It was from here that a car full of 'the boys' left to seek out their opposition and another famous shoot out took place. It seems two cars coincidentally pulled up side by side at a stop street in Boksburg and when the toughs in both cars recognised each other all hell broke loose. After the shooting stopped several people had been badly hurt and two passers-by killed. At the end of the ensuing court case, the father of my friend Braima Ismail was found guilty of something and later hanged. Mummy told us that it could have been Daddy. It was pure luck that he was out when the gangsters came by the house to get him to go along to Boksburg 'for a drive.'

Each time I found Daddy, the scene would be out of a Humphrey Bogart or George Raft movie or a Mickey Spillane detective story. He would be playing 13-card rummy in shirt sleeves and braces, his hat pushed back on his head, a cigarette dangling from his mouth, squinting at his cards, before slowly picking one up from the table, then discarding one from his hand. As I tried to get a word in about coming home, the other three men at the table, dressed the same as Daddy, would be doing exactly as he, squinting at their cards through a haze of smoke that filled the room.

Years later, I too would play 13-card rummy in the Broadway Billiard Saloon on Main Road in the Fordsburg dip. One month-end, soon after I had married, I lost my entire pay cheque before I even got home. Fortunately, the shock of that experience – having to lie to Hajoo and secretly borrow from loan sharks – killed the gambling gene in my body forever.

It was getting cold when we reached Mr K's gambling house and Mum and I talked in front of the Lebanese Orthodox Church next door: 'When you find your father, say loudly, so that everyone can hear, that Mummy is waiting outside. If he says go I'm coming, you say loudly again that you are not moving until he comes out with you. I'll wait in the van.'

The moment the man opened the door and called out, 'Hey Amie, your son is here for you!' it seemed I had stepped into another gangster movie and immediately forgot every instruction my mother had given me. There were men playing cards around four or five small tables, others were relaxing on sofas smoking and Daddy was sitting at a table chatting and eating from a tray of finger-foods while two women served cups and glasses of something on trays.

I expected Humphrey Bogart to walk in with Peter Lorre from the film Casablanca and say something stunning like: 'Champagne for everyone on me.' Maybe Pepe LeMoco would come in with Cyd Charisse. She would be in that magnificent green satin dress, and they would do the tango like it is danced nowhere else in the world but in the Casbah in Algiers. Even the gendarmes, who are about to raid the place, would stand in awe and dare not interrupt. Before I remembered what I had to say, someone called out loud enough for all to hear, 'Hey Amie, gaan nou huis toe man, jou vrou wag buite – Hey Amie, go home now man, your wife is waiting outside.'

When we came out Daddy went to the van, opened the door and said to Mummy something that sounded like 'Janub I lost the van and we must take the tram home.' Apparently he had lost heavily, borrowed from the loan sharks using the van and its contents as collateral, continued to lose and, with some very tough men standing by to ensure that he honoured his debt, signed a paper and surrendered the keys.

As we sat in terrible silence in the two trams back to Troyeville, I think something was dying between my parents on that ride. But what would a small boy know about such things?

Angry As Hell!

Mum and Dad were arguing a lot now and the pain and loneliness I felt, I came to understand later, was about being powerless to help them recapture the happiness of times gone by. This ache turned to fury that time, after we had returned from the boarding school, when fat-face Porky, Gavin and Peter shouted at the back yard gate, 'Coolie, come out and fight.' Boy was this coolie ready!

In the fields of the boarding school, there were no boxing gloves and no Marquess of Queensberry rules. There we fought bare-fisted and rough and tumble. The first time I bloodied Gavin's nose and split his lip the shock on his face was at least as great as the looks of disbelief and confusion on the faces of his brothers and their usual bunch of cronies. I was so angry I gave no thought to defence. I just attacked – relentlessly. Now he was on the defence and back peddling. Consciously or not, all of us in this bloody mix knew that something had changed forever.

After that first shock, they came back to fight a few times, but clearly Gavin was not as keen as before. It was his big brother prodding him. Then suddenly one day I realised there were no more calls to come out to fight. The brothers would still come to buy things at the shop, but there seemed to be less swaggering, less arrogance and a little bit more please and thank you to Mummy. The menace, however, was still palpable.

My street fighting continued in other places, but in Troyeville it came to an end only after I beat the arrogance out of Frikkie the bully boy and his two mates at the top end of Cornelia Street.

To get to madressa – Islamic school – we had to walk up Cornelia Street to Commissioner and take the F1 tram to Jeppe. These three boys hung around in front of the house at No. 5. They thought it great fun to block our paths, smack down hard on the crown of the fez – keffiyeh – we each wore, and smash it down over our eyes and ears. Then they would howl with laughter.

Actually, it really is funny to see a fellow floundering around with his ears bent over double by the keffiyeh and his vision blinded by the felt material. If you hit down hard enough the fez gets jammed on the bridge of the victim's nose for a while. Most madressa-going kids have done this in fun to each other. However, in Troyeville, when these horrors did this to Muslim kids in those days it was pure spite. Unfortunately, for them, after the boarding school and after Gavin, they had picked on the wrong coolie.

On this particular day I was on my own – no Enver and Dooli to slow me down. I did exactly what my Dad had told me I should do in just such a case, and the whole thing was easier than I thought. As the toughs stepped forward to block my path, I carefully placed my Quran, in its velvet jubdaan – a sanctified protective carrying bag – on the low perimeter wall of the house. Then, without warning, I stepped swiftly up and punched Frikkie full in the face. His nose gushed red so quickly I was startled. As he staggered away with both hands covering his eyes and nose, I rushed the second chap who was still in shock from seeing the blood flood. After two solid punches in the face he quickly went into a defensive crouch – a sort of standing foetal position – and was out of it. The third fellow had already run around the side of the house shouting for mama. I quickly collected my Quran, ran around the corner into Op de Bergen Street and was out of sight by the time the mother appeared.

That night, as we were serving customers, Mummy told me that Mrs So-and-So had come to complain that I had attacked her sons. I told her about these guys, how they regularly gave us a hard time, and what Daddy had said I should do to bullies. She said nothing more to me about this palaver, but I knew, from the light in her eyes, that she was okay with what I had done.

The Medell Family

The sunshine and joy in our lives in those months before we got out of Troyeville was my Aunty Sheila. When she turned up at the shop, she brought with her a special energy that lifted the depressing shroud hanging over us. We children would scramble around her for attention and Mummy's whole persona would light up as she watched her youngest sister hug and kiss each one of us in turn.

Aunty Sheila may have been around twenty at the time and, in the opinion of this ten year old, was simply the most gorgeous and exciting person ever. She had a radiant smile, an easy laugh and a bright, adventurous spirit and I adored her. She was the first person other than Mummy and Mrs Adams my teacher, who did not treat me as a brainless child.

Her visits were always much the same. She would suddenly appear on a weekend totally out of the blue and surprise even Mummy. If it was a Saturday, she would spend time helping out in the shop, and she and Mum would be talking and laughing almost all the time. If it was a Sunday, she would spend time in the kitchen with Mummy, cooking and telling each other things. We never knew when she was coming to visit and she never spent the night. But it was clear that she had come especially to see us all, and to visit with her mother, Grandma Medell, who lived around the corner.

Then suddenly it would be dusk and she would be gathering her things and getting ready to leave. None of us knew where she came from when she visited, or where she went to when she left. When I asked her, one time, where her home was, she didn't answer and offered me a piece of chocolate instead.

The last day I ever saw her was the Saturday she came to Troyeville and went to the koppies with us kids. She was the only adult who ever joined us in our escapades among those magical rocks. Then, all too soon, it was evening-time and she told me to get my jersey and get ready to walk her to the tram stop.

Her farewells were always the same. As the tram approached my Aunty would kiss me on both cheeks and bang on my nose and say something like, 'be good, help my sister in the shop.' But this evening it was different. Instead of kissing me goodbye, she gave me a mischievous smile and said, 'Get on the tram; you're coming with to town.'

As we clickety-clacked westwards, through Fairview, Jeppe, City and Suburban into the city centre, I could barely contain myself. And, at the tram terminus on the corner of Market and Loveday Streets, opposite the City Hall, Aunty Sheila gave me my first surprise treat. 'Do want an Eskimo Pie?' she asked.

Of course I did. An Eskimo Pie is, or was, a marvellous, solid rectangular block of vanilla ice-cream encased between two thick wafer biscuits. They look something like a really fat ice-cream sandwich and they cost a tickey – three pence. We sold them at the shop and these delicious ice cream sandwiches were one of the items we were expressly forbidden to choose for our weekend treat. 'You can have the penny suckers from the ice box but not the tickey or sixpence things,' Mummy always reminded us.

We got off the tram, walked around the corner to Solly Kramers and Aunty Sheila bought me a whole Eskimo Pie just for myself. Then she took me for my second unexpected treat.

In those days there were three cafe-bios on President Street between Rissik and Eloff. Aunty Sheila knew them all. Even after she explained it to me, I still didn't know whether a cafe-bio was a cinema with a cafe attached to it or a cafe with a cinema attached to it. Whatever it was, the concept was marvellous and I really regret these bios don't exist anymore.

We took a slow walk up President Street and checked all three cafe-bios to see what was playing. Then Aunty Sheila asked me to choose, 'What picture do you want to see?' It was easy – I had already decided: 'Let's see Captain Blood, the pirate picture with the sword fighting with Errol Flynn.'

Cafe-bios started at nine in the morning and ran pictures continuously, non-stop, till late at night. You could stay as long as you wanted, for the price – a shilling and sixpence – and see the same picture over and over again. Someone came along with a menu and, in the dark, with the help of a torch you could order what you wanted while watching the action on the screen. I think Aunty Sheila ordered chicken and chips and I had scrambled eggs and chips because the chicken wasn't halal – kosher. I remember we both had Ovaltine to drink.

What a fun time! I had seen Captain Blood before at the Rio bio and loved the story and the swashbuckling action of this seafaring buccaneer Robin Hood and his gang of pirates, stealing from the rich to give to the poor. Then, after we had eaten, and the picture was starting over again she said, 'It's getting late, time for you to go home.'

On our way to the terminus we stopped at a special sweet shop and this time Aunty Sheila shocked me by buying me a Frosty Twister for a shilling. That's a whole twelve pennies. This was an extravagance Mummy would never have allowed!

A Twister was a foot-long stick of solid, thick, chocolate, vanilla and Neapolitan ice cream encased in a kind of spiralled heavy paper wrapping. To get to the ice cream, you twist and twirl and peel off the wrapping inch-by-inch as you eat it. The more you eat, the more you twist and twirl, and the flavours change as the ice cream slowly disappears. I had seen Twisters before and, when I asked about them, Mummy told us that we didn't sell Frosty Twisters in Troyeville because only shops in town had customers that could afford such an expensive treat.

Now I was boarding the tram and Aunty Sheila was crying and wouldn't tell me why. As she hugged me, and kissed me again on my cheeks and on my nose, I had no idea all this adventure had been part of an elaborate goodbye. As the tram rocked on the track eastwards, back to Troyeville, I didn't know that I would never again see the face of this aunty that loved me so much. I didn't know that she had chosen to give us all up, marry a white fellow none of us would ever know, move to Southern Rhodesia and live as a white person.

Sheila Medell had chosen to disappear from our lives forever and when I found out the details, it broke my heart. I forgave her only many years later when I understood the difficult choices coloured people like her had to make in those days of race classification and re-classification.

The circumstances surrounding the lives of my mother's family was bizarre, and must have been painful, in the years when we lived in Troyeville.

Our Grandma, Christine Baines Medell, was a pretty, nut-brown woman with frizzy or, as the Americans would say – nappy hair, and obviously a coloured. It seems she was part Xhosa and part Scottish, but I could not verify this. She had moved from Cape Town to find work here, and lived in a single-car garage attached to the house of an Afrikaner family at No. 24 Eleanor Street, the next street from us.

Grandma was clearly non-white, Mummy was pretending to be white and Government inspectors were snooping around. When Grandma came to the shop, they would laugh and talk but stop immediately people came in and act as if they hardly knew each other.

Then Aunty Sheila would come secretly visiting her coloured mother and her 'white' sister – the one who had all these Moslem children fathered by her Indian shop manager. Surely Daddy also thought the situation weird. Here he was the non-white husband and brother-in-law of these so-called 'white' females, and the son-in-law of his white wife's coloured mother whom he could not safely acknowledge. His father-in-law, Joseph Medell, now deceased, would have added to the muddle. The man was raised as coloured, but was said to be the son of white nobility – the Italian Orsini family.

What a tangle. No wonder prominent conservative white church leaders supported any plan to straighten out this ungodly mixed-race miscegenation mess. A good, white, Christian apartheid government would defend racial purity and bring order where there was confusion. It would tighten the loopholes left by weak colonial laws and eliminate the evasions. By setting boundaries, erecting barriers, and imposing penalties everyone would know their place and stay there and people would be happier.

Laws were already on the drawingboards that would force countless fair-skinned coloureds to decide which side of the racial divide they would identify with – white privilege or coloured exclusion. Amazing opportunities could be yours on the right side of the tracks if you denied your heritage. Or you could choose to leave the country.

Grandma would be the first to go. She went alone, without any of her children, at the age of sixty-something, for a better life in London with her Church. Our mother married an Indian, raised us as Muslims and eventually also moved to England. Aunty Ruth married a European and moved to Australia to escape the stress and anxiety that life as a 'play-white' brought. Aunty Naomi married a Cape Coloured and made her life in Cape Town as part of the coloured community and Uncle Clarence chose to live as white in South Africa.

Is it possible to know what heartbreak these choices caused? Has anyone measured the collective pain or counted the tears? Who will add up the wounded spirits and the broken dreams? And who will tell me where my Aunty Sheila is?

Frozen Farts – My Weapons of Choice

After Frikkie, I did not fight on the streets of Troyeville any more. Instead, my resistance to our tormentors went under-ground.

Our shop was too small to accommodate a normal size freezer for the ice cream so we rented a small portable unit from the Good Humour people. It was a solid round insulated bag of heavy canvas with a plastic inside lining and used dry ice to keep the ice cream frozen. In terms of height and circumference, it was very similar in size and shape to a modern toilet.

Quite by accident, I found that it was a 'cool' place to sit on a hot day; so, when no one was around, I would sit on the freezer and cool off my bum. Then I wondered, how much cooler would it be if I sat *in* the freezer rather than *on* it? I unzipped the top, lifted it like you would a toilet seat cover and placed my behind into the freezer only inches from the dry ice. Boy was it cold.

Then I wondered some more. If I froze my balls could we sell them to the Dominie as iced lollies? If I froze my birdie, could we give it to one of the Inspectors as a present instead of the usual iced suckers or Eskimo pies? What if I farted into the freezer – would the fart freeze? Between Adam, Dooli, Enver and me, we farted a lot in the huge bed we shared. We could all fart in the freezer instead, and there would be enough frozen farts to supply all the horrible people in Troyeville. We could do a 'special' – Two Frozen Farts Free For Every One You Buy and Daddy could it write up on the shop window. Of course, we would exclude Sally's family, all the black people, the Chinese grocer and Jewish butcher and their families and those Afrikaners who treated us with tolerance and courteousy and who never gave us any trouble.

Whenever I felt I could, I would open the freezer and clandestinely drop my fart bombs. Then when customers came in to buy I would ask, with a smile, 'Does Mrs Ellis want an iced lolly today or an Eskimo pie? Are you having a sucker today, Mr. Pienaar?' In my mind I would add, 'Would you like to try the Coolie Poop flavour?' Over time I secretly produced and delivered hundreds of frozen farts to people who treated us without respect and never once was caught.

Those last few years in Troyeville were bad for all of us. We were living in dangerous times and I was keeping as far away as I could from people. When I was not at school or attending to customers in the shop, I was daydreaming on the koppies or disappearing into the secret world of my crawl space sanctuary from where I travelled far and wide through my books and Classic Comics.

In that period, it seems, I was marking time for something to happen and when it did, the move from this hateful suburb came not a day too soon.

6
CHANGING TIMES: SIX FOR THE BETTER – HALF DOZEN FOR THE WORSE

Inner City Street Kids

We were a family of eight when we left Troyeville that life altering winter of 1949 and moved into the two-bedroom, one-bathroom flat on the second floor of Jajbhai's Building on Market Street, a few paces west of Sauer Street, in Johannesburg's city centre. Space-wise we were still terribly cramped but for me, an impressionable 13-year old, this was an exciting place to live.

Our front balcony overlooked bustling Market Street with its constant hum of traffic and the clickety-clack of the pillar-box-red tramcars that careened past towards Newtown, Fordsburg, Mayfair and Langlaagte. From the relative quiet of our back balcony, we looked down on to a bright red courtyard kept shiny with regular applications of Sunbeam polish and elbow-grease. There was always a barely audible sound of soothing Indian music coming from one or other of the six floors and in the air hung an aromatic hint of cooking with exotic herbs and spices.

Half a block east, towards the city centre, on the corner of Sauer Street was the Johannesburg Public Library and Africana Museum. Inside the walls of this magnificent building non-white people could only visit as cleaners and night watchmen. Outside, however, the massive walls were regularly visited by anti-apartheid activists who, risking imprisonment used them as billboards to make political demands in big, black, angry letters:

RELEASE SISULU, DADOO, KOTANE!
DOWN WITH APARTHEID!

More and more these names had been appearing in the newspapers we sold at the Troyeville shop, usually in connection with organisations called the Transvaal Indian Congress, the South African Indian Congress or the African National Congress.

It seemed these people were in and out of jail a lot for marching or gathering somewhere illegally or saying something in public they should not have. I did not link their struggle with the struggle of my parents or my own battles in Troyeville. In any case I had no interest in such matters at the time. And why should I? In Ma's house Yusuf Dadoo's name had come up a few times during family talks about discrimination and passive resistance. Then someone would say that these Congress people were communist who would destroy Islam and confiscate private property and once that happened blacks would take over everything. At this point the conversation about 'politics' would dry up.

At home, Mummy and Daddy said nothing to us about the Congress movement and the subject didn't come up at school. So how important could it be?

Half a block west was Kort Street, a spirited place of spice shops and eating-houses that formed the eastern edge of Johannesburg's sprawling Asiatic bazaar. Black professionals, white liberals, communists and Congress activists, including people like Oliver Tambo and Nelson Mandela, came here to socialise and dine at the popular Kapitan's Café. This was the only good Indian restaurant in the city at the time that served people of all colours. You were welcome so long as you did not bring booze onto the premises and give the authorities an excuse to close the place down.

Towards the south end of tiny Kort Street was the International Club, which I heard in hushed tones, was established by members of the Communist Party. It was here that I met white people, socially, for the first time. Other than Sally van Rensburg, they were the first Europeans who talked to me with, what I understood later was, respect. It was also here that I saw my first play about race and experienced for the first time, in a very intense way, the power of the performing arts.

That first play was astonishing. There was no set. And *that* was the set. All the audience looked at was a pitch-black space and saw nothing. Then we heard two men talking to each other in the blackness, and still saw nothing. As they speak we realise that the clickety-clack we hear is the sound of a train in motion and that these are two homeless men – hoboes – in a railway boxcar heading nowhere. As the dialogue continues, the men recognise their common values, failures, hopes and aspirations and speak freely of them. Their common humanity binds them and they talk about friendship forever – brothers forever! The play ends when, at daylight, they see each other for the first time. One is black, the other is white. Will the bond of friendship they formed in the darkness be able to hold fast in the light? Will societal norms or their own social conditioning allow their friendship to endure?

My tears were for Friend Black and Friend White and for all the friendships, now and in the future, that would be stillborn because of ignorance and intolerance, as had happened to Sally, Simon, and me in Troyeville.

This was not Troyeville and I was thirteen, not eight. Our new friends welcomed us warmly into the community. Adam Limbada lived in the flat opposite us on the same floor. His family owned a shop on the corner of Pritchard and Diagonal Streets in Johannesburg's Asiatic Bazaar, diagonally opposite the Newtown Coloured School. The Limbadas specialised in the sale of Islamic literature. On display were beautiful copies of the Holy Quran, attractively framed rakams – holy texts in Arabic calligraphy – and a variety of religious artefacts from India and Arabia. I enjoyed accompanying Adam to the store on a Saturday morning when he had to help out. I spent the time browsing through the English-language newspapers from India and watching the colourful parade of people doing their weekly vegetable and spice shopping at the 'Indian market.' Even now, I remember the pleasant smell of agerbathi, the fragrant incense that filled that cool tranquil place with a faint smell of mysterious lands.

The city centre closed down after 1pm every Saturday and, until Monday morning, the empty buildings looked down silently over the deserted streets like brooding sentinels. The lovely Library Gardens were also virtually empty over the weekend and even though it was just half a block from our building, we couldn't play there. Mum and Dad had pointed out the signs that made things very clear: *Slegs Blankes – Whites Only.*

There were no koppies in this place. Nor was there a community centre or school programme in the neighbourhood that we could join. So, left to our own devices on weekends, Enver, Dooli and me – and our friends Adam Limbada and Essop Mayet – became adventurers on the rooftops and the new building construction sites in the area.

We had found a way to slide down the drainpipes on the outside walls of our building and onto the adjoining warehouse roof of L Suzman & Co. From the top of this large cigarette wholesaler, we had access to all the roofs between Market, Sauer, President and Kort streets. Secretly we would scrape together some eats and spend hours scrambling up over corrugated iron hills and down into concrete valley hideaways on the various roofs looking for a place to picnic. We would climb down into deserted yards and 'test-drive' the silent trucks that slept there. One time we found an open skylight but could find no way down into the warehouse. Because stealing never entered our minds we did not think this was trespassing that could get us arrested and sent to Tokai – that fearsome reform school for boys near Cape Town.

Our first adventure in a high-rise construction site was on nearby Fox street, where, for some strange reason, there were no mapoisas – watchmen. We spent one Sunday afternoon climbing up and down tall wooden ladders and half built concrete stairways between one dusty incomplete floor and another. When we reached the top – six to eight storeys up – Enver discovered a rope dangling from the centre of a long beam that had been laid across the 'canyon' high above what would be an inner courtyard.

We discovered that, holding onto the rope and taking a running leap, we could make a great swing, about 20 to 30 yards, from a two-storey high ledge on one side of the courtyard across to a ledge on the other side. I knew that if any of us could not swing hard enough to reach the other ledge we would be caught dangling in mid air. But I figured we could slide down the rope, gripping with our hands and feet, then let go and free-fall another fifteen or so feet into one of the piles of sand that dotted the courtyard floor.

Looking back, I can see the danger we may have placed ourselves in but, wow, what a time we had. Those pretty Library Gardens could never have been as much fun as that unfinished building.

Another Sunday we discovered the building site where Dooli nearly lost an eye. The place, on West Street, between Commissioner and Fox, was in the beginning stages of construction. Only the foundations had been excavated. The network of trenches, though soggy from a recent downpour, made for a super afternoon of trench warfare. This time there were about eight of us on this amazing battlefield ready to become war heroes. We all got filthy that day, crawling in the muddy ditches ambushing each other, taking each other prisoner and some of us being killed by the enemy, more than once, at the tops of our voices.

Then someone invented the mud hand grenade – sand and wet clay squeezed together. Soon clumps of earth were flying through the air and the good chaps were blowing up the bad ones. When Dooli screamed I knew he had been hit by a grenade. Then we realised that this was no play. A clay clump that contained chance stone fragments had landed with some force directly on his left eye and bits of sand and stone had lodged behind his eyelid between the skin and the pupil. Though he was in great pain, this brave soldier did not cry.

When he returned from the hospital, Dooli was bandaged up to look like a war hero. The operation to remove the sand and stone had taken a while and, for weeks after, Dooli proudly showed off the one side of his face as if it were a reddish-purplish-blue medal of honour.

Our rooftop adventures came to sudden end one day, because Enver and I foolishly allowed Dooli to follow us in the risky jump from the first floor balcony of our building onto to a parapet on the Suzman building next door. Dooli slipped and fell to the sidewalk, breaking both arms and suffering a concussion.

Labels, Boxes and Stereotyping

Moosa Matki, another new friend, introduced me to the Muslim boys who lived around the corner in a massive rundown tenement on President and Diagonal Streets. These fellows spent most Sundays playing boisterous games of cricket or football on the deserted streets and, because I was good at sports, I was quickly accepted into the crowd

My first fight in this neighbourhood was in Kort Street. It was a fair go, I won, and we shook hands and shared a bottle of SS Cola. Then it struck me – even in the heat of battle no one had called me coolie. This was incredible. In Troyeville, in every fight, that's all I heard; 'Moer die coolie! – Hit the coolie!'

Then a more profound realisation exploded in my head. I was not singled out as a coolie because here, in the Asiatic bazaar, we were all coolies. With that flash of realisation, I was introduced to the concept of 'group identity.' A pleasant, unfamiliar feeling of belonging enfolded me in a cloak of security I had never found in Troyeville and never felt in the Boarding School.

If only learning was always an agreeable experience. Unfortunately, some of our best lessons come to us in the most painful ways. I learned this truth when the feeling of closeness and belonging to a group, which I began enjoying, suddenly stuck in my throat and left a horrible taste in my mouth.

It was here, in the Asiatic bazaar, that I first became aware of the different Indian immigrant groups of Muslims from Gujarat and the importance they attached to these differences. My gang of weekend roof adventurers and street sportsmen thought of themselves not as South Africans or Indians, but first as Moslems and then as Surtees, Kanamias, Kholvidians, Miabhais, Alipurs or Koknees. We, the Carims, were Memons or, as we were often reminded, 'half-caste Memons'.

In jest or in spite there were snide put-downs for various groups. For example, Kanamias were stereotyped as ruffians and gangsters, Miabhais were lowly trades people and pottery makers, Kholvidians were preoccupied with the fairness of their skin, Koknees were dirty and Memons were money-grubbing liars. Now, instead of hearing nasty white boys chanting 'coolie poop no good' I heard Indian boys chant, in a kind of sing-song lilt, 'Memon ka bacha kabbi na bolê sucha – The children of Memons never tell the truth.'

These were my new buddies and so I bit my tongue, clenched my fists and decided to accept the teasing. But I did not stay friends with these fellows when the stereotyping became vicious and dangerous, as it did between these Muslim fellows and a Hindu family that had become very special to me.

On the ground floor of Jajbhai's building lived Manilal Daya, my genius friend. He was only two years my senior, but so much smarter that I always thought of him as 'much older'. Manilal was not what anyone would call a fun chap. He never came out with me and the other boys to play cricket or footie. He didn't join us on the roof scrambles and wouldn't come eat at our home. Instead, we would have long talks on the balcony about books he was reading or how to make Indian kites or other things, and I would have tea and bhajias – chilli bites – twice a week at his home, when this serious friend helped me with my school work.

I've always had trouble concentrating and studying because of my attention span problem or, as I learned later, what they call Attention Deficit Disorder. I did not get the extra help I needed at school and my parents were unable to assist. When Manilal realised this he invited me to do my homework with him. He was a patient fellow and a born coach, and he helped me enormously. Then one day our friendship and my free private tuition came to a terrible and painful end.

'My father says I can't be your friend anymore and you must stop coming to our flat.' The words were like heavyweight punches to my head. 'We are Hindus and you people hate Hindus,' he replied, when I pleaded why. Despite my urgent claims that I did not hate him or anyone, I could not change his mind, and when I knocked on the door the following day at the usual time Manilal told me grimly to go away and shut the door in my face. I was devastated. I realised later it was entirely my fault.

Without thinking, I had been drawn from a Sunday street game into joining the President Street Muslims in an impromptu march along Diagonal and Market streets related to a flare-up of violence between Muslims and Hindus in India that kept happening after India's recent partition and the establishment of the new state of Pakistan. The Muslim demonstration here on Diagonal Street was loud, ugly and clearly, anti-Hindu and half the shops in the area were Hindu owned. There we marched, me included, waving our fists and shouting 'Pakistan Zindabad! Hindustan Murdabad!'

I had inadvertently become a victim of unthinking 'groupthink', based on mindless group identity, which is often a precursor to mob action. And there, on the sidewalk, stood Manilal's father, watching me. And here I was, Mumdoo, his son's so-called friend – a boy who did homework in his house several times a week – shouting violent, hateful words against Hindus like himself and his wife and children.

I didn't understand what zindabad and murdabad meant, but I quickly understood, and bitterly so, was that I had lost a dear friend because of the same unthinking intolerance and hate that Sally, Simon and

I had experienced in Troyeville. I suddenly realised that some, if not all, of these boys were as ignorant and intolerant as Gavin and Frikkie although this time it was about religion not race. Manilal was to those Muslims in President Street what Simon and I were to most whites in Troyeville.

I couldn't bear the thought that South Africa had a box for Manilal and separate boxes for me and Sally and Simon and all the other children in South Africa. I squirmed at the thought that each box had a label that identified us as 'Hindu', 'Muslim', 'Christian', 'Black', 'Indian', 'Coloured', 'Chinese', 'White', and that we were all expected to remain imprisoned in the shadows of our own separate racial, religious and cultural containers.

In Troyeville this thing about identity was straightforward I thought. My tormentors were white, I was not and that was that. Here, things were more confusing. I was not black, not white, not entirely Indian and not entirely coloured. I was Muslim but could not identify with Muslims who discriminated against the gentle and kind Daya family.

After Manilal, I resolved, perhaps not consciously, that I would never generalise about people. I vowed that I would go it alone and march to a different drummer, rather than join any religious, political or social group that stereotyped entire sections of a community, put labels on them and self-righteously condemn them to separate segregated boxes.

I know, deep in my heart, that Simon Simelane a Xhosa boy and Sally van Rensburg, an Afrikaner girl, two Christians, had a lot to do with me, a Muslim, coming to this resolution, which was triggered by an Indian boy, Manilal Daya who was a Hindu.

7
JOURNEY TO ANOTHER WORLD

Our family fortunes ebbed and flowed like the South Atlantic tides at Sea Point and our personal experiences changed accordingly. One year we were attending Gold Street School, where many kids were so poor they depended on the school feeding scheme to stave off hunger. The next year Enver, Dooli and I were enrolled in Aitchison College, an elite school in Lahore, Pakistan, originally established by the British colonial regime for sons of nawabs, maharajas and senior British army officers. Here the principal was Mr Gwynne, who soon let us know that he was a direct descendant of Nell Gwynne, a renowned courtesan and mistress to King Charles II of England.

The journey from our ghetto in Johannesburg to this posh school in Lahore was an adventure in its own right – one that I will never forget.

The Pretty Girl, the Laughing Boy and the SS Karanja

'Pe, your Uncle Tar and me, we were deck passengers like those people down there when we left India and came to South Africa such a long time ago.'

It was December 1950 and we were standing at a railing on the steam ship, the SS Karanja that had departed Durban the day before. Daddy was pointing down to a deck where a number of families seemed happily spread out in the shade of a row of suspended lifeboats in what was an idyllic picnic scene. This was no picnic, Daddy explained. For 21 days these men, women, children and babies would not get to roll up their mats and cooking utensils and retire to a comfortable cabin. Instead, there would be days and nights when they would be exposed to the hot sun, stinging rain and wind and, though they would be allowed to seek shelter *under* the lifeboats, they would not be allowed to seek safety *in* any life boat if there was an emergency. Daddy also told us that there were life jackets for all cabin passengers but none for those that slept on deck.

A vision of a rain-swept deck 36 years earlier disturbed my thoughts. I visualised my father, uncle and grandfather huddled together and sheltering from the rain under the meagre protection of the lifeboats that were there for everyone's security but theirs.

I was 14 and my parents and Enver, Dooli and I were making the same trip my Grandfather, my Father and my Uncle Tar had made decades earlier – only now we were steaming in the opposite direction, north along the East African coast, as far as Mogadishu, then north-east across the Indian Ocean and the Arabian Sea to Karachi. The ship would then head south to Bombay. Three Johannesburg families were travelling together in a mutually supportive group – the five Carims, Aunty Amina Kotwal and her three sons Sonny, Khaled and Hilmi and several members of the Akhalwaya family.

This time the Carims were not deck passengers. We were travelling Intermediate Class, which was better than third, infinitely better than Deck, but not as good as first or second. Our cabin slept eight passengers in dormitory style on bunks. Hindus and Muslims were berthed in seperate cabins and the female section was on the opposite side of two parallel passageways with the laundry room, the bathrooms and the toilets between them.

There are few things more exciting for concrete-jungle street boys than clambering down steep stairwells and tiptoeing into mysterious hideaways that lurk everywhere in the bowels of a ship like the Karanja. Racing through the narrow passageways that seemed to run the full length of the ship and disappear far away into a dim lit twilight zone was thrilling beyond measure. Sonny, Enver and I were the oldest of this gaggle of children, and we were ordered to watch over the younger ones and keep them occupied. This was not difficult. Playing endless games of hide and seek and cowboys and crooks also gave us older fellows a chance to thoroughly explore the lower decks.

From time to time, I would get the urge to be on my own. Whenever a chance came, I would disappear up two or three flights of stairs, then along narrow passages and enter a world of beauty and wonder. This grand place – first class – was inhabited by what is today referred to in South Africa as the 'Previously Advantaged'. In retrospect I realise I never found the section of first class that was set aside for non-whites who were also 'Previously Advantaged'.

The decor in our Intermediate Class was of a dreary cream and bilious green. The metal walls, floors and stairways reverberated with the noise of running children, clanging doors and the dull thud of engines deep within the belly of the ship. The hushed world up above was one of gleaming rosewood panelling and long, deeply carpeted corridors, through which rang the silence of utter quiet. Occasionally corridors would open up into large bright spaces with brass table lamps and luxuriously deep sofa chairs. There would be people reading or having tea and tiny sandwiches while others leaned over a railing looking down onto a pool in which their children splashed and screamed in delight.

Each of these lounges was bigger than our entire living space at the back of the Troyeville Fruit Market, but I was not impressed. I saw no one reading Classic Comics in there. No one was having samoosas or bhajias with their tea. There was no running and jumping and laughing. What good, I wondered, would a dull place like that be to any boy?

My curiosity about the Deck Passengers grew by the hour. It seemed they had so much more freedom and fun than the passengers in intermediate class or those that sat in the sombre silence of the first class reading rooms. Each day I would look out for a particular group that included a boy and girl about my age. I hardly ever spotted them in the same place. They seemed to follow the warmth of the sun or the shade of the clouds. I saw them enjoying the morning rays one time, eating out of Tiffin pots under a canopy of flamboyant saris another time, and sheltering under the protection of the lifeboats yet another time.

It was clear that the deck passengers were all Indians – but were they Muslims on their way to Pakistan or Hindus enroute to India? If the pretty girl and the laughing boy were Hindus would it be okay for me to talk to them and ask them to come and play with us? What would the ship's officers say about deck passengers visiting the cabins? And what would be the reaction of the Muslim passengers? My experience with Manilal and the President Street mob still distressed me and so I hesitated to approach them. Not out of shyness, mind you, but from a fear of rejection. As a result, like Sally, Simon and Manilal, they too became like ships passing in the dark, their lights twinkling on the receding horizon and leaving only pleasant memories in my heart.

Madame Genghis Khan

In any event I had hesitated too long. By the time I was ready to approach those deck passengers with a brave hello I was forced into hiding in our cabin. For the last two days before docking in Karachi I remained out of sight for fear of being savaged by a lady who, I was convinced, was the terrifying reincarnation of Genghis Khan.

This is how it happened.

We were playing one of our endless games of hide and seek and Enver was chasing a group of the smaller boys down one passageway, while Khaled and Hilmi ran down another and disappeared breathlessly into the washroom area with me hot on their tails. On one side of this cavernous space was a bank of shower stalls. The entire opposite wall was occupied by a row of toilets. In a split second I saw that every door of every cubicle was ajar except one. Did these kids think I was stupid, I thought, smiling to myself as I advanced to scare the pants off them. Roaring in my most frightening voice, 'I've got you, you little horrors,' I rushed the door, jumped high, grabbed the top of the door frame, pulled myself up and looked over the top into the toilet.

Then I died.

We had run into the ladies ablution area and there, sitting on the toilet, doing her business, was the toughest, meanest old lady in the universe. She was the aggressive, self-appointed matriarch of all passengers who came into her orbit. Mummy, Aunty Amina and the other ladies were all intimidated by this terrifying Mongol warrior woman from Avenue Road, Fordsburg, and they did nothing to cross her. She had frightened all the kids into abject obedience from the moment we saw her. When she was in sight we stopped running or talking. We froze when she addressed us. If we saw her coming one way we hurried the other way, and if she was on the starboard of the ship, we made sure we were on the other 'board.'

Now I was staring straight into her face and she into mine. In this shocking rendezvous we were closer to each other than we had ever been – about three feet. In all eternity, I sub-consciously vowed we would never be this close again. She looked straight into my eyes and I knew, with the certainty of bladder-releasing fear, that she wanted me to drop back out of sight for just a moment so she could stand, pull up her lambi ijaar – the loose-fitting trousers Indian women wear – smooth down her dress and get her talons and fangs into my throat and neck.

I quickly dropped back out of sight, and for far longer than just a moment. For two excruciating days I hid and suffered from cabin fever as I trembled at the thought of her coming to find me. Thank heaven our paths never crossed again, but I only got my life back when we docked in Karachi port. Thanks to the turmoil and excitement of disembarking and the innate resilience of a teenager the fearsome spectre of Madame Genghis Khan faded into no more than a bizarre experience.

Chaos That Works

The systematic pandemonium at the Karachi docks was in startling contrast to the order and structure of life on a passenger liner. We South Africans watched in amazement as thousands of pieces of luggage spewed out of the belly of the Karanja and onto the backs of an army of porters. In a frenzy of disorder and linguistic babble of Urdu-English-Hindi-Sindhi, tons of baggage found its way, unerringly, to where hundreds of bewildered owners waited. We talked about it later: How on earth did a specific piece of luggage find its way to a specific owner in this mayhem? The same organised chaos reigned at Karachi railway station where we boarded the train for Lahore and at the other end when we arrived.

At the docks and at each train station we had to struggle with the porters who jostled each other to carry our suitcases and pettys – steel trunks. Partition between India and Pakistan had happened only three years earlier and there were still millions of displaced people on both sides of the border without homes and work, and all desperate for any means of making a living.

We watched in wonder at Lahore Station as one man loaded two of our largest trunks – the equivalent of two coffins – onto his back. Bent over double, he single-handedly balanced and carried the load from the teeming platform to the organised pandemonium that was the place of tongas – Pakistan's endemic horse-drawn carriages.

At each railway station we also had to force our way through swarms of beggars. We were appalled by the sight of a torso with a head that was supposed to be a child and horrified by the man whose arms were each the size of one of my fingers. I was baffled and angry when Daddy told me that many of these people considered these afflictions a moneymaking asset when there was no other way for them or their families to scrape out an income. It would take many years of working in countries like Nigeria, Ghana, Ethiopia and Somalia for me to come to grips with this awful truth.

My first ever ride in a tonga was in Lahore – from the train station to our hotel. I came to enjoy those two-wheeled, shaded, horse-drawn carts but, on this first ride, I was sick to my stomach all the way. I had been assigned to the luggage tonga and, because there was so much stuff, I sat on the front seat next to the tongawallah – the driver. That was a big mistake for a first-timer.

The sight and smell of fresh horse manure actually being produced inches from my face and under my nose, combined with the bobbing and swaying motion of this two-wheeled contraption moving rapidly in heavy traffic was disastrous. My breakfast and lunch raced each other straight up from my heaving stomach and were spewed forth over the side of the cart onto the smelly, dusty, manure strewn street.

I think learning to ride a tonga is like learning to eat with chopsticks. If you can persevere through the first one or two sessions, you will become forever proficient and comfortable with the new technology. By the time we went for tea with our future Principal, two days later, we had bobbed and swayed through hours of sightseeing by tonga and I and my stomach had become comfortable riding in these weird and wonderful carriages.

8
NEW HORIZONS

Perseverance Commands Success

As soon as we entered the gates of Aitchison College we left bedlam behind in a dusty brown haze, and entered 186 acres of peace and tranquillity. This was a hushed world of green manicured lawns, brilliant flowerbeds and scores of irrigation channels directing shimmering streams of water over thirsty beds and thirstier grass. Sometimes referred to as the Eton of Asia, Aitchison College, established in 1886, was named after the then governor of the Punjab, Sir Charles Umpherston Aitchison.

As our tongas clip-clopped down the driveway we passed attractive, u-shaped, sand-stone buildings in what a history teacher would later describe as Mughal-Gothic architecture. Each three-sided building enclosed a courtyard with a single massive evergreen shade tree and a verdant garden, all clearly visible from the roads through the open end of each 'u'. Three of these, we came to know, were student residences. Enver and Dooli would reside in Leslie Jones House, I was to be in Godley House and the third residence was Kelly House. Boys who lived with their families in and around Lahore were referred to as 'day boys' and were members of Jubilee House, which, obviously, did not have an on-campus residence.

Godley House

Godley House

Amir Zeb

Mr Goldstein

Assembly Hall

Right now we were heading for what was known simply as Assembly Hall, the main and most imposing building that also housed the administration offices.

Tea with Mr Gwynne was excruciatingly slow. The adults were talking about the history of the school and finalising financial and other formalities. As Mummy and Daddy had feared we were to be put back a year or two because of the higher standard of education here.

After tea we were taken on a tour of the school and of Godley House and Leslie Jones House, introduced to our house masters and shown the recreation halls, the libraries, and our accomodation. We were in awe when we saw the horses and the extensive stables, the swimming pool, the small hospital and the mosque. It was a thrill moving in the next day with our luggage and I remember no sadness when we hugged Mummy and Daddy goodbye after we were settled in. This was an exciting time for us. Enver and I were veterans of the infamous Boarding School and this looked like a great place in comparison – a piece of cake actually. And the two of us would take care of Dooli.

It was only after their tonga disappeared around a turn in the road on this first leg of their long journey back to South Africa via Delhi, Agra, Kathiawar and Bombay, that it dawned on me that none of us knew when we would see our parents and other siblings again.

Fun, Games and Discipline

Weekdays at Aitchison College were long and full. Lights out was 10 pm, which allowed for a good sleep and a 5am wake-up call by Hussein, our room attendant, a quick wash, a fast cup of tea and a brisk walk to the physical education location of the day. Our PE instructor, whom we respectfully addressed only as Major Sahib, which I gathered was due to his former rank in the Indian cavalry, tolerated no tardiness. He was notorious for handing out 'daggers' to anyone who was not ready to start PE at half past five exactly.

Stars and daggers was a system of reward and punishment that effectively kept us on our best behaviour. For good conduct a teacher or instructor may award you a 'star'. Unacceptable behaviour got you a 'dagger'.

The entire student body gathered each morning for Assembly. Any boy accumulating a surplus of five stars was invited to join the special Line of Honour for all to see and was hurrahed and roundly applauded as he stepped forward. The boys were so honoured and recognised as long as their stars out-numbered their daggers by five.

Conversely, a five-dagger surplus and you were made to stand in the line of dishonour where everyone could also see you. As these boys stepped forward the deliberate 'silence of shame' they heard must have been unnerving.

All the stars I ever got were for performance in sports, art classes and the debating society. My daggers came from poor effort and results in regular school work. Even in this posh school, during that first year, they could not help me with my attention span problem and I continued to switch off if a subject or teacher did not quickly capture my imagination. Each time I received a dagger in class, I made a super extra effort on the field, at the things I was good at, and soon earned a star, which then cancelled out the dagger.

Watching the boys in the lines of honour and dishonour day after day made an indelible impression on me. Stars and Daggers spoke loudly of cause and effect. Here the lesson was well learned that one's behaviour attracted visible rewards or punishment and that life was about living with the consequences of our choices. Because of the daggers I received, it took me nearly a year to accumulate a surplus of five stars before I was invited to the honour line. I was never in the line of dishonour and I learned never to be late for PE or for anything else that mattered.

In addition to regular callisthenics, PE varied according to the sporting events calendar. During the athletics season, for example, after the routine workout, we would break out into groups and train intensely in our chosen track or field event under the expert eye of Major Sahib and Mr Goldstein, who was the Director of Sports and also Master of Godley House. One morning each week we assembled at the stables and our instructor taught us the finer points of riding, which I took to fairly well. Then, during the run up to the Tent Pegging Tournament, training intensified. Riders selected for formal tent pegging trials practised hard to win a place on the college team.

If horseracing is the sport of kings then tent pegging is surely the sport of princes. Originally, tent pegging was essential training for the more dangerous tradition of the hunting of wild boars with lance on horse, as practised by the sons of India's Raj. It gradually became a sport in its own right.

Imagine you are on a frisky, well-trained horse. About 300 meters down the course in front of you is a small wooden tent peg with bright ribbons attached to it, hammered part way into the ground. Only the top half of it is protruding. Now imagine that you are thundering along at breakneck speed towards the peg, which you can barely see. Your feet are firm in the stirrups; you are leaning low in the saddle and to one side; your face is just above your knee and you are gripping a long steel-tipped lance with which you must pierce the peg and lift it clear from the ground.

The wind is in your face, the ground below is whizzing by in a blur, and suddenly the peg is rushing at you. It's the size of a hazel nut, then a walnut, suddenly an apple. At the time of impact it will be about the size of a man's hand. Too high and the lance will miss the peg completely. Too low and you could spear the ground and lose the lance, or even break it. If you hit well and lift high, the peg rockets up into the sky on the tip of the lance, its flamboyant ribbons dancing joyously in the air, heralding your success for all to see and applaud.

Even though I was nominated and practiced hard, I never made it to the tent pegging trials because of a bad fall from a skittish horse on a frosty Lahore morning that resulted in a lingering shoulder injury. I only began riding regularly again when Hajoo and I bought our first horse about eleven years later in Kano in Northern Nigeria.

Aitchison College was recognised throughout the region and in the UK for its high academic standards and sporting excellence. Mr Goldstein was a Cambridge Blue and a key driver of the sports and athletics programme. Under his guidance the school year was filled with sporting activities to suit all age groups, personalities and aptitudes from Kindergarten through Elementary, and Middle school to SC and HSC boys studying for Senior Cambridge and Higher Senior Cambridge.

My friends and close associates were all keen sports enthusiasts. Amir Zeb was my roommate. He was a Pathan prince and an heir to a princely state that was never conquered by the British. An asthmatic, Amir inspired the boys for participating enthusiastically in track, field and hockey, even though his breathing came very hard and required supreme effort each time.

Jehangir Khan had the handsome features of a Mongol horseman. He was a remarkable sportsman and the school champion swimmer. When most of us struggled to do thirty lengths in the pool, Jehangir easily did a hundred and would continue swimming long after we had showered and were sitting down to dinner.

'Hiya African buddy, move over so's I can sit next te ya.' The first time I ever heard a live American accent was when Jalil Alam pushed in next to me in the school auditorium during a science lecture. He was a day boy, a Pakistani with an American mother and he was born in the U.S. Jalil was the sort of fellow with whom one would would want to climb Mount Everest. He was confidant, on the brash side, and courageous. He caused a big stir when he appeared at the Godley House dining hall during dinner one evening and, in the presence of Mr Goldstein and some sixty bewildered boys, publicly called out the much bigger school bully and challenged him to a fair fight.

Zaheer-ud-Deen was my Bengali friend. He was my constant companion, perhaps because, like me, he did well on track and field and really badly in class. We motivated each other on the long, pre-dawn practice runs during the track season. I was uplifted decades later, when Raza Kuli Khan, an old boy visiting Pretoria, told me that Zaheer had done extremely well for himself and had risen to the rank of a Minister in the government of East Pakistan.

Students could elect to take part in cricket, field hockey, water and cycle polo and the numerous track and field events and, of course, tent pegging. Competition was keen and so each afternoon the playing fields, courts, tracks and the swimming pool teemed with sweaty boys eager to achieve a Star and perhaps be invited to try out for selection onto one of the school teams.

It was a great honour to represent the college in the regular games against Government College and the Forman Christian College. Occasionally teams would travel to Ghora Gali, near Murree, in the foothills of the Himalayas and compete against another great school, St Lawrence College. It was to this school where our family friends Hajoo and Rashid Garda of the prominent Garda family in Johannesburg would later send their sons Enver and Farouk.

'Perseverance Commands Success' was the Aitchison College motto. It was printed on the cover of all our books and I saw it so often I must have internalised it. By the time I left Aitchison I had won stars for coming second in the annual six-mile race, which I should have won but for an error in judgement, for being selected to try out for the cricket 'A' team and for Mr Goldstein selecting me as one of the boys he was personally grooming for inclusion in the Olympic tennis trials.

Considering the bad time I'd had with religious instruction in the Boarding School and other madressas back home, Islamic classes in Aitchison College captured my interest to a degree that surprised me. I enjoyed the enlightened balance between learning to read the Koran, memorising and reciting surats in Arabic and examining Islamic history and the socio, economic and political challenges that Prophet Mohamed faced in the Arabia of his time.

It was a revelation to think of our Prophet not just as a pious, religious figure, but also as a sage, a politically astute leader and a military strategist, and to hear of the events leading up to the Hijra – the migration into exile – from Mecca to Medina. I sat silently fascinated as classroom conversations took place about the battles of Badr and Trench, the unification of Arabia and the expansion of Islam until its influence stretched from India and Central Asia to Spain and from the Middle East, across North Africa to the Atlantic. I was enthralled to learn about the advances Islamic scholars had made in science, chemistry, astronomy and astrology while Europe lay stagnant in the Dark Ages.

From the beginning this school, this country and the people I met here had the capacity to shake up many of the unfounded ideas I had accumulated in fifteen years. It soon became apparent that Aitchisonians were being taught *how* to think, not just *what* to think.

When I told my classmates I was a Memon, what the devil is that, they asked. When I mentioned the other groups – Surtees, Kanamias, Kholvidians, Miabhais, Alipurs, Koknees – they were puzzled. 'I never heard of these people. Must be some of those Hindu tribes in Central India we converted to Islam during the time of our Mughal Emperors,' one boy asserted. 'In Pakistan Muslims are Pathans, Baluchis, Punjabis, Bengalis or Sindhis.'

In quick succession, other perplexing differences rattled the notions I had of how things were. There was my roommate, Amir Zeb: the first blonde Pathan and blue-eyed Indian I ever saw. I wondered how the Dominee in Troyeville and his flock would have acted had blonde Sally van Rensburg befriended a white, blonde, blue-eyed, Muslim prince who spoke Pashto and was a proud Pakistani.

Then there was the fact that no parent, student or governing body in this Muslim school in this Muslim country objected to Islamic history being taught by a white Christian American professor of Sociology or that the most popular House Master at the time was a loved and respected English Jew.

The first time the word coolie was used in my presence was when new furniture was being moved into some of the classrooms and I offered to help lift and carry. 'Not necessary,' a teacher said, 'the coolies will do it.' I flinched. A picture of Peter, Gavin and Porky flashed through my mind, and I restrained myself from questioning the teacher.

Later Amir explained that coolie was a word in India and China that describes an unskilled worker just as aya describes someone who takes care of children. 'You are obviously not a coolie and only ignorant people will call you one. Then, without wanting to embarrass me he embarrassed me: 'Didn't your school in South Africa have a dictionary? Was there nobody to explain?'

The truth is that Hajoo and I cannot recall a single time when any teacher, parent or student group ever used a dictionary, book or other tool to help children deal with the verbal abuse that was common in all South African communities: coolie, bushy, kaffir, mapla, charkie, yid, boerkie, pora, limey and gong. And so, when anyone called me coolie or bushy they got a bloody nose – or I did – and this was our style of conflict resolution.

The Foothills of the Himalayas

Lahore summers are long and awfully hot and the cost of flying Dooli, Enver and me to Johannesburg for the school holidays was too much for our parents. It was therefore arranged that we join nine other Aitchison boys at the Aitchison College Summer Camp in the foothills of the Himalayas, combined with a structured programme of academic tuition.

Early one morning twelve eager boys, two watchful teachers, a pile of luggage and our group leader, the beloved Mr Goldstein, were driven by tonga to the railway station. Excitement bubbled as we were shown to our compartments on the train that runs north-west between Lahore and Peshawar and across the frontier to Kabul in Afghanistan. At Rawalpindi, the then capital of Pakistan, we left the train and set off northwards, on a bumpy bus ride, up the Murree Road that led us into the clouds that cling to the western edges of the Pir Panjal Mountains. This is the same road that continues its climb to Muzaffarabad and then swings east to the trouble spots of Jammu and Kashmir. Before the day had ended we were unpacking our books and clothes in our summer holiday house, a spacious wood and stone villa that perched confidently on the side of a green mountain, about a mile along a winding road from the famous resort hill-station Murree.

The mountains and valleys here are magical places steeped in mist and mystery. During the train ride, we heard stories about Pakistan's Northwest Frontier Province that portrayed this region as a place of history, danger, intrigue and adventure.

For thousands of years, as Mr Goldstein told it, the people and culture of this region have been shaped by invading armies seeking the riches of India. After conquering an area, for example, Alexander the Great's generals would often marry the daughters of the defeated nobility to protect the peace and in this way influenced the culture and ethnic characteristics of the region. Conquerors came down through the Kush from Samarkand in the north or through the Khyber Pass from the west and through these valleys and over these mountains it was, that Islam came to India and the Mughal Empire was born.

Sara, Mother Superior and the Waiting Bench

With the chaperone-nun deliberately sitting close enough to hear everything we said it was a very strained conversation I was having with this extraordinary girl, Sara Meer, that special Sunday in the garden of the convent high up above Murree.

It was nothing like the laughter-filled bantering which groups of boys and girls had enjoyed the weekend before, at the Athletics Day competition at St Lawrence College in Ghora Ghali. Various schools that were at summer camp in the surrounding hills had come together for a day of fun. There had been a marching band from a nearby military college, a short tent-pegging exhibition and, as the athletic events followed, an air of festivity permeated the grounds.

The boys of Aitchison found themselves seated in the stands close to a group of lively girls and, in no time, we, the self-styled stallions of Lahore, were chatting with these lovely gazelles of the Himalayas. As I recall there was no co-education in Pakistan in the 50s and the occasions were extremely rare when girls and boys were able to meet. Not surprisingly, we took full advantage of the opportunity to socialise, talk and even flirt.

Sara was 16 and she challenged us boys with her vibrant personality, her confident wit and her laughing demeanour. She was obviously the leader of her group and her friends were all of a similar temperament – friendly and confident. All through this exceptional day, the boys from Aitchison and the girls from the convent enjoyed each others' company under the watchful eyes of a platoon of nuns and to the amusement of our own Mr Goldstein.

Sara's family were Karachi-based Christian Indians – now Pakistanis – and she was at summer camp at the convent, high up in the hills directly above the Aitchison summer residence. When she first told me her name it rhymed with tiara and I thought of a mountain princess. That we were all Moslems did not bother her or the other girls. On the contrary, that I was from Africa and made up stories about life on the 'dark continent,' actually added to my stock.

As the day came to an end and closing speeches were being made Sara looked straight at me and said, 'Come visit me at the convent next Saturday morning at ten – I dare you!'

This girl was a sparkler and I was fifteen and in a second I said, Yes, I'll see you at ten'. 'She asked you, not us,' was the response when I pleaded with the fellows to join me. 'Maybe you should ask Mr Goldstein for advice.'

As I huffed and puffed an hour up the narrow path to the convent, that Saturday morning, I appreciated Mr Goldstein's advice: 'It's no good planning unless you clearly understand what you are up against and plan accordingly,' he had said. 'First consider the obstacles and the pitfalls and anticipate what could go wrong. Then your planning will be more effective.'

Together with my mates, we considered the realities: the nuns might not allow a strange boy in to visit one of their girls. Wearing the full Aitchison College uniform might give me some credibility. Walking the long road through Murree and up the mountain would take hours and I would be dripping sweat by the time I reached the convent. And gifts would be good to take along.

With these thoughts in mind, I prepared well. I started out in good time and took the steep, heart pounding mountain path straight up. When I reached the driveway to the convent gate, a sweaty hour later, I ducked into the roadside bushes and put the first part of my plan into action.

I set the flowers down on the grass, opened the stuffed rucksack and removed all its contents, including the packet of English toffee. After a short rest, I stripped off my hiking wear, wiped off rivulets of perspiration with a towel and applied Mr Goldstein's cologne. I put on my grey pants, white shirt and tie, black socks and shoes and the navy blue blazer with its distinctive school badge. I gave my shoes a vigorous rub and brought up the shine. Then I stashed the rucksack in the bushes and, fresh as a daisy and cool as a cucumber, I approached the gate with the bunch of wild flowers in one hand, the toffees in the other, a knot in my stomach and a nervous smile on my face.

During the post-mortem that evening Mr Goldstein thought that my adventure had been a success because of good planning and because the Mother Superior, whom he knew personally, was the kind of person that admired a daring spirit, an open heart and youthful self-confidence.

The young nun who opened the gate had been taken aback when I told her I was 'expected.' She escorted me through a garden quadrangle to a vine-covered patio and asked me to sit on a long wooden bench and wait for the Mother Superior.

The nuns were obviously not expecting this unannounced visitor but it was clear that the girls were. Sara had asked me to come at ten and I was exactly on time. Almost immediately, girls began appearing from all parts of the stone courtyard, casually walking past close to where I sat, tittering and giving me looks and smiles. Then Sara walked briskly by, gave me a brilliant smile and disappeared around a corner.

The girls knew that the 'waiting bench', where I was sitting, was a place where heaven could turn to hell. And since anxiety and fear as you waited on the bench was the norm, the girls had all agreed to give me the emotional and spiritual backing they thought I would need.

When Mother Superior came and sat next to me on the bench, I was so nervous I did not hear what her first words were. Instead, I blindly put phase two of my plan into action. I turned slightly to make certain she could see the Aitchison College badge on my blazer. Then, in the longest sentence I think I have have ever spoken, I blurted out, 'Mother Superior, these flowers are for you, for your office, I am an Aitchison College boy, Mr Goldstein sends his regards and hopes that arrangements for the concert next week are progressing well, my name is Mohamed Carim, I am from South Africa, I have come to see Sara Meer, whom I met at the Sports Day at Ghora Ghali last week and she invited me to come see her at 10 am this morning and here I am'. Then I took a deep breath and looked down, not knowing what to expect, and noticed that my shoes were covered in dust again.

I must have said and done some of the right things because I was not asked to leave. I could see that Mother Superior's stern face had softened even as she laid down the law: 'Sara will be permitted to talk with you in the presence of a chaperone. You must leave in an hour. You are not to visit Sara again without my permission or the permission of her parents. We will see you Aitchison boys again at the concert next week. And please give my regards to Mr Goldstein.'

There was nothing aggressive or harsh about Mother Superior's manner. At that moment, I learned my first lesson about the effectiveness of well-controlled assertiveness, and the power of authority firmly and compassionately applied.

Sara was summoned to the 'waiting bench' and told that we could visit for a while but only in the garden quadrangle and only in sight of the chaperone and that I was to be shown to the gate at eleven thirty. 'Come find me and tell me about the invitation you extended to this boy,' she finished.

Soon as Mother Superior glided out of sight, Sara pulled me up from the bench and said, loud enough for the chaperone to hear: 'Let's walk in the garden where we can talk in private and have tea.' The nun really had been sitting too close. I was far more comfortable with her watching from a distance as we walked and talked in that very special quadrangle of Himalayan ferns and mountain flowers.

Sara and I talked our heads off, racing to get ahead of the minutes. She was delighted when I told her about my Mum and Dad – the Muslim Moor and the Alabaster Beauty from the convent – and told me about the disruption in her family when her Catholic sister brought home a Muslim boy that she eventually married.

The words we spoke raced each other to beat the clock and without stopping and hardly breathing, I told her about Sally and Simon and the pellet in my bum and the Dominee. She told me that Mother Superior was nothing like that and then we had tea with Scottish shortbread and Pakistani pakoras. Then she told me she would be a famous rider one day and had already won prizes for dressage. Then we walked among the ferns and I told her I would travel the world – then Mother Superior walked by on the path through the green quadrangle and smiled at us sweetly, and, what a coincidence, it was 11:30. Sara pushed the left over shortbread and pakoras into my hands and we talked faster as we walked as slowly as we could towards the gate. We promised to see each other next week at the concert and my mind was in a whirl as I waved goodbye and she waved back and I don't remember the climb back down to the house because I was walking on air. It was only when asked to return the rucksack did I realise that I had forgotten it in the bushes high up on the mountain top where heaven is a girl called Sara.

I never saw her again. She was not at the concert the following Saturday. She had been called away to Karachi to be with a brother who was hospitalised in a motor accident. As pleasant as the concert was, my spirits were down in my shoes. Soon we would be back in Lahore and none of the girls thought Sara would return to Murree before we left. I feared we had parted forever.

A lifetime later, I would be facilitating a strategic planning workshop for a government department in South Africa and a deputy director would ask for guidance. 'What do I say to a group of community organisers who demand resources from my directorate that we cannot provide and expect me to tell them each what they want to hear, which I cannot do?'

The advice I offered her that day came directly from the amazing experience I had near the Himalayas 45 years earlier, with a Housemaster, a Mother Superior and a girl named Sara: 'When you don't know how someone is going to react to what you say, and you don't know what to say to get the reaction you want, the best you can do is to say what you believe to be the truth.'

The last two weeks on the empty Aitchison campus before school recommenced were filled with thoughts of Murree. We, the-stay-behind-boys, rehashed the exciting times we had hiking and riding in the mountains, visiting the other schools summer-camping in the area and roller-skating in the cavernous hall in Murree town, with its highly polished wooden floors.

Sam's Restaurant, Murree

When no one was watching I would practise the dance steps I had learned from the band members who had befriended me at Sam's Restaurant where I had secretly spent time listening to music and learning to dance. In the beginning, I also thought a great deal about Sara Meer. Then, as we began to enjoy the glorious sights of Lahore – the Shalimar Gardens, the Lahore Fort and Museum and the Badshahi Mosque – with Mr Goldstein and his friends, thoughts of Sara and Murree began to take up less of my mind-space.

The school term started with a bang. Life was again a full programme of school, sports and homework. The daily tutorial sessions up in Murree had an effect I never thought possible. I began doing a lot better in Algebra and Geometry, and started enjoying English, Physics and Chemistry. To my surprise, I even did well in Maths and earned a star for an essay I wrote on our shipboard experience on the SS Karanja from Durban to Karachi that Mr Goldstein had suggested I write.

Enver and Dooli were also happier because of their time in Murree, except that Enver contracted malaria and turned an awful yellow from its effects. He was confined to the school hospital for four days and was under close medical supervision for weeks.

Then suddenly, within four months of returning from the summer holiday my brothers were called back home. It was a shock! I understood from Mum and Dad's letter that South Africa's currency had devalued and that they could now no longer afford Aitchison's fees.

The College made all the arrangements and one day my brothers were gone. Enver was thirteen. He was flying for the first time, and was responsible for the care of eleven-year-old Dooli. That night Jalil came to the Godley House rec room with a huge map. We spread it out on the table-tennis table and, with much rowdy debate a group of us plotted, argued and agreed the route my brothers would be travelling.

They would fly south-west from Lahore to Karachi and south-east to Bombay. Then they would head directly west across the Arabian Sea and south-west along the coasts of Oman and Yemen to Aden, where the Red Sea and the Gulf of Aden meet, near French Somaliland. From Aden, the flight-path would be directly south across British Somaliland, then over Ethiopia's Ogaden Desert, across Italian Somaliland and, as they approached the East-African coast at Mogadishu, they would veer south west to Kenya and disembark in Nairobi. They would connect with the South African Airways flight from London and fly over Tanganyika, Nyasaland and the two Rhodesias to Johannesburg.

That evening, thanks to Enver and Dooli's news-making journey and Jalil's map, we all received an action-learning geography lesson like no classroom ever offered. I was deeply touched when virtually all the boys voiced the hope that my brothers would somehow know that we were all flying with them in spirit.

For me schoolwork became easier as my attention span problem receded. The better I did at tennis, long distance running and sport in general, the more self-confident I became, and the better I did in the academic subjects. Things got even better when Mr Goldstein helped us understand the relationship between self-confidence and performance and showed us how to use success in one to trigger improvement in the other.

The Streets of Lahore

Before they left, Sundays at Aitchison were routinely filled with happy hours spent with Enver and Dooli playing table tennis in the Godley House rec room, swimming under the hot sun or walking under shady trees. A company of boys would visit the tuck shop and we would snack on salted pine nuts and sip fresh squeezed mango juice poured over shaved ice or suck on cold, flavoured sugarcane pieces. The three of us would sit quietly in the reading room going over letters from home. After my brothers returned to their residence – Lesley Jones House – I would disappear into the pages of my books and be carried off on wings of words to far off places until lights out.

The tranquillity of Sundays on campus was the perfect counter-balance to the buzz of the day before – my adventure filled Saturdays exploring Lahore's maze of narrow streets and lanes in the crowded, bustling Anarkali Bazaar.

To get leave on a weekend your homework assignments had to be up to date, you had to be dressed in full summer or winter school uniform, and you had to present yourself to your Housemaster for inspection at which time he would sign your chit granting you leave or not.

I remember my one and only rejection. My chit was written out as required, 'Please grant M. Carim leave from 9am to 6pm for shopping, exploring, lunch and cinema.' With his pen Mr Goldstein struck out the 9am, wrote in 1pm, and told me to spend the next four hours in the prep room completing my homework. The next time I saw Jalil, I asked him how Goldstein could know exactly what work I had not yet handed in. He laughed, 'These teachers are serious. What do you think they talk about in staff meetings?'

The following Monday there appeared on the Notice Board a message, in large print, reminding us all that off-campus leave was not an entitlement at Aitchison College. It was a privilege to be earned.

Saturday for me started on Friday evening. Hussein obligingly pressed my dark brown trousers, yellow shirt and off-white jacket. Early the next morning I was at one of the main gates collecting my rental bicycle from the cyclewala. Then, quickly back to the House to get a shower, dress in uniform and present myself for inspection. Once the leave chit was signed I would be on my way. Near the gate I stripped off my summer uniform – white shirt, khaki shorts and stockings and brown shoes – and changed into my smart Saturday outfit, which I had earlier stashed in the hedge near the gate. Much as I respected Mr Goldstein, I was definitely not going to the dance at the Railway Institute where I was sure to meet older girls and be dressed in shorts like a little boy.

It is said that in South Africa today public taxis carry more passengers than all other means of transport – motor cars, buses, trains, airplanes and ships – combined. The same may have applied to bicycles in Lahore in the fifties. There are no steep hills or valleys in this city on the desert and cycling was easy. So everyone owned or hired bicycles and they were everywhere – thousands on the roads and in the narrow lanes, thousands more parked in neat rows in front of shops, government buildings, restaurants and cinema houses.

I would leave my bike at a central location, pay the few annas to the attendant, collect a numbered tag and begin walking the streets. The first few hours were spent poking around in tiny mysterious shops, down little side streets, even though I had no money to buy things. It was easy to make conversation in broken Urdu and English with talkative craftsmen as they cheerfully created beautiful objects from bits of brass, leather or cloth. From a street-side cart or seated on a bench in a hole-in-the-wall eatery I would enjoy a brunch of warm naan and kebab – a thick, chewy, round flat bread and spiced mince balls with sweet and sour chutney or chicken-tikka – hot, grilled, chicken strips wrapped in a chapati – a thin, flat bread. All this would be washed down with iced freshly-squeezed juice or hot spiced tea. Then it was time to head for the show at one of the picture houses in the cinema district.

At home, Saturdays were bio days and there were four we could choose from – the Rio and Good Hope in Doornfontein and the Majestic and Lyric way across town in Fordsburg. In Lahore I could take my pick from some 20 cinemas, and they were all packed in one four-block area.

On Saturdays these movie houses were all jammed to the rafters with passionate enthusiasts.

When the hero saved the damsel in distress and broke into song as they rode off into the sunset the audience jumped to their feet and roared their approval. When the cruel king or the conniving mother-in-law appeared on the screen and the girl and boy again sang, this time in despair, the hoots and curses would have frightened the devil herself. I loved it all, applauded, and swore as loud as the loudest.

After the movie, it was usually roadside dessert – a syrupy pastry or fresh fruit juice over shaved ice then a slow bike ride to the matinée dance at the Railway Institute.

The first Saturday I walked into the Railway Institute I thanked Allah I was not wearing my short pants school uniform. The band was fast and loud and the place was packed. There were pretty girls everywhere, and I was as smartly dressed as any of the boys. I whispered a heartfelt thanks to Allah for guiding me to this place to meet these beautiful people.

In South Africa most Anglo-Indians would have been classified as non-whites. As a group, they looked like any collection of South Africans of Indian, coloured and Malay descent, with the same mix of ethnic features and complexions that ranged from nut brown to coffee macchiato to tan to alabaster. I felt an immediate kinship with them.

It's agonising when you're a teenager and you badly want to dance but you don't know anybody in the place and the first girl you ask says no and the next two also say no. And it's absolutely marvelous when the fourth, an older twenty-something woman, says yes and she is the most beautiful of all. The Aitchison motto had proven true again that afternoon, Perseverance Commands Success.

The chaps from the band at Sam's Restaurant in Murree – all Anglo Indians – had told me to practice and then go to the Saturday matine at Lahore's Railway Institute. They assured me that the girls there would dance with me and it was true – I was never refused again after that first time.

So there I was, all week, practising the fox trot in the shower stall, the toilet and anywhere no one could see me; one-two-together, one-two-together, one-two-together. When I tried it that first time on the floor at the RI with an experienced dance partner, it worked beautifully until we approached the end of the hall. Then I couldn't negotiate a turn. All I knew was this one step, which kept moving us forward in one direction. Ralph, at Sam's Restaurant, had said nothing about how to change direction and how to avoid crashing into someone or something.

Thank God for mature women. Before I realised what was happening my partner took momentary charge, did some magic, and steered us firmly away from a collision with the stage. Within seconds, we were dancing down the other side of the hall – one-two-together, one-two-together – as smooth as any other couple on the floor and she took charge without once making me feel foolish or bruising my ego. No one could have guessed that this was my first ever real dance experience.

And I had my first lesson in how to correct someone's mistake without humiliating the person.

As the weeks passed regulars in the cinema district began recognising and greeting me, and at the RI people would invite me to join their table. I enjoyed the company of one Anglo-Indian family in particular – a boy my age called Mark, his older sisters and their spouses. They reminded me so much of the Douglas family back home who once lived on Siemert Road in Doornfontein. James Douglas was in my class in Gold Street School, his sister Dawn was a class below us and their older sisters were married to two great chaps. The similarity between these two families was uncanny and, in a strange way, it was a connection to home that added a lot to my happiness.

Life at school in Pakistan had become a pleasure. I was excelling in athletics and tennis, my schoolwork was going well and my Saturdays in Lahore were as much fun as the times I had spent on the koppies in Troyeville with Simon and Sally. Even the cyclewallah was reserving the newer, smoother-riding bikes for me.

No matter how much I enjoyed myself on the streets of Lahore or on the dance floor at the Railway Institute, I was never late reporting back to Mr Goldstein or his appointed prefect. I was always dressed again in my school uniform and I was always back five minutes to the hour or earlier. In Godley House, boys were expected to be five minutes early to anything – otherwise one was considered late.

The Diamond Market

My last Saturday in Pakistan was spent in Lahore town with Jalil Alam and the officers of the Hira Mandi police station. It was the best way I knew how to deal with the pain and anger that engulfed me when I found out that I was being recalled to South Africa; that soon I would no longer be an Aitchisonian.

Three weeks earlier Mr Akram, the school Purser, and Mr Goldstein had given me the shocking news – I would be flying back to South Africa when the summer holidays began and would not be returning. As gentle as they tried to be, the news was devastating. I ran out of the office, out of the college grounds and along the canal crying uncontrollably. Did my parents not know how much I loved this school? Did they not want me to try out for the national tennis squad next year or sit for Higher Senior Cambridge examinations in a few years? How could they do this terrible thing to me? Would they change their minds if they knew how well I was now doing? I cried, raged, and swore that I would never forgive them!

The letter from home arrived a few days later. Mum and Dad did, indeed, know how well I was doing. They had been receiving regular reports of my progress. They said they knew this would be a hard thing for me to accept and pleaded that I understand that the family could simply no longer afford to keep even one of us at this expensive school. This time there was no mention of currency devaluation and, as the days passed, my pain subsided and I came to accept my misfortune.

That last Saturday in Lahore with Jalil Alam and the policemen was unusual, even for me. We met at the school main gate and cycled directly into the Walled City through the Roshni Gate. Here the narrow city streets got even narrower and the crowds thicker. We were on our way to the local police station in the red light district called Hira Mandi – the Diamond Market – where the Station Commander was helping to improve the quality of Jalil's personal collection of homing pigeons.

Earlier Jalil had explained that his father, the Commissioner of Police, championed the idea of police stations expanding the use of carrier pigeons to communicate with each other. In a place where telephones were scarce and hardly ever worked and where even bicycles could not get through the thick traffic quickly enough, Commissioner Alam sought ways to make more effective use of pigeons. This form of communication had worked extremely well for the Mughal Emperors, the British Raj and for the Allied Forces during World War II. The Hira Mandi station commander was a big supporter of the idea and he and Jalil had become carrier pigeon buddies and had been exchanging the best homers and breeders.

The prostitutes started teasing us as soon as we reached Hira Mandi. Pretty girls, some possibly not older than us, were standing in the doorways and leaning out of the windows of the wood frame houses lining the street. As we passed, they called out laughingly for everyone to hear: 'Does your mother know you are visiting Hira Mandi?' 'Come rest your bikes here you little boys and I will love you both for half price'. Jalil seemed used to this and had fun filling the gaps in my Punjabi: 'The one in blue says she will do both of us for the price of one and also do a Mujra dance for free'. The women were having a good time, Jalil was obviously enjoying the banter and I wasn't sure if I should laugh and join the fun or be embarrassed.

The roof of the police station was a perfect place to breed and train the flock of 50 or so pigeons from which Jalil would today receive another pair to take home. He and Captain Muzzafar spoke animatedly in a mixture of Urdu and Punjabi about pigeon things. Then they released the tumblers and the acrobatics these birds did high up in the sky was amazing to see. My interest in tumblers and homers waned, however, when I looked down into the street the way we had come and could see the girls we had passed earlier in their blue and yellow Punjabi suits.

Where did the laughing women come from I wondered. And what was a Mujra dance? I dared not ask. Jalil would surely tell the fellows at school and I would be ragged to death. So I kept quiet and would learn years later that Mujra was an ancient erotic dance form for which Hira Mandi was internationally famous.

No one would ever know the sick feeling I carried in my stomach that last week before school ended. We were all packed by the Thursday and on the Friday, after Jumma Masjid, the main Friday midday prayers, boys were embracing outside the mosque, saying fond farewells and departing: 'Have fun, salaams to your family, see you next term and bring photos'. I was the only one of my group not returning. My heart broke over and over again, each time I realised I would soon be flying out of Pakistan, probably never to see Aitchison College again or the streets of Lahore or the Pir Panjal Mountains.

South, South-West & South Again

The flight from Lahore to Karachi that Friday was the first time I had ever flown, and it was terrible. The cabin attendants were stiff, unsmiling men not the gorgeous hostesses that my mates said would be treating me like a prince. The turbulence was awful, and the DC-3 bobbed and swayed and shuddered far worse than any tonga. Sitting in the window seat over the wing, I saw flames spurting from the engine and, when I called urgently for the cabin-attendant and reported the danger, I was irritably told it was 'normal'. By the time they served us a snack in a box, I had thrown up into the stupid paper packet and messed my shoes.

I was flying the same route as Enver and Dooli – Lahore, Karachi, Bombay, Nairobi and Johannesburg. After Karachi, everything improved – the weather, the size of the planes and the food. And, thank heaven, the cabin crew were now attractive, smiling females.

The flight from Bombay was uneventful. Like an attentive Aitchisonian at a lecture, I listened carefully to the cabin crew and read through all the information cards on the Pakistan Airways DC-6 to Bombay and the Air India Lockheed Constellation to Nairobi. I checked the location of all the exits on both aircrafts and felt certain I would be able to assist the three young unaccompanied boys who were travelling to Mombasa for their holidays. They would be met at Nairobi airport by their parents and, here on the aeroplanes from Karachi, I was their self-appointed guardian.

We landed in Nairobi in Kenya and, chattering like happy monkeys, my little friends were whisked down a corridor in the airport terminal towards passport control, and the welcoming embraces of their parents no doubt. I was the lone passenger who went down another corridor to the transit lounge.

As I sat waiting for my South African Airways connection to Johannesburg pictures of my family came flashing onto the screen of my mind, and I wondered what life would be like back in Johannesburg.

9
BACK HOME

As I walked towards my seat on the South African Airways Constellation from Nairobi, I was bowled over by one of the stewardesses – a tall, stunning version of Sally van Rensburg, the Blonde Bomber from Troyeville. My breath caught in my throat and my heart raced as she took my carry-on bag and with a smile – just for me – stowed it above my seat in the last row in the very back near the toilets and the kitchen. Astonished by this apparition of Sally I gave no thought to any implications my seating allocation may have had.

I later learned that non-whites who flew South African Airways were seated starting from the very back rows. Whites were seated from the front. In this way, if the flight was not full, the races would never meet in the middle somewhere. If the flight was full, someone had a big problem indeed. I was told later that the crockery and cutlery, as well as the cloth headrest covers on the seats, were of different colours for easy identification, so they would never be mixed together and could be washed in separate facilities or disposed of in different containers.

But I knew nothing of all this and, I suppose, I should have been grateful that I did not have to fight a Gavin or a Frikkie for a seat to Johannesburg.

A story would be told during the Mandela presidency of a woman who objected strongy to being seated next to a black man on a flight to London. 'I'll take another flight if I have to,' she had stormed. Having explained, in vain, that the flight was full and that nothing could be done, the intimidated cabin attendant consulted the captain and returned with a message for both passengers: To the woman she said, 'If you wish to disembark the Captain suggests you do so immediately because we will soon be preparing for takeoff and there is no other seat available. We will be happy to assist you off,' she added sweetly.

Then she turned to the black passenger and said, 'The Captain apologises to you for this incident and asks that you kindly allow us to move you to First Class where you will be more comfortable. Please accept our apologies for this unpleasantness.'

35a Terrace Road, Fordsburg

For me, returning home to Johannesburg that cold July day in 1952 was no simple 'live-happily-ever-after' matter. For a long time I was beset by a muddled mix of conflicting emotions. Each time I heard my sisters sing or laugh and my brothers rollick together I would be pleased to be home. I was unhappy to see that the joie de vivre Mummy and Daddy had rediscovered on the SS Karanja and in Pakistan was lost again, replaced by insecurity and turmoil. Now I was caught, again, in the storms between the two people I loved most, same as had happened in Troyeville, and I avoided the stinging hailstones by finding shelter in the streets.

A sports item in the news, a picture of mountains or the sound of an aeroplane overhead and memories would flood my mind. I would see again the fields of Aitchison College, the streets of Lahore and Murree and the faces of Sara Meer, Mr Goldstein and my school mates and my spirits would drop into my shoes. Time would heal the pain and thoughts of Aitchison would fade, I was told, but that never happened. For decades, a lump would form in my throat or a smile play on my lips as I remembered a game, a word or an adventure. Then one day, more than a half century later, the phone rang and a voice from the past opened a floodgate of memories and longing, and and I was right back in Aitchison College again.

INTERLUDE

Raza Kuli Khan Khattak

It was August 2005. Hajoo and I were wondering how we would spend our 48th wedding anniversary when the Police College in Pretoria called: 'Are you Mohamed Ahmed Carim?' Yes, I answered. 'Were you a student at Aitchison College in Lahore, Pakistan in 1952?' 'Yes,' I answered again, bewildered at the questions. 'Please hold'. Then the voice came on: 'Hello, Carim, this is Raza Kuli Khan Khattak; we were together in Aitchison College when we were teenagers.'

Suddenly I was transported back to cycle polo, tent pegging, Olympic tennis trials and misty mountains. Out of the blue came a picture of a convent high up above Murree and girls in bright Punjabi suits. I heard again the shouts of boys on playing fields and heard the laughter of the beautiful people at Lahore's Railway Institute. But, although I clearly remembered the name Raza Kuli Khan the decades had dimmed the face.

South Africa was hosting an international tent-pegging tournament under the auspices of the South African Police College Riding Academy with teams from New Zealand, Italy, the UK, South Africa, Kenya and Namibia participating, and Raza was managing the Pakistan team. 'Would you and Mrs Carim please come to the Tournament as special guests of Team Pakistan,' Raza was urging, 'or at least to the final practice day? The boys will be very pleased to meet an Aitchison old boy from South Africa and it would be so very good to see you again.'

Almost every boy on the Pakistan team was an Aitchisonian, and, as Raza formally presented them to Hajoo and me, we could see they were pleased that an old boy of a half century ago would come out to show support.

Success in polo and tent pegging is, in large measure, about synchronised energy between horse and rider. It's this synergy that makes the difference between winning and losing, and it's important that the two spend time together and become comfortable with each other. While the riders were introducing themselves to their allotted horses, saddling up and getting ready for their final practice runs, Raza talked to us about the college and about our former teachers and school mates.

We took to Raza immediately. He was a gentleman of the old-school, erudite and urbane and a sensitive host who made Hajoo very comfortable by making a point to include her in the conversation. The next few hours of tent pegging practice were, for Hajoo, a series of astonishing revelations, for me an exciting memory jogger and for us both an extraordinary way of spending the first day of September 2005, our 48th wedding anniversary.

Raza was a Pathan – a Khan of the Khattak clan – and a successful businessman and industrialist. For years he had been directing the affairs of his family's vast business interests, based in Peshawar. He had also kept in close touch with Aitchison College and, as I recall, sat on its board of advisors or governors. Now he was leading the team to this tournament.

As Raza spoke, I was startled at the things I had forgotten and pleased as punch as I watched my stock rise in Hajoo's estimation. He would say to Hajoo something like, 'Did your husband tell you that Mr Goldstein, our House Master and the college sports director, was grooming him to try out for Pakistan's Olympic tennis trials?' Or to me, 'It's a pity you did not return to the tent pegging training after your accident. We all thought you would have done well and possibly make the team.'

As much as it is an adrenalin rush to actually ride oneself, it is also a great thrill just watching tent pegging in action. This was the final practice morning in Pretoria and there was a buzz in the air. The crowd was small but enthusiastic and the riders – a mix of boys and girls, smartly fitted out in full riding habit – were flushed with the excitement of meeting counterparts from around the world.

Each time the peg was lanced the roar of approval from the small group of supporters reminded me of Lahore 50 years before. I was then the same age as the younger of these Pakistani riders and felt again the immense power of the horse between my thighs and relived the thrill of the ride. Hajoo revelled in the thunder of hooves on sod and the rapid and precise action of horse and rider. She was visibly animated by the unusual sights and sounds of this equestrian event.

We drove back to Johannesburg in a state of gloom because we would not be able to spend more time with Raza and the boys. Team Pakistan would be caught up in the tournament, attend a formal dinner and awards ceremony and visit a game reserve to all of which we were invited, but could not attend.

As we embraced at the airport the following week Raza and I expressed brave hopes of seeing each other again in Johannesburg or Peshawar even though we both knew it was unlikely that we would see each other again in this life time. But, in this small world, who really knows?

After Lahore settling back into life at home, in the early 1950s was confusing and bitter. I was angry with my parents for sending us on an adventure with so much promise then ending it so suddenly. Anger would be overcome by guilt for not remembering how generous Mum and Dad had always been. Surely, they had done what they did only because they could not do otherwise.

Guilt would be followed by sympathy. Like Sisyphus, they repeatedly pushed the boulder high up the side of the mountain in Cape Town and then again in Troyeville, only to see it roll back down each time. In Jajbhai's Building and now again in Fordsburg, they were toiling up steep slopes to make life good for us but the odds were against them. Their endless battle was choking the fun out of their lives and turning their laughter to bleakness and I was incapable of helping bring back the joy.

We had lived here in Terrace Road a short while before our voyage to Pakistan in December 1950 and, in that time I had made some friends and learned how to handle myself in this tough new neighbourhood. Here, now, my life would be as different from Aitchison College as tent pegging is to street football or Punjabi is to kitchen Afrikaans and, in terms of the quality of the education at our local schools, as sugar is to shit.

At the first opportunity, I got out of the house and connected with my friends Yusuf Asvat, Solly Essop, Enver Miller and Ronnie Felix who all lived nearby. Soon we were sprawled out in Sol's room talking about anything and everything and laughing a lot. By the time I went home late that night the chaps had taught me their new passion – chess – and I had been brought up to date on matters of importance to us all.

Football

The Pioneer Rangers, our local football club, had become a touring team while I was away. This Sunday there was a game in the Benoni location and I could play if I wanted to.

We were an informal 'pick up' team and like most touring teams not affiliated to the race-based Indian, coloured or African football leagues. This meant that each Friday Issy Daniels, the club's driving force, would, say to us something like: 'The fellows in Rustenburg want to kick ball with us on Sunday at one o'clock. Abie's truck can carry fifteen and he wants seven pounds roundtrip so its ten shillings a head plus the two shillings for the club kitty. We leave at ten sharp.'

Our job, as core members, was to 'pick up' anyone who wanted to play or just join us for an inexpensive trip to see country towns we would not otherwise visit and meet people who were usually friendly and generous.

If we were playing against the sons of relatively affluent small town shopkeepers in a rural Asiatic bazaar win, lose or draw we would be treated to a super curry lunch. Few of the chaps ever got such luxurious meals at home and the twelve shillings we paid for the trip could never buy the biryanis, samoosas, kebabs and other treats anywhere. If we were playing in a coloured township, the catering would be more modest but there would be music, dancing, beer and lots of girls – usually the local hockey or netball teams – to help entertain us big city boys.

Make no mistake. These pick up games were no Mickey Mouse affairs. When we played the strong Evaton team, for example, we played a man short and still won. Yusuf and I had 'picked up' the Gilmour brothers from Coronationville – a coloured township west of the city. Boy Gilmour once captained the Coloured Football Association's South African eleven. His younger brother Willy Gilmour, popularly known as 'Willietjies' – Little Wheels – played on the coloured national team for several years. Donny, the youngest Gilmour boy would have joined us but he was doing more important things: he had been recruited by a Spanish team and was playing professional soccer in Europe.

Boy and Willie Gilmour decided, at the start, to lay back and allow the rest of us to shine. They did this brilliantly by turning the football into a game of chess. Through tightly controlled dribbling and lightning short-pass combinations, they dominated possession of the ball and all the while drawing the opposition away from their defensive positions. Then, when one of us was in striking position, they would make a magical through-pass that set us up to score. With their mastery of the tight game, these brothers galvanised us into playing a match that got us invitations to play serious games from near and far.

On long trips to places like Kimberley or Mafeking we would leave early Saturday morning, play one game late the same afternoon, party into the night, play another game Sunday morning and leave for home after lunch. We slept wherever there was space: in the staff quarters of a large general store, on the floor of a school class room, in a warehouse filled with bags of sugar, flour and rice. Sometimes each one of us was taken home by our opposite number and warmly received by their families.

But the law kept us away from the African teams in the South Western Township of Orlando, Jabavu, Moroka and White City where we could learn really good football. It was illegal for non-residents to enter an African location without a police permit, especially these political hotspots that later became known as So-We-To – Soweto. Large signs on the access roads screamed messages forbidding entry.

Later I would join Father Sigamoney's team, Vredons, play in the Transvaal League, train extremenly hard, and even be selected to try out for the provincial Indian Association team.

Vredons Football Team: Reverend Sigamoney, centre, me front left

I've often wondered what my football mates would have said, if anyone had told them that one day I would co-ordinate a 12-day tour through the Middle East of Edson Arantes do Nascimento, the greatest football player in the history of the game, better known as Pele – the Black Pearl. I suspect the response would have been: 'Voetsak man!' – 'Get out of here!' 'Never in a million years.'

With Pele Istanbul airport

Pele with Hajoo and Sandy Albright

The fact is that Hajoo and I, and our sons Xavier and Zane got to spend quality time with Pele, his coach Julio Mazzei and his business manager Senor Xisto. We were living in Beirut at the time and I was the Business Promotion Development Manager for Pepsi-Cola International's Middle East and Africa Division.

But that's another story, for another time.

The Gestapo, Gangsters & Marshall Square

Things weren't safe on the streets when I returned from Pakistan, and violence was top of everyone's mind in Fordsburg, Fietas and the outlying townships. Stretched out in Sol's room, I learned that the Time Square Boys in Fietas had become the most dangerous gang west of the city centre. They were now marauding in Fordsburg, were still clashing with the Kajala Boys and were now being challenged by the Les Harvey Boys – a new alliance of tough guys from Fordsburg, Malay Camp, Bekker Street and Fox Street. 'We must tread carefully, chaps,' Sol said darkly, 'and be ready for anything.'

As it happened, when Yusuf and I were attacked and he was stabbed in the head, the violence came from an unexpected quarter and had been triggered by an incident that had taken place in the notorious Marshall Square police station weeks earlier.

It's a bizarre story, which was triggered by the launching of Uncle Joe Kajee's International Dance Club – for international read multiracial – which was far ahead of its time and caused us much grief.

The trouble began on the Saturday night when our group was attending a dull Bridge Association fund raiser dance in Delvers Street in the city centre. Someone suggested that some of us go check out the white band playing at Uncle Joe's new club on the corner of Avenue and Mint Roads in Fordsburg. None of us had ever heard a white band play live, and, if they were as good as peope said, we should come back and fetch the others.

As Basil, Ginger, Yusuf and I lined up in front of the ticket office we were captivated by the marvelous big band sounds that came pulsating out of the club and were oblivious to what was happening behind us. Suddenly without warning we, and the people ahead of us in the line, were violently pushed, en masse, from behind, by a phalanx of police. As we stumbled or fell through the double doors into the the club, one of the cops yelled into a bull-horn: 'This is an illegal gathering. You are all under arrest! You will be taken to Marshall Square and formally charged. Move out quickly – Now! Now! Now!'

Before we knew it, weekend revellers of all colours were being pushed and prodded down the stairs by armed, baton-wielding police and forced into trucks, vans and squad cars. The shock was stupefying. As I screamed about the Gestapo-type country we were living in one of the policemen punched me hard in the mouth. Then he slapped handcuffs on my wrists and snapped them closed so tightly that I writhed in agony the twenty minutes to Marshall Square in Ferreirastown.

By the time we were herded into the charge office, both my wrists were badly swollen. The pain was terrible until the cops removed the handcuffs. Like us, many people had some cash but not enough to pay the three pounds admission of guilt and get released. So I went around saying to people: 'If you koozat with us – pool your money with us – two of us will go find the cash to get you and our friends released.'

Four couples trusted us with what cash they had. But two tough looking fellows from Albertsville angrily opposed this idea. They made a fuss about us all sticking together, not admitting guilt, and going to court instead. We ignored them.

Soon Yusuf and I were bumming a ride back to Mint Road where we had left the borrowed car. Then we raced back across town to the dance in Delvers Street. We needed thirty pounds to release Basil, Ginger and the four couples who had trusted us. This was a large sum, but it didn't take long to raise. Soon as we explained things people gave angrily and generously and soon we were racing back to Marshall Square with enough cash to release eighteen people instead of just ten.

The two bruisers from Albertsville were still loudly insisting that no fine be paid, but when they heard we had extra money they shoved and pushed in front of the others and virtually demanded we pay to have them released. Again, we ignored them, but one of the ladies who had koozated with us gave them a tongue lashing: 'Youse got a bleddy cheek, man. Youse don't wanna koozat, youse talk rubbish about going to court, now youse expect these manne to help you out, voetsak man – get out of here !'

The violence happened a few weeks later and it was so fast neither of us saw it coming. Yusuf and I were standing in front of the Majestic bio on Central Road looking at the forthcoming attractions on the posters. Suddenly, out of nowhere, one of the toughs from that night at Marshall Square was lunging at me, swinging a screwdriver. We all agreed afterwards I could have been killed had I not ducked as low and as fast as I did. Then he went for Yusuf as two of his mates grabbed and immobilised me. It was like watching a movie in slow motion. Yusuf slipping, the attacker swinging the screwdriver at him and also slipping, the two of them falling in a heap like wrestlers, the guy coming to his feet, Yusuf also coming to his feet a little after, and the guy swinging at Yusuf's head and then, suddenly, a bright red gush of blood as the fellow continues swinging and Yusuf miraculously deflects the blows and suddenly I'm screaming: 'Stop him, you bastards, he's going to kill him,' and suddenly its over. My captors had let go of me, grabbed their mate and dragged him away to a nearby car, as I helped Yusuf stumble away in the opposite direction.

We were never sure why that guy attacked us so violently. 'That woman who shouted at them in front of everyone: you don't do that to guys like the Desmond brothers,' Yusuf said. 'They must have thought the big mouth lady was one of us,' Basil added. Brian and Boet Desmond were feared in Albertsville we learned later. Had we helped release them from Marshall Square, we would have enjoyed their protection in the area they controlled. Instead, Albertsville and Sophiatpown had now become no-go places for us.

We finally put this whole thing behind us when Sol teased Yusuf, 'Ag man, it wasn't so bad. Flesh wounds bleed like hell and they all look worse than they really are. If those guys were really out to get you manne, they would have come with knives and guns – not scratch around in the car for a screwdriver. Only seven stitches? Shit man, you lucky you not dead. '

Struggling With the Struggle

Before I left for Pakistan there had been little interest shown in politics by my family and friends. I remember no conversations about liberation; there was no reading of progressive publications apart from the odd Spark one of us was handed in the street, and I don't recall any of us attending anti-apartheid meetings.

Now I was surprised by the interest being shown in the Defiance Campaign that had been launched in June 1952 – a few weeks before I returned from Pakistan. 'Don't talk shit man, this was not a sudden thing,' Sol was saying. 'It must have taken a lot to plan that meeting we went to. It was the first time Africans, coloureds, whites and Indians joined together like this.'

I learned that the mass meeting they had attended on the Red Square in Fordsburg, less than a block from our house, was just one of many that had taken place around the country earlier in the year, on April 6th. People had marched in their thousands to each venue, leaders had called for 10,000 volunteers to defy all unjust laws, and on June 26 the first group of volunteers were arrested, including the new head of the ANC Youth League and volunteer-in-chief – a rising politico by the name of Nelson Mandela.

Across the country the pattern of defiance was the same. Nana Sita, for example, a veteran of Gandhi's passive resistance days, led a group that tried to enter Boksburg's black township near Johannesburg without permits. They were met by heavily armed police, refused orders to turn back, were arrested, and without resistance, taken away and locked up. In court they refused to recognise the authority of the magistrate, were sentenced to jail or a fine, which they refused to pay, and chose instead to do the time. Later the nation learned that some 8,500 volunteers were imprisoned, most receiving sentences much harsher than what the statutes called for.

The argument in Sol's room that day was about my friends mustering up the courage to volunteer to go to prison and then being told to attend political education classes instead. As usual, Sol clarified things: 'I didn't hear anything about age limits,' he was saying, 'it's just that Congress didn't want youngsters to be arrested without some understanding of the politics of the defiance programme. Many people got a few weeks when they thought the sentence would be only a few days'.

My friends didn't fear taking chances with the police and were willing to paint slogans on walls, distribute pamphlets and sell anti-apartheid publications, but they didn't like the idea of political education classes. 'Too much like blerry school'!

It was not clear who was behind these classes – Congress or the Communist Party or both – in any case, for some of us, they were dreary events. As one fellow complained, 'I thought maybe they could help me go on a training course so I can get a job, but they just go on and on about all kinds of things I never heard about. Do you manne know what is something called dialectical materialism?'

Later I attended a few of these semi-secret lectures myself at the madressa room on Mint Road in Fordsburg, opposite the Kacholi Mansions.

The sessions were indeed tedious. Though the struggle obviously had great relevance to the lives of ghetto teenagers, these lectures did not convey this in a way that was meaningful to young, unemployed school dropouts from troubled homes. I think the facilitators were tactically misguided in allowing heavy Marxist theory to overshadow straightforward bread-and-butter issues.

If the objective of political education was to stimulate lateral thinking, promote dialogue, encourage a level of self discovery and develop politically informed people, these 'teachers,' in Fordsburg, in the fifties, failed miserably with me, my friends and many other young working people.

INTERLUDE

How Best To Support the Struggle

As time passed, I would place a high value on the struggle for liberation in South Africa but, rightly or wrongly, I would always place a higher value on family life and the safety and security of my wife and children. I chose to support the struggle rather than be a militant in it. And I never apologised for that.

It was in 1973, in Addis Ababa, that the late Oliver R. Tambo, then President of the ANC, sensed our desire to do more for the struggle and explained how Hajoo and I could increase the value of our contribution in ways that we were best suited for and with which we were more comfortable.

O.R., as he was affectionbately called, was in Addis with a delegation to address the Organisation for African Unity and launch the ANC's campaign: 'The Decade for the Release of Political Prisoners in South Africa'. Hajoo and I helped the group with transport, drove them around, helped sort out bungled hotel room reservations and were invited to join the delegation at the official launch at OAU headquarters. During visits to our home O.R. explained how we could do more qualitative work for the movement.

'Don't join the ANC,' he advised, 'your names will quickly appear on some Bureau of State Security list in South Africa and you could be in danger. Because of the presence of the OAU, the Economic Commission for Africa and other UN agencies there are more embassies located here in Addis than in any city in the region. We need someone here who can put us in touch with key officials that we can talk to informally, ex-officio. But whatever you do,' he cautioned 'don't risk losing your job. You won't be much help to the struggle without it.'

Later we had other houseguests. Alfred Nzo, then Secretary-General of the ANC, passed though Addis and talked to us about securing educational scholarships for ANC youth, and Uncle Reg September, Chief Representative of the ANC in the UK, suggested we find ways to help strengthen local anti-apartheid support groups.

In the years that followed, without ever joining the ANC, that's what Hajoo and I did.

Hajoo organised a lunch where Alfred Nzo was introduced to our close friend Wilbur Jones, who was head of the African-American Institute's East Africa Region based in Addis Ababa, and who operated a significant scholarship programme. When I reminded Nzo of the rumour that the AAI was a CIA funded organisation, he responded in his usual quiet manner: 'The ANC is aware of these allegations. We will manage the situation accordingly. Please arrange the meeting.'

At the time of this writing, I contacted friend Wilbur in New York and asked if he remembered how many scholarships he and Nzo arranged in Addis Ababa in 1973. 'I remember meeting Alfred Nzo in your house twice – once with Oliver Tambo. I remember talking to them about the AAI scholarship programme, but I don't remember precisely what came of our discusssions all those years ago.'

By day I worked for Pepsi-Cola International in Africa, based in Addis Ababa and Athens; in the Middle East based in Beirut and Dubai; in Canada based in Toronto. After hours, with Hajoo's indispensible backup, we did what we could to help strengthen the organisational effectiveness of support groups wherever I travelled.

Uncle Reg had put us in touch with Barry Fineberg and Ramini Naidoo of the International Defense & Aid Fund of South Africa (IDAFSA) in London who provided us with an excellent anti-apartheid presentation package. I remember going to Islington to collect the slide show and our first batch of handout literature and was taken aback to learn that Ramini, because of the serious threat of danger from South Africa's Bureau of State Security, was obliged to sit and work behind bullet-proof glass in a shop on a busy London street. And I remembered O.R.'s concern about the threat of BOSS operatives in Addis Ababa.

Armed with the anti-apartheid slide show and support literature from IDAFSA I addressed church groups, Rotary clubs, trade unions, schools, teacher associations and every anti-apartheid group I could reach. Many years later, as Executive Director of the Nelson Mandela Fund in Canada, IDAFSA would supply us with material, for publicity purposes, including photos of a meeting between OR and the recently released Nelson Mandela.

Attempting to fix Oliver Tambo's passport problem was probably the most important task Hajoo and I undertook.

In 1973, O.R. was travelling on an Algerian passport which contained 25 pages and was valid for three years. Because of his hectic international travel schedule all the pages were filled with immigration stamps long before the passport itself expired. O.R. was then effectively 'grounded' until he could get a new book, and since these were ex-officio passports, issued under 'special circumstances', the hassle to get a new document often took 'forever.'

At that time, I was also travelling on an Algerian passport with the same 3-year validity – but mine had fifty pages.

In 1968, presumably because they thought I was an ANC militant or something, the authorities in Pretoria decided not to renew our South African passports. Hajoo, Xavier, Zane and I began travelling on temporary Certificates of Identity issued by Ghana's Immigration Authority in Accra. Then, after we relocated to Addis Ababa, we applied for more permanent UN refugee passports from the United Nations High Commission for Refugees.

Months later, when our Algerian friend Ambassador Mohamed Ahmed Sahnoun – Deputy Secretary-General of the OAU – learned that we still had no refugee passports he enquired on our behalf and made a startling offer: 'The UN High Commision is swamped with refugee applications and cannot cope. Because you have jobs and an income, you are considered "settled refugees" and therefore not priority cases.

Forget about them. I will clear things with the ANC first and arrange for the Algerian ministry to issue you with four special passports. And Mac, because you travel extensively, I'll arrange for your passport to have fifty pages. You'll have the passports within two weeks.'

When O.R. heard this, he wasted no time: 'Please see if you can arrange for senior ANC personnel to be granted 50-page passports. Comrade Nzo or someone else will be in touch with you in this regard. Can you manage this?'

Trying to get 50-page passports for the President of the ANC and other senior ANC officials meant that Hajoo and I had to further strengthen our relations with our Algerian contacts. This meant a series of dinner parties that Hajoo organised and meetings that I attendend, all of which would culminate in an 'ex-officio' gathering between senior Algerian officials and Secretary-General Alfred Nzo.

'You have done well. Thank you very much.' We were dropping Nzo off at his hotel after his meeting at our house with an Algerian delegation that included Ambassadors Sahnoun and Ben Hassine and Farouk Lamini from the Foreign Ministry in Algiers. Mr Nzo shared no further information.

Protocol in matters like this requires that facilitators like us bring the parties together, make them comfortable and allow them complete privacy, with no questions asked afterwards. Hajoo and I never knew how many 50-page passports were issued to leaders of our liberation struggle – if any.

10
DROP – OUTS

By the time I returned from Pakistan the last of my friends, some as young as fifteen, had dropped out of school and were apprenticing in the furniture trade as carpenters, cabinet makers, upholsterers or French polishers and my best friend, Yusuf Asvat, was driving trucks for various delivery companies. I was the only one still in school and hating it.

Compared to Aitchison College the Johannesburg Indian High School in Fordsburg was dismal. The sombre, dark-brick buildings resembled the fortress-like Fordsburg police station directly opposite and, instead of peaceful green tranquility, the school sat in a dusty triangular sand patch bounded by noisy Central Road, Bree Street and Burghersdorp Street. What passed for a playing field was being swallowed up by prefabricated classrooms meant to accommodate the overflow of pupils from distant Indian townships where no high schools existed.

The teachers here were a mix of Afrikaans and English-speaking white South Africans with a handful of European Jewish teachers – Mrs De Kat, Mrs Drits and Mr Picardie among others – who, we understood, were refugees from Nazi Germany and who were by far the best and most popular instructors in the school.

Opinions of the local teachers were in sharp contrast. Sister Zarina's thoughts reflected what most of us had felt: 'They're here only because they're unqualified to teach at the better paid white schools.' She was almost expelled for shooting a water pistol at a teacher in response to a racist slur.

Hajoo talked about one Mr Engelbrecht, a maths teacher, whose busy schedule left him no time to teach. There were five crowded standard six classes, and he would race into each one, write bewildering algebraic hieroglyphics on the board, make a few demands and be off to another class. Engelbrecht offered no guidance and helped no one who may have been falling behind. Towards the end of the term, he suddenly demanded to see everyone's books. Hajoo remembers clearly one of his comments:

'You people say the Government is treating you unfairly, but when I see the low quality of your work I think you deserve it.'

Humiliation like this fostered anger and sometimes violence. There was the time when brother Dooli punched up a teacher for beating our brother Adam mercilessly with a cane. Dooli quit school and Adam was expelled soon after for insubordination. He had refused to apologise and admit to something he didn't do. Brother Enver, though he was a great student, was slowly slithering down the path of booze and pot.

But what stands out most in my mind is the time, in October 1952, when classmate Marimuthoo Pillay pulled a knife on Mr van Zyl and petrified us all.

Mari was a sullen angry loner who was falling far behind in his schoolwork. He had been on van Zyl's shit list for weeks. On this day he was being humiliated worse than usual for not answering quickly: 'Kan jy nie praat nie, domkop – Can't you speak, dummy?' van Zyl was yelling. 'I don't know what to do with you people anymore, maybe school is not for you.' It was painful to watch as as this horrible man relentlessly lambasted Mari and the boy became more confused and tongue-tied.

Suddenly Mari jumped up from his bench, face distorted and, in a split-second, had a knife pressed to the soft underside of van Zyl's chin. I remember clearly a slender dagger with a beautiful cobalt blue handle and a stiletto blade, five or six inches long and the teacher standing paralysed with his head stretched up and far back as possible, straining to avoid the needlepoint piercing his skin.

'Don't do it Mari,' someone called out quietly, 'it's not worth it.' That voice of caution may have saved Mr Horrible's life. For a few moments, the protagonists stood there frozen. Suddenly Mari stepped back, plunged the knife deep into the top of his wooden desk and lurched out of the class, leaving the stiletto quivering wildly in the desk as if alive with his hate and anger.

I never saw Mari Pillay again.

The visibly shaken van Zyl collapsed into Mari's seat, sat there trembling in silence for some very long minutes as we watched in stunned silence. Then he stepped to the front of the room, picked up his car keys from the table and, looking straight ahead, marched stiffly out of the class. I never saw Mr van Zyl again either.

Troyeville Fruit Market today

Halim family from left: Joey, Ayesha, Ma Mabel, Bashir with little Enver, Bobby, Farida with Ferosa, Dicky and Mr Halim

Restating our vows – 50 years later

Celebrating our 50th with us – Monika Hagen, Grace Jones and Jeanette Judkins

Brother Enver with Ruth

Brother Dooli with Tima

Lt-Colonel Abdulla (Dooli) Carim – SANDF

Brother Adam with Cecilia

Xavier and Zane – African brothers

Gypsies returned

A week later in my sixteenth year, in 1952, and within three months after returning from Aitchison College, I dropped out of school without bothering to write the end-of-year examination. Instead, I self-enrolled into what I would later hear people refer to as the College of Hard Knocks in the University of Life.

Claustrophobia and Wanderlust

In his book, *The Power of Now*, Eckhart Tolle opines that there are really only three ways to deal with an unhappy relationship or a bad situation: Change it, walk away from it, or accept the circumstances and learn to live with it without negativity. The book was a present for my 70th birthday from our son Xavier and our new daughter, his wife Amita, and I recognised that what Tolle advocated I had done in Fordsburg, more than half a century before.

I hated school, I couldn't change it, and I wouldn't accept it, so I 'walked away'. I simply told my parents straight out that I would start a cabinet-making apprenticeship at Steel and Barnett, a furniture factory in Alberton and that I would hand over half my wages to my mother for board and lodging. Money was scarce at home and Mummy was obliged to agree. Daddy supported the idea: 'If Mumdoo is going to leave school then getting an apprenticeship in a trade is the best thing.'

It was not. Certainly not for me.

The job was almost four hours both ways by tram and bus and the starting wage was less than two pounds a week. This left very little after deductions and transport. It would take four years for me to become a journeyman cabinetmaker and top pay would then be twelve to fifteen pounds a week. Later I would make more than that in my first week as a bread salesman for Crystal Bakery in Doornfontein.

After two weeks as an apprentice cabinet-maker a supervisor congratulated me for the good work I had done filling millions of tiny cracks on hundreds of wooden headboards with a concoction of wood putty and glue and then sandpapering the edges smooth. Within four weeks, I had mindlessly hammered strips of wood onto the sides of a few zillion kitchen dresser drawers and I did this almost blinded by clouds of sawdust and nearly deafened by the buzzing of heavy cutting machines.

The claustrophobia was awful. I daydreamed about the Pir Panjal Mountains, tennis trials and the spray of windswept seas. Within six weeks, I had two warnings for dozing at the bench and sleeping in the toilet, and before I had served two months, I quit the job.

Then Daddy fixed me up with an independent contractor in the plumbing trade who demanded that we all wait at a corner in town at six in the morning so we could be on site and working by seven. I started my apprenticeship with Martin's Plumbing on a cloudy Monday on a dreary job site surrounded by a high rusty fence. In this confined space I joined waste-water pipes together by applying a foul smelling epoxy to the inside of the wide end of one section of pipe and the outside of the narrow end of another section and pushing the so-called male joint into the female joint until I had the required lengths. Then it started raining, work came to a stop and we packed up and were driven back to town.

It rained the rest of that week. Each morning I would arrive at the pick-up point, sometimes soaked to the skin, only to be told – 'No work today.' Then the following Monday the boss handed me an envelope containing a day's pay for the entire previous week, less a deduction for transporting us to the job site. When I questioned the unexpected deduction, he responded with words that influenced my job expectations for the rest of my life: 'No work, no pay and no free ride.'

I tore open the envelope, saw that there was just enough for bus and tram fare back to Fordsburg, quit on the spot and walked off the job thinking to myself – 'To bloody hell with you.'

Was it the wanderlust in me that triggered the claustrophobia in confined spaces or vice-versa? In any event things improved during the first half of 1953, when I started travelling and apprenticing as a trainee shop-assistant in farm stores across the Transvaal. Daddy's new idea was that I should follow the family tradition and learn the retail business from the ground up. I would then one day take over his fabric store, the dreary General Job Buyers & Sellers in Barclay Arcade on the corner of Market and Diagonal Streets, opposite Pe's old shop.

And so, I became a teenage migrant worker. I would arrive at a country store with a small suitcase and a bundle of books, be assigned a lonely room or a bed in a noisy staff dormitory, depending on the size of the business. I would be taught aspects of the retail business stay a while and then move on.

I learned shopkeeping at Bob's Bazaar in Louis Trichard, Dadabhai's Store in Vereeniging and shops in Vlakfontein, Carolina, Ermelo and a few other small towns. The usual deal was very low pay, plus room and board and on-the-job training in return for a 55-hour week.

11
VLAKFONTEIN

Mr Sale was the owner of the general store in Vlakfontein. He was a demanding boss but also the best coach I ever had in the retail business. He believed that good service was a basic right of customers, not a favour granted to them; that the secret to success was customer satisfaction not just customer service; that real customers are people and their families who shop with a store all their lives not just occasionally.

The Vlakfontein General Store was a beautiful shop. It had bright red linoleum floors and pale green bins in the grocery section holding bulk sugar, salt, flour, rice and maize meal. The pine shelves in the textile and clothing sections were all highly varnished and offset by white walls and ceiling.

The store stood in solitary isolation on a dusty sand road surrounded by hundreds of square miles of cultivated trees in a district of pristine lakes and wetlands. To get to this beautiful area I took the overnight train from Johannesburg to the Eastern Transvaal rail terminus town of Breyten. Then I boarded the connecting South African Railways bus that shuddered further east along the rutted highway, past Lake Chrissie, heading for the Swaziland border post at Oshoek-Ngwenya. Somewhere between Breyten and the border, we passed the Jessievale Sawmills. Soon afterwards, I was standing in the dust in front of a collection of buildings in the middle of nowhere, with nothing in sight except trees, a few pick-up trucks and a boy – a year or two younger than me – named Skep Kunene.

As we watched my suitcase and books being offloaded with the South African Post Office mailbags that icy July morning in 1953, I learned that Skep's job was to collect the mail and the deliveries and that this was not just a general store – it also housed the area post office and the district telephone exchange. Later I met Mrs Faith Muller, a kind lady who managed the post office and the exchange and also cooked for the Sale family and the shop assistants.

I learned to like Vlakfontein. I had my own private room and the food was good. The only other occupant in the staff quarters was Mr

Francis a sixty-something Christian-Tamil from Natal. He ran the small convenience shop that stayed open seven days a week. It sold things not offered in the main store like newspapers, cigarettes, bread and milk, as well as cakes, ice cream, sweets and fresh fruit and vegetables. The evening of my arrival, when I went to his room to greet him, he snorted, harrumphed, and made it clear that I should keep out of his way.

The next morning Mr Sale showed me the ropes and I started work in good spirits. I served customers, carried boxes of groceries to their vehicles and, when there were no shoppers, priced the goods, stocked the shelves and wiped bottles and cans till they sparkled. The rule was never to be idle.

I weighed sugar, rice, flour and maize-meal in two, six and twelve-pound paper bags and stacked them neatly in readiness for rush periods. I swept the floors, polished and shined the counters and bins. Mr Sale always closely inspected what he expected. Later I would learn to order new supplies, check the shipments on arrival and approve invoices for payment.

Another rule was to stop whatever we were doing the moment a customer walked in. We were not to wait for them to seek help but approach them, smile, keep eye contact and offer assistance. We were not to chew or smoke in the shop, jingle coins in our pockets or slouch over the counters and there was to be no idle chatter or laughter in the presence of customers.

Today, I am often shocked at the unhelpful, bored attention customers get in most retail stores, including the major chains. Senior management obviously haven't learned that while customers rate efficiency high, they value warmth and a friendly smile a whole lot more.

At Vlakfontein there were no confined spaces and no chance of claustrophobia. The shop was spacious, bright and airy. Outside there were thousands of acres of pine and eucalyptus gum trees. The plantation hills and valleys were criss-crossed with miles of winding service roads, mysterious pathways and cascading streams flowing into rock pools – all waiting to be explored. The Sale family spent most weekends with their friends in Carolina and Ermelo but I prefered to remain in Vlakfontein. I enjoyed being alone and read and walked a lot and soon was exploring this amazing rural area with my new friend Skep.

Skep and I had connected that very first day. He had insisted on carrying my suitcase and books from the railway bus, and I had insisted on helping him carry the postbags and other packages. He was the shop's general factotum and often helped me in the shop during rush periods. Soon we were spending time together on Saturday afternoons and Sundays and I was introduced to a side of life that few outsiders get to experience.

Rural Friendships

Our adventures together started on a dusty football field near the Jessievale Saw Mills. It ended with me 'kidnapping' Skep and taking him to Johannesburg where we both thought he could have a better life.

The goal I scored that first day – a good shot from a pretty long distance – caused a hubbub in siSwati and isiZulu that I did not understand. All I heard was the word 'umhlungu' over and over again, and I realised these chaps took me for a white boy. Skep explained in his kitchen Afrikaans and fanagalo – a kind of patois – that the hullabaloo was about whether I could formally join their club. Some feared this might cause trouble with the local whites and the police and others thought it would be okay for me just to play without formally joining. It seemed I was the first non-black to have played here and though I was clearly welcome, the phenomenon caused anxiety.

Getting to Jessievale on a Sunday morning was an adventure in itself. Sometimes we walked along the dusty main road and usually a logging truck would give us an exhilarating ride high up on the logs as far as the mill. Other times Skep had an errand to run to a small kraal – a collection of huts – deep in the bush, and we would take the 'shortcut' on the long trek to the football field. At these times we walked along snaking forest paths deep in the shade and clambered across sparkling streams, hidden in the freshness of pine and the muskiness of eucalyptus.

There could be as many as four ninety-minute games on a Sunday, with players coming, and going, and some of us panting and puffing through every game. After football, the fellows would sit around and talk. Although I understood very little, I enjoyed the robust exchanges, the gwara-ing – teasing – that I sensed was going on and the occasional arguments. My race, colour and religion were far less important to this group than my skill on the football field.

It was with these chaps that I had my first taste of ntomboti or skokiaan, the indigenous African beer, and got happily drunk for the first time at 16. It was okay. We all just lay back relaxing on the grass, catching the afternoon sun and dozing for a while, till it was time to go.

Through my new friends I also met the vibrant Talitha, a thirty something Swazi woman – a good friend of the boys and generous with her favours. They would provide a rabbit or some kind of wild fowl they had trapped and after a game we would come back to her place for maize-meal pap – an African polenta – with a tomato-chilli breedie – a kind of spicy salsa sauce – and roast meat. This was washed down with mageu, a thin gruel also made with maize meal, water and sour milk.

When it rained, we would gather inside some dim family hut and my eyes would water from the smoke of the cooking fire as the fellows continued talking. I noticed that none of the huts had water, electricity or sanitation – not even the bucket system – and when nature called us, we all simply went to nature.

Beauty & the Blond Terrorist

Vlakfontein was turning out to be a good place for me. I had the work under control and thanks to Skep, my weekends were a delight. Then suddenly violence ripped through the serenity of this beautiful forestland and revealed the ugliness and terror behind the facade.

It was a late Sunday afternoon and Skep and I were returning from football. Even before we emerged from the trees onto the road near the shop, we could hear women screaming and wailing and a man pleading: 'Nee baas! Asseblief baas! Hou op baas! – No boss! Please boss! Stop boss!' Then we saw a scene that had me crying for days.

Imagine about eight people in a thin circle, watching a black middle-aged man being beaten up by a white boy, so badly that he can barely stand. Each time the older man sinks to his knees he is pulled upright, carefully positioned, and again a fist is smashed into his face – over and over.

I didn't know the man but I had seen him in the shop. The young blue-eyed, blonde policeman I had never seen before. He was three or four years older than I was. His muscular suntanned biceps strained in the short sleeves of his khaki shirt and his legs were bronze logs stretching his tight shorts. And he was wild: 'Ek sal jou wys, jou verdomde kaffir, jy moet leer om gou te antwoord as ek jou iets vra – I'll show you, you stupid nigger,you must learn to answer quickly when I ask you something.'

The anguished wailing and moaning rose and fell then suddenly stopped. In silence we all watched as the sweating white, blonde terrorist stepped back, letting the bloody man with the now unrecognisable face drop to the sand in a heap, get into the police van and drive off.

For days after, Skep and I hardly spoke. He wore that Sunday look for days – face grim, jaws clenched, eyes hard – and when we finally spoke we both cried.

The victim was a family friend whose nose and jaw were broken and a cheekbone fractured. The man who pleaded with the policeman to stop punching was Skep's father, an elder in the bush community.

That frightening scene changed my feelings for God's beautiful countryside forever. Now, when I drive through South Africa's rural areas, I wonder what terrible things happened behind the silent trees and shimmering lakes in those bad old days. But as awful as that experience was, it was not the only reason I asked Skep to run away with me to Johannesburg.

Laughing Children Flying

Black drivers of logging trucks usually gave lifts to black children who would otherwise walk huge distances to and from school each day. The kids waited on the side of the road and when the truck stopped as many as twelve boys and girls clambered up and sat on the logs and away they went. This day things went horribly wrong. Instead of driving straight past the general store, with his load of laughing children, the driver suddenly changed his mind and swerved into the slip road onto the shop property. Then he slammed on his brakes and six children came flying off the logs, through the air, crashing into the gravel directly in front of the entrance to the store.

When Mr Sale and I got to the scene, a crowd had already gathered. There was wailing and crying and shouting, but no first aid was being administered. In Troyeville, until I was told not to come back, I had attended a few St John Ambulance first aid classes at the whites-only school at the bottom of Cornelia Street, so I did what little I remembered.

I asked Mr Sale to get blankets and cover the kids to minimise shock, while I checked for broken bones. His response was to ask who would pay for the blankets and made no move to get them. I shouted for someone to bring a basin of warm water as I ran into the shop, to our little pharmacy, and grabbed antiseptic, cotton wool, bandages, ointments and plasters. While I was doing this, Mr Sale asked again, 'Who is going to pay for all this?'

Later, he came to tell me that my personal account had been charged with the cost of the bandages and stuff and that he didn't think I could pay for the blankets so he did not bring them. I silently wondered why the shop would not pay to help the children whose parents were our customers.

Suddenly an accumulation of negatives began souring my taste for Vlakfontein. Besides the terrorist policeman and Mr Sale's attitude towards those injured children, I now remembered that I could not eat in the Breyten Hotel when I went to get a sandwich. I was instructed to go around the side of the building and into the back yard, where I could place an order at the kitchen window, from a crummy menu. If I wanted to, I could eat at a picnic table in a grungy corner of the yard under a leaky tarpaulin.

Then Skep told me that we could not swim in certain rock pools in the forest, because the best places were reserved for white farmers, plantation managers and their families. Later I noticed some of our regular black customers being refused credit during desperate times, on the grounds that they were a credit risk. I remembered how proud Mr Sale was that the shop was able to give white customers long-term credit during even riskier times.

The Frightened Convict

It was around seven that morning when Skep and I first saw the ex-convict. He was huddled on the cold cement stoep, near the corner of the building, in front of the shop. His feet were bare; he was dressed in filthy khaki shorts, a ripped shirt that showed more skin than cloth, and he was trying to keep warm under a skimpy prison-issue blanket. The thing that struck me most was the forlorn look on his face. It was the look of a person forsaken, desperate and frightened, and so I spoke to him while Skep fetched hot tea and bread.

His name was Petrus Sindelo.

As he munched and sipped, we heard his sorry tale. It was a story similar to one that black men all over South Africa had told before and would tell many times again.

Some three months earlier, he had mistakenly left his pass book in his room and could not produce it when the police stopped him on the street where he stayed, some distance from Middleburg. He was arrested, processed and transported to the Jessievale Prison. Skep had pointed it out to me one Sunday, as we walked through the forest. It was a grim place, hidden behind a facade of tall trees, down a shadowy road that slinked into the valley from a point diagonally opposite the Vlakfontein General Store.

INTERLUDE

The ordinary struggle

Those were very dark days for black men. No indigenous South African man, sixteen years and older, had the right to remain outside his area of official domicile for more than 72 hours without a police permit. Every African man had to carry a pass or reference book on his person day and night. Failure to produce it on demand by the police, meant immediate arrest and a spot fine or jail. Not having the right stamp in it also meant arrest and a fine.

By colluding with the prison system, white farmers were able to exploit cheap convict labour. For black men this meant that non-payment of a pass-offense fine could get them shipped to distant places, with no family members being informed, to serve a term of forced farm labour, usually under terrible conditions.

The nation and the world were shocked when it was revealed that potato farmers in the region were literally getting away with murder. People like Bethal ANC branch chairman Gert Sibande, journalist Ruth First and a priest, Michael Scott, exposed the inhuman conditions in a publication called New Age. Later, in 1952, the story was taken up by the influential Drum Magazine.

Eye-witness reports told of young children, adults and convict labour digging for the potatoes with their bare hands in winter and sleeping on naked cement floors wearing only potato sacks. There were accounts of workers being beaten to death and left to die, and stories of bodies actually recovered from unmarked graves in the potato fields.

All this prompted the national Potato Boycott of the Bethal farms, initiated by SACTU (the South African Congress of Trade Unions), which paralysed the potato farming industry. My friends and I actually supported the boycott by monitoring fish and chip shops in Fordsburg and demanding or ensuring that they sold fish, without the chips, during the boycott.

My parents must have known about what could happen to someone arrested for not having a proper pass, because when our own domestic helper – Malola – was arrested and taken away, Mummy panicked. Malola was cleaning the family car parked immediately in front of our house. Two things still stand out in my mind from that experience: The policeman refused to allow him to fetch the pass book from his room in the back yard just a few steps away, and that the hard-hearted constable was a black man just like Malola.

Daddy urgently pressed three pounds into my hand and told me to drive fast to the Fordsburg police station, pay the admission of guilt fine, and get Malola released.

Petrus couldn't say how long he had been working on farms in the area. He was released at four that morning and was now waiting at the shop for the railway bus to Breyten station where he would take the train to Middleburg. As he responded to our questions it became clear this fellow was in deep trouble.

He hadn't eaten since the afternoon before. His own clothing had been stolen in prison and now all he had were these rags, the prison-issue blanket and a government travel voucher for the bus and train. He would have to wait here another nine hours for the bus that arrived at 4pm and would reach Breyten after dark. And he had no clue when the train to

Middleburg departed. Nor was he sure how to get to his family once he got off the train.

By the time Petrus boarded the bus that afternoon we had fed him well and provided him a parcel of padkos – travel food. He was wearing my striped woollen shirt and Skep's khaki long pants. He also had on a warm jersey, thick socks and canvas shoes – which I had taken on credit from the shop.

Cash was the problem. Skep and I had none. Mrs Muller lent me some and so Petrus had a pound – twenty shillings – to help him get from the Middleburg Station to his home if he could find the way.

Skep Comes To Jo'burg

Skep couldn't believe that the coloured man on the Johannesburg train was actually making up a bed for him. He stared in silence as brass handles were pulled and twisted, and the shiny wooden wall of the compartment collapsed and magically became a bunk bed. He gaped when the porter opened a canvas bag and within seconds had unrolled and spread out the luxurious blue blankets and lightly starched white sheets between which he would be sleeping.

After the porter left, Skep silently stroked the soft bedding then a fantastic smile slowly cracked his face wide open. Skep had never in his life been further than Lake Chrissie, Lothair or Lochiel – a few miles from Vlakfontein – and this evening he had eaten in the back yard of the whites-only Breyten Hotel and was now on a train to Johannesburg – Egoli – the City of Gold. As the enormity of the escapade sank in he started laughing, then he laughed louder and soon we were both laughing and jumping madly around in that little compartment like souls possessed.

My decision to quit Vlakfontein was made the day after the Petrus affair. Mr Sale had returned from a trip and called me into his office. He told me that some white customers were saying that my mixing with Skep and the kaffir boys in Jessievale location could create problems and that I should stop. In a flash, I was back in Troyeville and in trouble because of my friendship with Sally van Rensburg. Now my crime was my friendship with a bunch of black fellows. My response was polite: I wouldn't stop playing footie with my friends. Then he said I must stop if I wanted to work here, and I told him I wouldn't stop and would rather leave Vlakfontein at the end of the month.

My decision to take Skep to Johannesburg had been made earlier, the instant I learned that he worked all month for just ten shillings. And when I told him he could earn much more working in our family home or at my father's shop near Johannesburg's city centre, if he would come with me, he immediately agreed.

The plan was simple. I would take the Tuesday afternoon bus from in front of the shop and he would board the bus at Jessievale. The night train from Breyten would get us to Johannesburg early on Wednesday morning and we would then walk from Park Station to Fordsburg, since there were no trams for blacks to Fordsburg. To avoid suspicion Skep was to give his father his pay – the ten shillings – in the usual way and not pack any clothing. The plan worked perfectly – I thought – until we got home and Mummy shocked me by saying, after the hugs and kisses, 'This must be Skep.'

Bloody hell! Mr Sale had phoned while we were enjoying the train ride and told Mummy what I had done. He also said that he would be visiting Johannesburg on the weekend and would fetch Skep on Sunday, unless we preferred the police to come and collect him. Bloody hell again! What a crappy plan I had hatched. Mr Goldstein would not have been impressed.

Mummy was happy to have me back home but grim-faced about Skep, until I explained things to her, then she seemed okay with it. Daddy's response was angry. 'You did a stupid thing. The boy must go back with Mr Sale. I want no trouble!'

I was devastated, but Skep didn't seem to care. I think he knew this adventure couldn't last and that he would soon be returning home. Meanwhile he was revelling in the moment.

He had never been to a cinema in his life before, so he and I went to the Lyric and the Majestic on Central Road in Fordsburg two matinees in a row and sat in the 'native section'. I had to stop him from jumping up and shouting out loud, as I myself had done at the movies in Lahore. His foolishness in the bioscope was matched only by his utter stupefaction as we walked through the bustling streets of Johannesburg's city centre. Every few paces he would stop and stare into the shop windows at the colourful displays. As we ambled along, he would strain his neck and gaze up at the skyscrapers. Meanwhile I kept an eye out for the police who could arrest Skep at any time.

There were no hard feelings between Mr Sale and us when he came to collect Skep. Mummy apologised for my actions and he said something about boys being boys. Then, looking straight at me, he explained: 'Skep is soon sixteen and without a pass he could end up in prison or as a contract labourer on a farm. His family is very worried and want him home.' I thought of Petrus the ex-convict and the truth of the point Mr Sale had made was like a nail in my head.

Years later Eddy Sale, who had taken over the shop after his father died, told me that thousands of black people had been forcibly moved from the area and resettled in KaNgwane – a tribal Bantustan that had been established in 1977. He confirmed that Skep, his wife and children had also been moved to KaNgwane where he had later died.

I never saw Skep again after he climbed into Mr Sale's car that day in front of our house, but I can see his handsome face anytime I want to. I remember the good times we had in the bush, on the football field and during his great train adventure to Jo'burg. But what I remember best is the radiant smile that lit up his face, as our eyes met for the last time, seconds before they drove off back to the timberlands of the Eastern Transvaal.

The last thing he said to me in his odd mix of Afrikaans and siSwati was a simple 'Dankie kakooloo, Mac – Thank you very much, Mac.'

12
STRIKE THREE – YOU'RE OUT

The House Always Wins

While I was away at Aitchison College gambling had gripped our father. Then later, while I apprenticed in country stores across the province, that grip became a stranglehold. By the time I returned home from Vlakfontein, our family fortunes were in serious decline. Betting on chance was choking the fun, laughter and Daddy-hood out of my father's life, and Mummy's struggle to maintain a certain lifestyle for us was draining her life of joyousness.

Although none of us knew it at the time, we had entered a dark period in which we would begin, imperceptibly, to unravel as a family unit. The stage was beginning to be set for our very own physical and spiritual Diaspora.

But all that would come later. Meanwhile things had been getting better, after we left Troyeville, before they got worse.

Mummy and Daddy had anticipated our forced departure from Troyeville and Daddy had searched high and low for business premises, but the few decent locations in Indian and Coloured areas had long been cornered by well-established trading families. New shops in the expanding white suburbs north of Johannesburg, like Bryanston and Randburg abounded, but were off limits to us, and our parents were now too afraid to risk starting up illegaly again in a forbidden area. It had become a case of 'twice bitten forever shy'.

As a result, with his characteristic boldness and help from Mr Schneider, Daddy entered a new world of horse-racing, betting and bookmaking. He gathered scores of testimonial letters and signatures from respected individuals in support of a petition for a licence to operate legally as a bookmaker. He even had the endorsement of an Afrikaner magistrate.

Sorry, said the law, bookmaking is another business off-limits to non-whites. Frustrated and desperate, Amie yelled, 'bloody racist bastards!' and angrily decided to become a 'bookie' anyway. This was the only time I ever heard my Dad rant against the apartheid government for his circumstances. He began operating 'underground', illegally, out of his fabric shop in Barclay Arcade on Market Street, and paid the police and the gangsters for protection.

As long as he only took bets as a turf accountant – his preferred business description – and did not gamble himself, money flowed in because, as everyone knows, 'the house always wins'. Thanks to Daddy's chutzpah, our family prospered and things between him and Mummy improved once again.

So long as there was money, our parents spent it generously. At Mummy's insistence, one or other of us was always taking lessons – tennis, piano, accordion, voice or ballet. I was coached by a Jewish tennis professional at the white's only Nugget Street public courts in Doornfontein. To gain entry I had to 'play white' and pretend I was Lebanese. Some of us were members at the Bantu Men's Social Centre in Eloff Street Extension near the City centre. Fortunately, membership here did not require that we 'play black'. I took tap lessons from one of the popular Manhattan Brothers, a marvellous group of black township songsters that would leave South Africa and find fame and fortune in more liberal social climes.

Then Mum and Dad moved us out of the cramped space in Jajbhai's Building into the spacious Terrace Road house in Fordsburg. This was when they enrolled Enver, Dooli and me in prestigious Aitchison College in Lahore and personally escorted us there as part of their once-in-a-lifetime tour of Pakistan and India.

Gradually my parents had become so-called 'socialites' – big fish in a small non-white pond. Now they were going dancing at gala balls and awards dinners at smart venues in white suburbs, like Northcliff and Buccleuch, in support of the Association for the Blind, the Transvaal Tennis Association, the South African Bridge Association and others. Of course, all these were institutions separate from the 'official' white South African bodies.

Daddy was brilliant at cards and became a champion bridge player. He once beat the British bridge champion Boris Shapiro in a friendly match, and then beat him again in a return game, which was not as friendly. His popularity grew and though he won recognition in bridge

The socialites

circles across racial lines, he was still not allowed to play on the white's only South African team.

When young Sydney Poitier came to visit our home in Fordsburg in the fifties, I doubt if anyone around knew that this Negro actor would one day become one of the most award winning film stars in America; and be an inspiration to black people all over the world, just as Joe Louis had been.

He and Canada Lee were in and out of South Africa making the film of Alan Paton's book 'Cry the Beloved Country'. Mr Lee had the lead as the aging Stephen Kumalo and Mr Poitier would be the young Reverend Msimangu. Because of Prohibition most white people, in those days, had no idea how to socialise with black celebrities, especially if they were connoseurs of fine liquor. Dicky Naicker, a friend of the family, was assigned by the production company to 'look after the Negro visitors'. He asked Mum and Dad to assist – hence an evening out with the Carims and an illegal nightcap at our home in the ghetto.

If we had asked, I think Daddy would have said that he was happiest when he was nominated for the position of President of the Johannesburg Memon Welfare Association.

Memons are a tribal or ethnic group who may be found in areas that stretch from the Sindh, which is now a province of Pakistan, to Kutch and Kathiawar in India, and who have became well known for their entrepreneurial aptitude. Our paternal ancestors – the Poonjanees – spring from the Kathiawar branch in Gujarat. We grew up listening to Pe and Ma and our uncles and aunts talking in sing-song Memoni, a unique language that I later learned was a mixture of Sindhi and Kutchi.

I imagine Daddy's proudest moment came when people began addressing him as Pe – Amie Pe – the title of recognition and respect accorded to an elder in the community. The same title his father had earned before him.

Gamblers Eventually Lose

Then, suddenly, Daddy changed from a restrained, thoughtful turf accountant to a high-risk, high-stakes gambler, and Mummy's ambitions for a more gracious middle-class life for our family began to fall to pieces.

What caused this? Was it desperate impatience to succeed, a shift in his inner fault lines, or fear, anxiety and the spectre of failure as a husband, father and provider?

Daddy would get a tip – 'a sure thing'– bet large portions of the day's takings from the 'bucket shop' and lose. Other times he would get a call and fly to Durban or Cape Town for card games reserved exclusively for 'big shots.' These marathon gambling sessions could last up to five days, and he would take along the significant winnings from the 'bucket shop' as his stake. He won often enough to be beguiled into thinking he was ahead, and lost often enough to destroy his and Mummy's dreams.

His last big blast of glory as a gambler came when Mowgli won the Durban July Handicap in 1952, and Daddy miraculously won the coveted Triple Crown. Incredibly, the three horses he bet on to win in two different races in the UK and South Africa's July Handicap at Greyville in Durban all won. As the winning from one race was automatically bet on the next, the compounded payout that Daddy brought home was huge.

Our parents went on a splurge, which centred on Mummy's flair for interior decorating. As Daddy watched proudly, she had our house transformed. The old floors were removed and the sub-floor space filled with concrete and overlaid with solid burnished wood. The piano was retuned and its wood exterior beautifuly restored and polished. All the rooms were brightly painted and the living area tastefully wall papered. Then she installed a revolutionary new, perpetual, anthracite-burning Esse stove, replaced the old washing machine with the latest Hotpoint and bought a contemporary dining room suite with a circular table – additions rarely seen in our neighbourhood.

While the house always wins, punters almost always lose and their families suffer. Everyone knows this to be the truth except the gamblers themselves. They live in a world of delusion. Life inevitably crumbles down around them and they are often the last to know what's happening. So it was with Daddy. Mowgli was his last big win before the downward slide began.

Before long financiers, spurred on by one of his brothers, edged him out and took over the business. Quickly hangers-on, fair-weather friends and some of his extended family abandoned him. Dad's desperate efforts to regain his position in society drove him into ill-conceived, under-financed ventures that all failed.

Mummy tried to stem the decline. She worked as a hotel switchboard operator and as housekeeper for a wealthy white family in the northern suburbs. She started up a fish and chips shop on Main Road, Fordsburg with her friend Aunty Amina Kotwal, then a haberdashery store in Adam's Arcade in town. She even tried cooking convenience foods for sale to factory workers, with Hajoo helping with the cooking and the actual selling. None of these initiatives lasted, simply because people with little money selling goods to other people with even less money have little chance of success.

Now our mother was back on the treadmill she thought she had left behind in Troyeville. Fatigue, frustration and anger mounted and the acrimony between my parents was now, more than ever, mainly about money – or, rather, the lack of it.

The Anger of Despair

Daddy was little different to many other ordinary heads of families in South Africa who had seen their capacity to provide for their families stifled or destroyed. In the process, they had become desperate, angry men and toxic husbands and parents. Their wives were similarly infected as desperation stilled their laughter and hardened their hearts. It is fairly common knowledge that whereas success tends to make a person amenable and generous, too many barriers and failures often leads to bitterness and sometimes to violence.

In classic form, our father first lost his self-confidence and then his self-esteem. Like most uninformed victims, he did not even know this was happening. He searched for his lost prestige in the wrong places: false bravado, high-risk gambling, younger, good time dolly-birds and VAT 69 whiskey. When he still could not find the person he once was, he took his anger out on some of us.

When he beat me for the delinquent I had become, even my toughest friends were shocked. He would tie me to a bed headboard and lay into me with the rubber hosepipe from the washing machine, and later with a piece of thick rubber-coated electric copper wire bent over double and twisted into a lethal weapon that drew blood. 'Why,' I would silently sob, 'does my Daddy hate me?' 'Where is Mummy?'

The years would help me understand the source of my father's anger and violence and I could empathise. But I still can't figure out what kind of deliverance he thought he would find from shouting, as he hit me, that I would never amount to anything; and that I would not go far, not even to nearby Benoni, on my own steam. And why, after each beating, would he drag me to the Lyric Hairdressing Salon on our corner and have Tony the barber shave off all my hair?

Those were the years when the cool of jive and boogie-woogie was making room for the 'wall of sound' that was rock and roll; when marabi-turned-kwela rhythms were sweeping in from the backyards of the black townships, and Spokes Mashiyane's Penny Whistle Blues gave people new dancing feet for our very own outrageous 'makeppie-special' jive.

Boys who could were sporting a hairstyle made famous by the rising New York movie star, Tony Curtis. Mirrors in homes everywhere reflected fellows smearing gobs of Brylcream or Brilliantine onto freshly washed hair and brushing the sides flat and smooth. Then, with the tip of a comb and, with practised flicks of the wrist, painstakingly twisting and pulling the front into a curly tuft which, to be 'really real,' should dangle nonchalantly forward over the forehead radiating a cheeky attitude that declared: 'Watch out – here I come!'

That was also the time when my friends and I were convinced that we were hot, because, each Saturday, the hottest girls in the hottest dance venue in Johannesburg – the Springbok Hall on the corner of Delarey and 23rd Streets, in Fietas – told us so, and showered us with their friendship and their favours.

Like Tony Manero – the disco king character played by John Travolta in the 1977 movie, Saturday Night Fever, and his group of friends – we too, were hotshots on our ghetto dance floor in our day. Just as Manero blossomed under the disco lights, here, at the Springbok Hall, we too, were admired and respected. When we sauntered in on a Saturday, dressed to kill in our buy-now-pay-later charcoal-grey hopsack suits, pink Van Heusen shirts and ox-blood Jarman shoes, heads would turn, fellows would call out greetings and girls would become all aflutter and atwitter.

I hate the thought that my father could have known all this; that he cut off my hair because he knew the humiliation of losing my 'Tony Curtis' would be as painful for me as any beating. I prefer to believe that, in some misguided way, Daddy was trying to send me some kind of wake-up call for my own good.

The seven shillings and sixpence we each paid for admission to the dance hall did not permit the truth of our lives to enter the hall with us. We left that outside on the sidewalk. And, as we thrilled to the raw, pulsating music of Pieterjie – Short Peter – and the Mascots, I could push behind me the anger and unhappiness at home, and the mind-numbing boredom of my going-nowhere jobs. The softness of my many dance partners and the sounds of their happy laughter helped me avoid dealing with those strange feelings that persistently percolated up from my subconscious and unsettled me.

These disquieting thoughts were notions that I should raise my sights. They murmured that there were more mountains for me to see besides the Pir Panjals in the foothills of the Himalayas and more ships to explore besides the SS Karanja in the Indian Ocean.

The whispers from my future urged me not to lose heart. They assured me that I would meet people on my road who would continue to teach, expand and inspire me, as Father Sigamoney and Mr Goldstein had done in Gold Street School and Aitchison College. They promised me that the vision I had shared with Sara Meer on the waiting bench, in the convent in the sky, would translate into a great journey across oceans, continents and many cultures, and that I would share this journey with a life-partner who would be my life support for more than half a century.

13
THE COLLEGE OF
HARD KNOCKS

Like my Dad, I too seemed to have lost my way and my self-esteem was steadily sinking down into my shoes.

After being torn from Aitchison College and then dropping out of high school, I had found myself in the murk between one aimless distraction and another. I had roamed around the Transvaal working in a variety of country shops and, in between jobs, had fun touring dusty rural football fields with the Pioneer Rangers. I'd had more girl friends than breakfasts – and took pleasure in their company to the deepest extent they would allow.

I skipped from one place of employment to another in troubling succession, and the dreariness at work was only relieved in the electric atmosphere of the weekend dances in the Springbok Hall and at lively house parties, wherever they happened. I was always on the go and into new things in different places. In its deceptive fullness, there were disquieting voids in my life that each distraction was meant to fill – but never did.

In those days, I had heard nothing about setting life goals and I recall no talk about consciously planning and creating the kinds of lives we wanted for ourselves. No one asked me where I thought I would be in five years. All everyone seemed to do was react and respond to immediate circumstances.

Mummy and Daddy's road had led them, haphazardly, from the broken promise of happy times in Cape Town, to the lost potential of Troyeville, then to the relative prosperity of the early days in Fordsburg and now, thanks to bad laws, bad luck and bad judgement to a place of desperation and fading hope.

For me the Muslim Boarding School had been a painful disaster, withdrawal from Aitchison College a crushing disappointment and attempts at becoming a cabinet maker, plumber or retail shop assistant, a misguided waste of time.

Without an experienced mentor and a structured programme, the College of Hard Knocks in the University of Life seemed to be leading me nowhere. So there I was – the eldest sibling – drifting without a rudder, earning rubbish wages and unable to give Mummy the financial support she needed. Worse: Because of my temperament, I was *between* jobs almost as often as I was *in* one and I was in trouble a lot thanks to the devil and idle hands. The ever-present 'Now' seemed slowly to be smothering me and, like my Dad, I began searching, in different and distant places for... I knew not what.

One time four of us – Sol, Ronza, Yusuf and I took a train to Kimberley, in the Cape Province, to spend the Xmas holidays with friend Eddy Glass and his family. This was a helluva lot further than the Benoni my father had said I would never reach on my own steam, and we had a whale of a time.

A family in our third class compartment shared their homemade pickled fish and fried chicken with us, and we shared our shop-bought masala chip rolls and samoosas with them. We provided the gin and they the orange juice, and together we sang old Cape Ghoema songs – 'Die blikkie se boom is uit en kyk hoe lekker slaan die ghoema... Keena kana kina, keena, keena ho... Hier kom die Aliebama...' – till sleep took over.

Mrs Glass opened her heart and her modest township home to us and the local girls wrapped us in their warm welcomes, while their fellows had mixed feelings about our presence.

In those three weeks, I saw much of Kimberley and made pocket money to boot, working with Moos – a new friend – delivering bread for the local bakery to shops in the city's famous maze of crooked streets. Each one of us fell in love over and over again, and we danced and laughed with new friends at the season's house parties, club dances and the annual New Year's Eve Grand Ball in Kimberley's City hall.

Another time three of us –Yusuf, Dicky (Hajoo's brother) and I ran away from home and headed for the South Pole. The article and the pictures in the Outspan Magazine, about brave young men – non-white boys included – shipping off to Antarctica on whaling expeditions and earning pots of money, fired our imagination. We decided to cycle to Durban, join the whalers and hunt the icy seas for valuable ambergris.

What a pipe dream.

The biting wind that winter's night, combined with the weight of our heavy coats and backpacks made cycling a nightmare. We left Jo'burg soon after dark on a frigid Friday and before we even reached Heidelberg - some thirty miles away – the marrow in our bones had iced up, it seemed, our brains had frozen and we could not go on. We crawled in between two circular poured-concrete dams we saw standing on their sides in a farmer's field and huddled together for warmth. We tried to make a fire with damp cow dung, which smouldered and smoked but would not burn. The wet smoke succeeded only in making us smell like piles of barbecue-smoked cow poo.

Dawn saw us and our bikes lying in a muddle on the back of a God-sent truck piled high with crates of vegetables that were being transported to the Johannesburg Central Market on Bree Street in Newtown – just a few blocks from our homes in Fordsburg.

We three valiant fortune-hunters had fearlessly departed for the far-away polar region at around six the evening before, and were back home so quickly – feeling and smelling like dung – that no one even knew we had left.

Stop Or I Shoot!

Many years later, as I lay on the filthy floor of the acrid, piss-soaked, police station cell in central Beirut, with my nose pressed to the crack below the door, gasping for acid-free air, my mind went back to another cell near Johannesburg, long before. I would remember being backed into a corner, fighting off a ferocious attack by inmates and being saved from grievous harm by three tough, small-time gangsters – tsotsis – from Sophiatown. It was a time in our neighbourhoods when it was virtually impossible for most red-blooded teenagers to keep out of trouble unless they locked themselves indoors or joined a monastic society.

A case in point is the Friday night Yusuf and I decided to go to a snowball in Coronationville that was raising funds for the Rangers hockey team. How could we have known, when we decided to attend, that Yusuf would have to disappear into hiding from the police and that I would end up in a tough boys' detention centre where I would be in danger of losing my life?

The Rangers was a community team made up of possibly the prettiest girls in Johannesburg. Snowballs were small dance parties that cash-strapped sports teams or community groups organised to raise money from friends and sympathisers who were mostly just as badly cash-strapped. Club members and their families would donate food, refreshments and gifts for raffle prizes. Someone always offered the use of a house or back yard for the party. Invitations would go out by word of mouth, and supporters like us would to come to dance, eat and have fun.

The idea is to generate income starting with a small entrance fee. Then, as the evening progresses, the funds are 'snowballed' through the sale of food, refreshments and raffle tickets. Unemployed or underpaid as many of us were, we could usually scrape together the half-a-crown per head entrance fee, the sixpence a serving for soft drinks, tea, coffee or cake and the three shillings for a plate of mutton or chicken curry and rice or roast chicken, chips and salad. Alcohol was never on offer – those being prohibition days, but boy, did we dance – with or without the booze.

None of the other guys wanted to go to the snowball that night. 'Naa man, the last bus from Corrie is at eleven and the party will only be hotting up then,' Ronnie reminded us. 'I don't want to walk three hours back to Fordsie at two in the morning – you manne always say we'll get a lift but it never happens.'

'There'll be lotsa ruckshuns if those Lulu Belle guys from Newclare pitch up,' Sol added, 'you know the Coloured manne can't handle it when those Tamil chaps start dancing with their women. There'll be lots of shit flying and we'll be in the middle – naa, I'm also not going.' And so it was just Yusuf and me.

We got into serious trouble much later that night, but it had nothing to do with the snowball.

Sol was right – those guys from Newclare did pitch up. There were four of them – big, tough looking Tamil and Coloured chaps. But there was no trouble. They came with their own girls and with enough illicit booze to share behind closed bedroom doors or in the dark corners of the back yard. They were surprisingly good company and added to the gaiety. Before long Yusuf and I were dancing with their ladies and there were no problems.

At dances, in those days, dancing with a woman you did not know could be dangerous. If you did things right, no one got hurt. You first respectfully asked the guy for permission to ask his lady to dance. If he said no – that was that. If he responded positively, you then asked her – also very respectfully. If she said no you thanked her and backed away. If she agreed, you offered her your arm, escorted her to the dance floor and the two of you showed off your moves.

One dance only and it might appear that you did not enjoy the lady's company. Three dances and her boy friend or husband might think you were enjoying her company a little too much – and the shit could hit the fan. So, after the second dance, you escorted her to her seat and thanked her and her fellow politely. So the evening passed and a really good time was had by all.

It was one in the morning when Yusuf and I decided to start the long walk back to Fordsburg. As we collected our jackets from under the large pile in the bedroom, three fellows from Ophirton – far south of the City – asked if they could join us on the long trek. Clearly they felt they would be safer with us walking through Brixton and Mayfair (Afrikaner territory), Fietas (Time Square and Kajala Boys territory) and then Fordsburg (our territory), where, they had heard, we were fellows to be reckoned with.

Our group was certainly not made up of gangsters or tsotsis. We were not even recognised by anyone as a gang. However, it was obvious that people knew we were not to be messed with. On several occasions, real gangs had tried to shove us around. We had stood up to them in street fights in Fordsburg at the bioscopes and in Fietas at the Springbok Hall. We knew, if we didn't push back our lives would be a misery everywhere we went. And so, yes, we were not a group to be taken lightly – but we were not ruffians looking for trouble.

Like I said before, there is hardly ever just one reason for something significant happening. I ended up in the Apex Detention Centre for Boys for four reasons: Tired legs, wanting to be helpful, poor judgement and my ego needs. I should never have agreed to drive the stolen car no matter how tired I was. Particularly since Yusuf and I were only a few blocks from home. But, I pitied our companions who still had a long, tiring and dangerous way to walk to Ophirton.

The shortest route for them was the 'back way' from Fordsburg, across the Main Reef Road and along the narrow, mine service road through the mine dumps, but this was far from safe in the dark at three in the morning. The less hazardous way was the longer route through the city centre then south on Sauer Street through Selby and Park Central until they reached the relative safety of their own turf. These poor guys still had five or six more miles to walk and I felt sorry for them. Driving them home seemed the right thing to do. When they started trying the doors of the cars parked on the street I did not object as hard as I should have. And, when they found one unlocked and hot-wired it, I should never have agreed to drive it.

The lone policeman appeared out of nowhere on his bicycle while the chaps were still pushing the damn car and I was struggling to get it started. 'Klim uit die kar uit!' the cop fired at me in Afrikaans – 'get out of the car'. 'Who owns this vehicle?' he demanded to know, 'Show me the keys!' In a flash Yusuf knew the jig was up. He made a lightning dash for it, shouting: 'Run manne,' and we all scattered.

In the rush, the constable grabbed the sleeve of my jacket but I jerked free, and flew up some side street with him in close pursuit. Had I been running on the track at Aitchison College I would surely have broken some record for the 100-yard dash. Within seconds, I was a half block ahead of him.

'Stop or I shoot!' I didn't think the policeman could see well enough on that dim-lit street to hit me, so, instead of stopping, I ran faster, in an adrenalin-induced zigzag. Soon as I turned the corner, I had a fast decision to make: Could I be out of his sight around the next corner, before he turned *this* corner and opened fire? I wasn't sure. I jumped a fence into someone's front garden, then climbed a wall onto their dark veranda and hid there, panting and sweating. Within minutes, I heard the cop open the garden gate. He walked straight to my hiding place and said, quietly, in Afrikaans, 'come out slowly, or I shoot you dead!'

Later, as I sat handcuffed on the back seat of a squad car I heard my captor laughing as he described the chase to his colleague, the driver: 'Yessus Boet, the coolie can run, man. I couldn't keep up. When the bliksem turned that corner, I had to stop running I was out of breath. The fool should have kept going. I would have lost him. Die mense is so dom – these people are so stupid – don't they know it's always the breathing that gives you away when you're hiding. And blerry hell, I didn't even have my revolver with me.'

The journey to Apex took forever. After the chase Corporal Sarel had silently walked me back to his bicycle and handcuffed my one arm to the carrier-rack. Then, after taking down particulars of the vehicle, he casually cycled the few blocks to the Fordsburg police station, puffing on a cigarette, with me running behind him like an obedient dog. There a police van transported us both to his own base-station somewhere in Mayfair-West where, between slaps, I was questioned.

'Waar is jou vriende? – Where are your friends?' Slap. 'They not my friends Sir, they all from Ophirton. I only met them now walking from Coronationville.' Slap. 'You lie, you coolie swine, what were youse doing in a white area so late'? 'I was walking home from a dance Sir – I don't know where they were coming from.' Slap. 'You think us blerry fools hey.' Slap. 'They your chommies – friends – so you tell us now, before I break your blerry jaw, where they going?'

I knew Yusuf was under a one year suspended sentence for punching up a nasty boss. I also knew that the guys from Ophirton would take the road home through town which was longer but safer – so I had made up my story in the back of the police van. My first priority was to keep the cops away from Yusuf.

Now I started a good rendition of sobbing and stammering, 'They said they, they, they going home Sir,' I whimpered. 'They said they taking the short cut to Ophirton through, (stammer) through, (stammer) through the mine dumps, Sir, because they afraid to be seen in town, Sir.'

Corporal Sarel may have thought that he was so smart and I was stupid because I did not know about that heavy breathing thing when I was hiding. The fact is that he and his partners were as thick as two planks. They never got close to Yusuf and those three fellows from Ophirton.

I was arrested around 3am that Saturday morning and only delivered to Apex in Benoni some twelve hours later. For what seemed ages Corporal Sarel and his partner Boet had vainly scoured the dark, narrow, mine-dump, back roads south of the Main Reef Road. I just sat quietly, like the Sphinx, with a Mona Lisa smile in my eyes, handcuffed on the back seat of the squad car. The cops were thorough in their hunt, but completely off track. They never once thought of looking for the chaps on the longer route through the city centre.

Afterwards I was transported to the notorious Old Fort Prison

Complex on Hospital Hill, a frightening place popularly known simply as Number Four. There I was dumped in a large empty room where I lay on the floor, for hours, with my arms stretched above my head, handcuffed around one of eight thick, intricately carved wooden legs of a huge conference table.

As the pain in my back cut deeper and I twisted and squirmed to find a less painful position, I did not know that, in history's own time, the nation and the world would find out about this terrible place. Here thousands of South Africans had been incarcerated, interrogated and punished; here many famous political figures had been detained, including Mahatma Gandhi and Nelson Mandela. I did not know that one day we would see this evil place physically and spiritually cleansed and regenerated. It would be renamed Constitution Hill, would house our Constitutional Court and become the place where the basic rights, freedoms and hopes of all South Africans would be enshrined.

It was from this hateful Number Four that I was finally processed and carted to Apex in a police lorry, the next morning, with fifteen other boys including a tsotsi called Bomba, whom I didn't know but who smiled at me as if in recognition.

Shit started happening as soon as we arrived and I was targeted before I got to the reception counter in the administration block. 'Hier is ń amper-baas vir julle – here is an almost-boss for you,' announced the Afrikaner official to the black inmate-boss-boys who had started herding us into the building as soon as we jumped off the truck.

In this context, in those days, all whites were seen as baas or boss. Indians and Coloureds, though not white, were not black enough and, because of the racial pecking order of the times, were often referred to, with anger or contempt, as 'almost-boss.' And so I had become an 'amper-baas' – fair game to be got at.

'Die wittes in die kantoor sal alles steel – the whites in the office will steal everything,' one 'boss-boy' said, as we moved towards the building, 'give me your cigarettes and cash now, quickly, before you are searched. We will share with you inside or you will lose it all.' I and a few others parted with our cigarettes and other items of value and never saw any of it again.

Then, during the regulation arrival-shower, one of the boss-boys whacked me hard on my wet behind with a plastic belt for no reason. As I spun around in anger, one of them glared at me: 'Ek sê will jy rol? – I say do you wanna fight?' In a flash I was back in Troyeville with those white bully boys Peter, Gavin and Porky. I heard again the hateful call, 'Coolie come out and fight!' this time in a different context from three black bully boys instead

I didn't respond to the challenge in the shower and, for some reason, they had backed off – or so I thought. After showering and cleaning the shower and toilet areas, all our things were taken from us and we were issued clean short trousers – far too big for us – a shirt, and two blankets. Then we were herded to the lock-up, carrying our folded blankets on one arm and holding up our trousers by hooking two fingers of the other hand into a trouser loop – since we were not given belts.

The sight of maybe a hundred and fifty boys – almost all black, with a smattering of Coloureds and not an Indian in view – is forever chiselled on my mind. The lock up was a massive hall, with a shiny, green concrete floor and a high roof. Wherever you looked there were boys walking around with a finger hooked into a trouser loop, stretched out on narrow sleeping mats or sitting in groups talking, smoking, and passing around stompies – cigarette butts. The loners seemed nervous or afraid and the small groups of tsotsis – vicious small time thugs – were rowdy and loud, and their leaders all had belts.

The weekend I spent in Apex would have been pure hell had it not been for Bomba. Most of the new arrivals had found floor space near each other, and, as we were settling down, Bomba had smiled again and signalled me to come lay my mat closer to him and his mates Fanyaan and George.

The second Bomba started talking my anxiety eased. 'Ek sê biza, moenie wurry nie, alles is dolie, ek ken jou – I say friend, don't worry, all is okay, I know you.' His next words, in Afrikaans, blew my mind. 'Howz your brother Keppies, is he still dancing the Makeppie Special?'

If we weren't working at some part-time Saturday morning job or away on an errand, it's more than likely you would find one or other of us Carim boys on the corner, just steps from our Terrace Road house, jiving with the street kids to the blistering kwela rythms blaring from Tony's barber shop. The music was loud, people on Main Road were alive with a vibrancy that was pure Fordsburg and the young dancers received spirited applause each time one of them showed off a new outrageous movement that no one had seen before.

I was there the Saturday mid-morning when Enver – Keppies – danced and did his wacky new step. Bomba and George told me they were also in the group of onlookers that morning and had also koozaed him – shouted their encouraging approval. Then they enthusiastically joined in the dancing to learn Enver's 'special' moves, which they afterwards took back home with them to the lively street corners of Sophiatown.

When the bully boys attacked before dawn the next morning they came at me with belts flailing as I stepped out of the lavatory stall. In seconds, I was bleeding from cuts on my face and arms. With no time to think I back-peddled down a short corridor into a deserted dead-end corner in some dim lit, dusty storage area piled high with banged-up metal folding chairs, sleeping mats and assorted boxes.

Please don't say it: Of course I should have known better than to go to the toilet alone at that hour. But what should I have done? I didn't know Bomba and the others well enough to wake them from their sleep, I didn't realise the extent of the danger and, as they say in the pictures: 'When you gotta go you gotta go!'

The toilet and ablution area was deserted and the assault was silent. All you could hear was the swishing of the belts and the smack each time plastic or leather connected with naked flesh. I fought back, also in silence, swinging a chair and keeping them at bay as best I could. I lost my shorts when I grabbed the chair and now the belts were biting into my thighs and buttocks.

Then I saw the malevolence in the eyes of the smallest of the three and realised he was rewinding his belt around his clenched hand, this time with the buckle at the business end, meaning to do me severe harm. I panicked, started screaming for help and began swinging the chair even more ferociously, knowing I would soon tire. It was at that instant of impending hopelessness that Bomba burst into the room. He was yelling obscenities as his flying belt buckle cut the air and bit into the neck of the small guy. Fanyaan was close behind, belt whirling, buckle-end also slicing up the space. The fight was vicious and quick, and when George arrived and waded in with a length of broom handle, the attackers tore out of that room faster than I can swing a metal folding chair.

Bomba explained what happened as he cleaned away the blood from the cuts and welts on my body with water-soaked pieces of my shirttail. Fanyaan had wanted to go to the lavatory and had prodded Bomba awake as back up. Their street antennas began vibrating the moment they noticed my empty mat and, as they approached the dimly lit toilet and shower stalls, they heard my screams. Like warrior protectors sent by my guardian angels they were on my assailants in an instant. The yelling had also electrified George into action. It was he who said the next morning, as we dunked our stale bread into the watery coffee, 'Jy is dom, man, maar die God, Hey kyk agter jou. Nou is jy met ons –You are stupid, man, but God looks after you. Now you're with us.'

It seems I had inadvertently come between two rival Sophiatown tsotsi gangs. I had been targeted not only for being an amper-baas but also for appearing to be part of the Bomba faction. Now the only safety for me was to stick as close as possible to my watchful protectors until Monday morning when we would be taken back to Johannesburg to the Magistrate's Court.

The case was heard in quick time and I can still hear the magistrate's drone as he sentenced me: 'Six months in a boys' place of detention, suspended for two years in the care of a remand officer – next case!'

Blood on the Pavement

Even now I can see Bomba's rebellious grin as I walked past him and Fanyaan and George on my way out of the court. He gave me the thumbs-up sign which said: 'Alles is figzup – all is well,' and the moving-fist-in-front-of-the-eyes sign, with the index and pinkie finger extended, which meant two things, 'Kuik uit. Ek sal jou weer noch my biza! Keep your eyes peeled. I'll see you again, my brother!'

I never ran into George or Fanyaan again and the next time I saw Bomba – maybe a year after Apex – he lay bleeding on the pavement in front of the Lyric Hairdressing Salon. I did not know, as I kneeled beside him, speaking softly and dabbing at the blood trickling from a tiny hole in his chest with my handkerchief that he was dying.

I did not cry: Not when the ambulance medic pressed a finger onto the bleeding hole and a fountain of Bomba's blood, red like mine, shot a foot into the air and ran into the cracks in the pavement. Not later, when the medic announced to his partner, as a matter of fact, 'Hey man, die okie's dood. – Hey man, this chap's dead.'

I would cry another time, but now I just remembered... everything. What a fellow, Bomba! Here he was, my tsotsi friend from Sophiatown, dead - stabbed through the heart with an ice pick or a sharpened spoke from a bicycle wheel. I wondered then, as I wonder now: To what extent did his fierce defence of me in Apex contribute to his death? I wondered then, as I wonder now: Does he feel my grief for my loss of his friendship? Does he hear my thanks for the lesson he taught me: That love and courage and friendship can emerge from the most unexpected quarters, in the darkest of times, and that it can reach across the widest and most complex racial, cultural and religious divides.

From that time, my thoughts and actions have been guided by what I learned from Bomba: the good or evil that people do comes from what is in their hearts and souls and characters, not from their station in life or from the colour of the pigmentation granules in their skin tissue that determines their complexion.

Yusuf, Basil and Ginger

Yusuf Asvat was my best friend in the world at the time and when I agreed to accompany 'Spooks' Duplessis to a party in Denver one Saturday night, I had no idea that I would meet Basil Maynard and Ibrahim (Ginger) Bhayat, my next two best friends.

I've always had a 'best friend in the world' – one who was sent by the Universe to walk with me through a particular chapter in my life. Cousin Zohra is the first. When we made chutney together in Ma's back yard she showed me that I would learn best by actually *doing* – not just by reading or listening. Then there was Sally van Rensburg in Troyeville, who defied her community to keep up her friendship with the coolie boy from the shop. This Afrikaner girl was my messenger of hope for a future South Africa free of racial divisions. None of us could even imagine such a society in those days. Our friendship, in all its innocence, was too far ahead of its time. From Simon I learned about unconditional compassion and from Manilal the value of reading that stayed with me all my life.

Spooks and I had danced and laughed together at a Saturday afternoon church social in dusty Noordgesicht – a sprawling Coloured township southwest of Jo'burg across the highway from today's Soweto. I had led a square dance that he was part of, and he was bowled over by the high-octane movements and by how much we had all enjoyed ourselves.

'Ek sê man, you kwaai man – I say man, you're terrific, man,' Spooks was gushing, as we left the church hall heading for the train station. 'You must come with to the jeet – the dance – tonight and lead our square!'

This gregarious fellow was taking the train home to Denver, a tough, treeless neighbourhood far away on the eastern edge of Johannesburg – opposite Malvern – on the bad side of the railway tracks. I was on the same train heading for home and would leave it at Braamfontein Station. Now Spooks was persuading me to continue on to Denver with him. 'The snowball's gwana be hot, and there'll be lotsa lekker cherries.' I agreed when he added the clincher: 'And after the dance you can dos – sleep – by my pozie.'

The dance was going full blast when we arrived and Spooks introduced me to my future best friends in his usual enthusiastic style: 'Ek sê manne ou Mac here gwana lead our square.'

Basil, Ginger and I were just getting to know each other when a charge of excitement surged through the spirited crowd and stopped us short. The unique Ghoema-sounding burst of musical fanfare from the band had announced, in the language of musical notes: 'Get your partners, get ready, the squares are about to begin.'

Suddenly people were scampering about and forming animated groups of four couples with one person as the dance leader. Spooks appeared with green-eyed Olive and her sister Claudette and introduced them as our partners. Within seconds, Basil and Ginger appeared with their partners. And there we stood – a square of four keyed up couples facing each other, among other squares of four couples also facing each other – all eagerly waiting for the music of the first set to blast off and lift the revelry to more exhilarating heights.

As I led my square through the first set, calling out and signalling the basic movements – 'arm-in-arm', 'corner-swing', 'glacé', 'halfway', 'swaai' and 'huis-toe', I had no idea that the squares we were dancing were a combination of two very old dance forms – one from Europe, the other from our very own Cape Province.

First, there was the Quadrille that originated in Spain when groups of Spanish cavalry horsemen performed intricate square-shaped formations and movements during military parades. These displays were so impressive that soon people began developing 'cuadrillos' – Spanish meaning four or the Latin 'quadratus', meaning square – without horses. Gradually the four-couple-square evolved into an intricate dance form in its own right. It moved to the grand ballrooms of France and England between 1760 and 1808, and later caused a so-called 'epidemic of quadrille fever in South Africa's colonial society'.[2]

In South Africa's Cape Coloured community, the quadrille was fused with the commercial which, as historian, educationist and executive director of the Western Cape Theatre Company, Peter Voges opines, may have been developed by the Cape's slave musicians. These local artists emulated the music and dance formations of their European masters and blended it here, on the sun-drenched tip of Africa, with their own homegrown rhythms.

What I also didn't know was that the indigenous Cape music had, much earlier, been infused with exotic sounds that came with the sailors, adventurers and slaves off the ships from the spice routes of Ceylon, India, Indonesia, Malaya, Madagascar and Mozambique. These multi-cultural cross-pollinators had arrived here, after 1652, at Jan van Riebeeck's halfway refreshment station as free men or slaves. They brought with them the richness of Eastern cultures and the words they spoke would gradually fuse with words from local and European languages. Together this melange would seep into the Dutch and transform it into a creolised patois that would become their new language – Afrikaans.

These cross-pollinators had also intermingled with the local people and with each other, and had given birth to the vibrant and attractive Cape Coloureds of South Africa, of which my mother and my future mother-in-law were among their loveliest descendents.

In the heat of the dancing that night, I was not thinking about history. Instead, I was assessing the level of square-dancing talent of each of the seven other dancers. I needed to know how far and fast I could mix in more complicated formations, and the best part was the 'dance within the dance'.

---

[2] See A.F. Hattersley: An Illustrated Social History of South Africa

The music would suddenly change from a ghoema or quadrille beat and we would be surprised into slowing down completely and doing a conventional tango, slow waltz or fox trot. Then suddenly, in a kind of spontaneous combustion, the tempo would explode again into the ghoema beat. In no time, the girls were shrieking with joy and we were all breathless and damp, our faces glistening and radiant and our carefree hearts bursting with fun and high-octane adrenalin.

I am convinced that no dancers in the posh ballrooms of 17th and 18th century Europe or in the cotillions of the colonial Cape of Good Hope, could have enjoyed themselves more than we did that night in 20th century Johannesburg.

I must have done something right because, immediately after the first square, Basil took charge: 'After the dance we going for a bite and then take these cherries home. You'll sleep at my house tonight and tomorrow we'll drive you home – I'll tell Spooks.'

From that night we became a clique of four – Yusuf, Basil, Ginger and me - and we were inseparable.

Basil Maynard (right) and me

From left: Yusuf Asvat, Basil, me

From left: Sham, Yusuf, Basil, Spinner Eaglehof and Ginger Bhayat

Basil and the ever-popular 1949 Chevvy

These Denver boys were well groomed and sharply dressed. They had a quality about them that young people today describe as 'cool'. Yusuf and I agreed later that Basil and Ginger had added a new level of style to our image. Best of all Basil had a car – a shiny, green, 1949 Fleetline Chevrolet with white-wall tires. This automobile expanded the boundaries of our pedestrian lives.

Now, making long walks home from a party that was just 'hotting' up became a thing of the past. We could now stay as late as we wanted, offer to drive a load of laughing girls home from a dance after the last bus, enjoy a hamburger at my Uncle Pietie's Crescent Cafe, and usually also enjoy a smooch at the Zoo Lake on the way home. It was now no big deal to drive to distant Pretoria and party with the popular Moosa brothers Hassen and Issie. Or go on a holiday break to faraway Durban for good times with socialites Spinner Eaglehoffe, his wife-to-be 'Eskimo', and Davy Martin and his group of fun-loving, dance crazy friends.

Such good times became the norm, but, I quickly realised, this could only last as long as I had steady work and made good money. I needed to earn enough to help support the family and still have cash to pay my share of a fast-paced weekend.

Thanks to Yusuf, Basil and Ginger, I sharpened my street smarts and my ability to move safely through our tough neighbourhoods. From Yusuf I learned when to stay cool in a face-off and when to come out punching first, before saying even a single word. Later in life, this instinct would get me out of hairy situations more than once.

From Basil I learned to identify potentially dangerous situations and to either defuse them or steer clear, which, in our tough neighbourhoods, was a vital skill. It seems he picked up this know-how while he and Ginger assisted Mannie, his older brother, to provide a safe environment for their mine-worker customers in the most successful shebeen in Denver.

The richest gold mines on the Witwatersrand were concentrated along a reef that stretched from Randfontein in the west, through Johannesburg's southern suburbs, to Springs in the east. The black migrant workers who dug up and processed the gold were housed in huge male-only hostels in desolate compounds and lived lonely lives, without their families, in atrocious conditions. Their desperate need for relief from the monotonous compound life was the catalyst for the presence, in every mining town, of shebeens – South Africa's famous illegal drinking houses. These establishments provided the miners a space to relax, meet friends and generally socialise. Unfortunately, the money miners brought into the shebeens also attracted the criminal elements – the tsotsis with their crime and violence.

Management by Avoidance

The Maynard family shebeen was located in a sprawling old house on a large property close to several mine hostels. 'I don't give a damn what the church says,' Mannie once fumed, 'If things were different I could own a licensed restaurant or a pub any where in the Transvaal and these workers could come have a quiet drink in a safe place – but the laws say we can't. These people need somewhere on their off-days. We'll give them a clean, safe place to relax and socialise. If the government gives us a licence, we'll do it legally – otherwise to hell with them!'

Mannie knew that the key to success in the tough and dangerous shebeen business was safety and security of workers carrying pay packets. So, he trained his people to protect the customers from pickpockets and muggers and the violence they brought with them. His approach was something I would call 'management by avoidance.' It was all about defusing potentially dangerous situations before they escalated into violence.

Basil, Ginger and selected staff were coached to take frequent walk-abouts in and around the shebeen in a state of heightened awareness. They would look closely at the dynamic between groups of patrons in the various rooms, the verandas and in the front and back yards. The trick was to read body language, check facial expressions and listen to tones of voice. At the slightest hint of tension, my friends would engage with the patrons and assess the situation more closely.

'Ootini biza?' 'Is hoe my broer?' 'What you say my friend?' 'Howzit going brother.' Then they would take the appropriate action; either defuse any threat if they could or call for back up. Suspected trouble-makers were quickly and roughly escorted off the premises.

We used this management-by-avoidance technique often. Whenever we attended a snowball, a dance or other public function where we didn't know the people the routine would be the same. We would first casually fan out through the crowd, observing intently and listening closely. In minutes, we had a sense of whether or not we should leave. On more than one occasion, we knew we had 'read' the situation right when people said afterwards, 'You manne were smart to leave – there was big trouble later and people got hurt'.

No Attitude of Entitlement

These Denver boys loved a good time as much as any of us, but they also demonstrated a healthy balance between work and play. They were never unemployed, while some of us were constantly between jobs and they were always upwardly mobile. Ginger was training as a furrier, a highly specialised field. Basil was becoming a master cabinet-maker with plans to own his own furniture factory – which he eventually did. And, no matter how hard we played on weekends, they never missing a day at work. 'Look,

I love the good times as much as anyone,' he once said, 'but nothing comes free. We must work and be able to pay for it. '

A lifetime later, in 1994, Basil's street wisdom helped save a confused boy from a dead-end life.

I was on a research visit from Toronto and learned that Hajoo's nephew Ridwan Halim had dropped out of school and Brenda, his mother, had pleaded: 'Talk to him, please, Mac. He has a useless job offloading crates from trucks for R700 a month. He must at least finish matric to get a decent job'.

Riddie and I had a chat over spicy masala chip-rolls and tea in Fordsburg and talked about cars, smart clothes and good stereo equipment. He knew the big brands well and knew exactly what he wanted. We talked about travel and he said he would visit us in Toronto one day. When I asked if he was the marrying kind: 'Ja, sure,' he responded enthusiastically, 'I want my own family and a nice house with a garden for the children.'

Then we got to the money part and talked about the cost of owning a car, visiting Canada, supporting a family and buying a house and the boy was sharp. He quickly realised that R700 a month would not buy much.

Fourteen months after our chat Ridwan Halim earned his Matriculation Certificate and graduated as a Lotus Software Engineer a year later in 1996. Then he moved up from one good job to another, bought a car then a house and, in 2006, married lovely Cindy de Wet. In 2008, he called me during the christening party of their first child Connor: 'We're sorry you couldn't make it Uncle Mac, I just want to thank you again, for making me understand about the culture of entitlement, and for reminding me that nothing comes free – and that only good knowledge and skills would get me the kind of job and income to pay for the things I want'.

Ridwan doesn' know the extent to which Basil Maynard's street philosophy influenced his personal growth and development.

14
SATURDAYS WITH HAJOO

Fordsburg

It was a Saturday evening, the first of September 2007. Hajoo and I had renewed our marriage vows in friends, Gillian and Biagio Longano's amazing garden in Johannesburg, under trees ablaze with pink and white peach blossoms, while a gipsy ensemble serenaded our guests. Then we dined and danced with a hundred and twenty family and friends in celebration of our 50th wedding anniversary. Much later, as I lay restless in the still of the early morning night, waiting for the adrenalin to stop its mischief, a vision came to me of another Saturday, 52 years earlier, in 1955. That was the day when seventeen-year-old Hajira Halim talked and laughed with me and, in a flash, sparked a rebirth of purpose that ignited within me a positive discontent with things the way they were.

That distant Saturday, like every Saturday in Fordsburg, the neighbourhood was abuzz with shoppers and dawdlers. From Bree Street's small family-run Indian spice and vegetable markets, to Main Road's Jewish hot-bread-and-rolls Atlas Bakery and tiny Lebanese mom and pop stores, to Tony's raucous Hairdressing Salon, the morning streets were pulsating with energy and enthusiasm.

In the afternoon the Saturday excitement shifted to the north-west edge of Fordsburg and mingled with the crowds of snazzily-dressed people that thronged the Cinemascope shows at the Majestic and Lyric bioscopes – cinemas – on Central Road and the lively eating establishments in the vicinity.

Bioscope was one of the few affordable pleasures many in our community had in those days and, for us teenagers, the most exciting time to arrive on this pulsating Saturday scene was in the early afternoon. This allowed adequate time to rub shoulders with the beautiful people as they did their leisurely fashionista promenade from the Majestic Cinema, past Solly's Corner on Bree and Central, past the Lyric Cinema and the Kentucky Milk Bar, then around the corner into Burghersdorp Street to the popular Cisco's Fish & Chips and our Uncle Joe Kajee's vibrant Crescent Cafe. This little strip of weekend magic was where we rendezvoused with friends, shared the news, and had a bite together. Then we would saunter back to queue for the four o'clock show at one of the bios – unless of course we were headed for the matinee dance at the Springbok Hall in adjacent Fietas.

I can still feel the eagerness during that early spring day in 1955, as I laid my sharpest trousers out on the bed, chose the contrasting shirt and matching socks and belt, bathed, fixed my Tony Curtis hairstyle, and checked my cash. I did not know, as I left the house that my life was about to change forever.

I was driving my Dad's 1948 Chevrolet and cruising with Basil, Yusuf and Ginger in the vibrant Central Road and Burghersdorp Street area when suddenly there she was – Hajoo Halim – on the sidewalk, in a group, in front of Cisco's Cafe, smiling radiantly, and then suddenly laughing at something someone said. In that instant, I lost my heart. I also lost control of the wheel momentarily and would have scraped the cars parked in front of the Crescent had Yusuf not grabbed the steering and yelled at me, 'Blerry hell. Stop ogling the cherries and look where you driving'

I parked, and, trying to appear as cool and collected as I could, walked over to the group, gave Timie, Hajoo's gorgeous older sister, a warm hello and nodded politely to their smartly dressed escorts, Salim Musson and Sayed Patel. Then I looked into Hajira Halim's eyes and, mustering my appealing best, spoke to her, what I thought were words that would dazzle, 'It's good to see you again, Poenie.' From the way she smiled in return, I convinced myself I had made a good impression: 'It's nice to see you too, Mac,' she said quietly, her dark-brown eyes sparkling with amusement at my brass.

Man, how she had blossomed! She was a quiet twelve year old the last time I had seen her. I was fourteen. The Halims were one of the families I had liked well enough to pay a special farewell visit to before I left for Aitchison College in Pakistan, in December 1950. I remember Hajoo at that time as a shy, smiling, brown-skinned girl with two plaits that hung far down her back, wearing a navy blue school gym, white shirt and socks and black school shoes.

Now, five years later, she was a striking beauty, dressed in a sky blue grosgrain jacket and skirt, with shiny black hair set in the fashionable poodle-cut of the time. Her skin had the texture of Duke Ellington's satin-faced-baby, which, years later, Deribe Siné Georgis, my friend and colleague in Addis Ababa, would describe as the dusky shade of the best Ethiopian coffee with the perfect amount of milk – 'bunna be witit'.

Hajoo

All this, combined with the radiance of her smile and her serene, modest manner that hinted at a deep melancholy, touched places in my soul I didn't know I had.

The chance encounter with Hajoo in front of Cisco's happened in the spring of 1955 and, in the months that followed, I was lost to my friends, my family and my neighbourhood. How could any of us have known that the sincerity in Hajoo's unpretentious response: 'It's nice to see you too, Mac,' would have the power to draw us together and carry the two of us – then three, then four of us – on an adventure-filled odyssey that would take us onto three oceans, nine seas and across four continents?

All that would come later. First, I had to face the daunting task of getting 'house permission'.

Mr Halim, and his oldest daughter Ayesha, who managed the Halim household since the divorce of their parents, believed that 'decent girls' did not meet boys on 'street corners', or anywhere outside the house. Gentlemen, they insisted, should 'come calling'.

Hajoo told me later that, when we met, I had a reputation for being a wild one; that I was running with an unruly bunch; that we were often in trouble, and that I had a string of girls in tow. It must have surprised many when I formally asked Mr Halim for house-permission and he formally allowed me to visit Hajoo at home as often as I cared to. She was also permitted to go out with me once a week, on a Saturday afternoon – and without a chaperon!

Hond se Bêk

The person who coined the phrase 'roses in a dung heap' must have been thinking of the lovely, gracious Halim girls living in that gritty corner of Doornfontein, commonly known as Hond se Bêk – Dog's Mouth. The tiny suburb was so named for the crazy barking of the dogs each time squads of police raided this tough, dangerous neighbourhood.

The four streets in this area were dreary, dismal and bereft of flowers, grass or trees. Instead, they were pockmarked with drab commercial buildings and ugly galvanised iron warehouse-sheds that cast shadows of gloom over a sprinkling of twenty or so humble dwellings that people called home and which they bravely struggled to keep as tidy as they could.

The Halim home, at 2b Beacon Road, was one of a terrace of four small houses all painted a matte-white. They stood out from the dark, miserable appearance of the other structures on the street like lush green palms on a barren desert plain. The pale finish of each of these houses contrasted attractively with their narrow red verandas which lay behind low white walls that were topped with a glaze of the same red surface. All this redness gleamed from regular applications of Sunbeam Stoep Polish.

It seemed as if each veranda stood as a buffer between the neat house and the dreary pavement and street. What I noticed immediately about the Halim home, when I began courting Hajoo, were the lovely white lace curtains in the large old-fashioned sash windows that looked out over the stoep. Despite their delicate prettiness, these curtains seemed determined to soften the environment and protect the family inside from the danger and ugliness outside.

This neighbourhood was a multiracial mix of Coloured, Indian, Malay and African families who were Muslims, Hindus and Christians. In neighbourhoods like this, despite occasional flare-ups that come from the pressures of a difficult existence in close quarters, there was a cross-cultural sense of community. Here the 'aunty' up the road would feel free to pinch your arm or twist your ear for swearing in the street. Or you could be klapped on the head by the 'uncle' on the corner when he caught you smoking in one of the lanes.

Here parents eked out a living as best they could; children played on the street dodging fast cars, and adolescents often dropped out of school soon after they entered their teens to look for work and supplement the family income.

Here police vans prowled the streets continually, for Hond se Bêk was a place where danger constantly lurked.

I saw this danger first hand when I turned the corner into Beacon Road one Saturday and walked straight into a life and death battle.

There, in the middle of the street, in front of the Halim house, was a large Zulu man stomping, snorting, and brandishing two deadly knobkierries – fighting sticks – one in each hand. He was facing off a small and far younger chap, a tsotsi, armed with a vicious-looking slim-blade dagger in his right hand, his jersey protectively wrapped around his left forearm as a shield and a look in his eyes that was chilling.

As the group of onlookers watched silently, these fellows weaved, bobbed, and circled each other grimly, each waiting for an opening to do serious harm. The big fellow was a Zulu, and because of his height advantage and metre-long kieries, he was on the offensive. He kept jabbing forward with the left-hand stick, lifting the right one high in the air. Then suddenly the right arm would swing and we could hear the whoosh as the heavy stick cut down through the air, intent on destruction. For an instant, I remembered my father's boxing lessons in Troyeville: 'Straight left, straight left, straight left, watch for the opening, and then a quick follow through with a right cross.'

Each time the heavy stick whooshed down, the nimble tsotsi would back-peddle out of range with the speed of lightning, then just as fast he would jump back in to stab at his enemy, then in a flash, back out of range again. So they danced, back and forth, round and round and when the end came, we could hardly believe our eyes – it happened so quickly.

The big stick had whooshed down; Tsotsi had jumped back, then quickly forward again. When the stick whooshed down the next time, instead of jumping out of range again as Zulu-man expected, Tsotsi jumped forward, fast as greased lightning, ducking low under the descending arm and suddenly there was blood gushing from Zulu-man's neck onto the street. As the big man stumbled and dropped his kieries the silent crowd evaporated, but I think we all saw the incredulity on Zulu man's face as the boy stabbed him twice again, and he fell to the tar.

The massive male-only mine hostel on Van Beek Street that loomed over the west end of Beacon Road was so close to the Halim home, you could throw a ball from their stoep against its forbidding outer wall. It housed hundreds of migrant mine labourers who, like the miners in Denver and in all such compounds on the Rand, lived in terrible conditions.

In mine hostels everywhere, the miners' desperation for relief from the monotonous compound life was the catalyst for the presence of the usual shebeens. Nearly a third of the houses in this tiny area of Hond se Bêk were actually illegal drinking houses and, as usual, the cash money miners brought into the shebeens attracted the tsotsis and their thieving violence.

The Halim house shared the lane behind their backyard with one of the shebeens. As Hajoo recalls, from their yard they could smell the sourness of the skokiaan and hear the miners coming and going and sometimes brawling. 'We all learned to live with this,' she said, 'but the late night barking of the dogs and the screaming when people were beaten with police batons and dragged away, were sounds I never got used to.'

Hajoo's life-long passion for flowers and gardens and for clean, quiet, orderly spaces clearly came from growing up on that drab, dusty street that did not have a single garden or tree and barely any grass. Her intense dislike and unforgiving attitude towards aggressive people, insensitive, bullying behaviour and rough language came from seeing men bleeding and staggering past her front door almost every weekend.

Our life-long friends the Veerappans, a large family of flower-sellers, lived in similar circumstances around the corner on Siverwright Avenue. Decades later, in Toronto, as immigrants, we would reminisce at family gatherings about the good-old bad-old days and, although we laughed a lot, the recollections would be bitter sweet and tears would be just behind the eyes.

Hajoo's memories of the grit and grime of a depressing street would transmute into a gifted ability to transform ordinary spaces into oases of peace, tranquillity and beauty. She succeeded in doing this when we lived in a converted storeroom, in Kano, on the edge of the Sahara Desert, and in other countries that were going mad in the throes of coups, counter-coups or civil wars. In each of the homes she made for us, the first things that went up after the fridge, the toaster and the coffee pot were connected, were the snowy white curtains to keep danger and ugliness out.

Poenie

Hajira Halim was born in a tiny flat in a double story building in Fordsburg at 69 Avenue Road. It was here, at the age of three, that she dramatically demonstrated her fondness for travel, and got the nickname Poenie.

As the story goes, little Hajira (or Hajoo) had suddenly disappeared one afternoon, causing a major family panic. She had taken off, alone, and, without any qualms, walked into the open door of the the home of a Tamil lady – Poenie – several houses away, around the corner. That was the first of many solo excursions the toddler made to Poenie's house. In time, amused neighbours began referring to her as 'Poenie se kind – Poenie's child.' Soon they began actually calling her Poenie, and the name stuck.

Years later, after the family moved to Hond se Bêk, seven-year-old Poenie fell in love with the big musical spectaculars. Whenever her mother could spare it, Hajoo cadged a sixpence for the cheap seats in the first four rows at the Rio or Good Hope bioscopes and a tickey – three pence – for the new king size cola drink called Pepsi. There she, often with her friend Ruth Hill from around the corner, would be enthralled by dancers like Fred Astaire, Ginger Rogers and Rita Hayworth or Gene Kelly, Judy Garland and Cyd Charisse. In her sixties, she was still mad enough about musicals to go and see the blockbuster Kander and Ebb musical Chicago four times – first with her best friend Grace Jones on Broadway in New York, then three more times in Johannesburg at different venues. 'I'll go as often as I can to see choreography by Bob Fosse,' she would enthuse.

School for young Poenie was a very happy time and her favourite teachers were Gang Naidoo, Mrs Adams and Mrs Scharnek. 'I could feel how much our teachers cared for us,' she once affirmed. 'I did well because of them and usually came first or second in class.' Then, laughingly, she told me that she cried bitterly the first time she came third. 'I loved the books we got as prizes every year. When they told me the school could not afford to also give prizes to those who came in third I just burst into tears.'

'The best book I won was *Heidi,* by Johanna Spyri,' she recalled. 'As I read the words, I would lose myself in the tall grass and flowers on the hillsides of Switzerland. Sometimes I thought I could actually smell the fresh mountain air and taste the goat's milk cheese. Then I would daydream about leaving Hond se Bêk and wandering with Heidi and Peter the Goatherd through the green mountain meadows.'

Hajoo's dream of walking in the those mountains came true in the Swiss summer of 2001 when she visited our son Xavier and his wife Amita, in Geneva and made memorable trips to beautiful Evian-les-Bains and Montreaux on Lac Genéve and Chamonix on Mont Blanc in the French Alps.

I joined her in 2004 when she visited Geneva again. We often drove through quaint villages and walked along mountain paths high in the green hills around Lake Geneva. One special morning I caught a look on my wife's face that reflected pure joy and I remembered the melancholy in her eyes, all those years ago in Hond se Bêk, when she talked about a neighbourhood without grass and trees, where dogs went mad, people screamed and blood stained the pavements.

Hajoo is happiest today when we drive in the cool of the Drakensberg Mountains, walk under the flamboyant bougainvillea and the tranquil jacaranda trees in Pretoria, cruise through the pretty seaside towns on the Garden Route to Cape Town and stop anywhere we choose, for a coffee or lunch or a night's lodging.

During one of our many talkathons on the stoep in Beacon Road Hajoo said things that helped me understand how she, a prize-winning pupil, whose work was highly commended in primary school, suddenly could not cope and dropped out of high school before she reached her teens.

From childhood, she had dreamed of finishing school and becoming a ballet dancer or a concert pianist, but her father did not see any value in academic or artistic advancement for girls beyond the basics. 'He wouldn't allow me to join the girl guides when Saris Naicker asked me to, and ballet or piano lessons were out of the question. He gave me the two shillings and sixpence for school fees each term but only after lots of shouting and delays.

Hajoo spoke in a matter-of-fact manner, never complaining: 'I knew we were poor. I accepted having to push pieces of cardboard into my school shoes because of the holes in the soles. I felt lucky when it was my turn to wear the one good dress that I shared with Yvonne February, a girl Mummy took in, because of her alcoholic parents. I didn't grumble about such things, but I hated not having the school fees and being reminded week after week to pay up. It was only the understanding from Father Sigamoney and our teachers that got me through.'

Things got worse at the Johannesburg Indian High School. Now this aspiring artiste needed a pound – twenty shillings – each term for school fees. She also needed two shillings a week for the tram coupons to get to school across town in Fordsburg. She couldn't get it: 'You're only wasting my money!' her father would rage, 'You won't amount to anything anyway.'

What would be worse for a teenager, I wondered, as her voice dropped to a virtual whisper and I choked back the tears: the terrible words of her father or the crushing embarrassment when the school secretary publicly came after her for the fees?

The administrator would interrupt Hajoo's class, march her to the Principal's office in full view of her chums and demand: 'Its two terms now you haven't paid. Stop making excuses. When can we expect the money?'

I gleaned from various family members, over the years that Mr Halim did not believe in education for girls. It seems he expected his daughters to find work, bring home money and be married as soon as possible. 'Each sister left school and was out working for a wage by the time we were fifteen'.

There is no telling how different life would have been for everyone had Mr Halim moved his tailoring business to the booming northern suburbs around Sandton and Randburg; a suburb of affluent people with enormous disposable incomes. With their reputation for fine, bespoke tailoring, and their proven ability to work hard, the Halim Tailors would certainly have prospered. But, these upmarket areas of opportunity were off limits to people the colour of the Halims and Carims.

In order to comprehend the plight of Indian entrepreneurs – South African citizens or new immigrants – at the time, one needs to understand the combined effect, on this group and on their South African born offspring, of the Alien's Act of 1937, the Group Areas Act of 1950 and the Immigration Regulation Act of 1953.

The purpose of these laws, as well as the intent of the Immigration Selection Board, was to severely restrict the right of Indians to travel, trade and own or occupy property in South Africa.

My parents could not legally successfuly re-establish their busines after Troyeville and the Halim family business remained trapped in a depressed over-traded area.

Mabel Merckle-Halim-Williams

Hajoo's humiliation at school took place at the same time she was grieving at home. Her parents' marriage had broken up and she was silently bearing the pain of her mother's departure.

I got a measure of young Hajoo's sense and sensibility when she told me about this. 'I felt Mummy's loneliness for a long time as I watched her sitting all alone, smoking at the kitchen table or on the stoep, night after night and week after week. My father would come home from the shop each day, wash up and read the paper while Mummy got his dinner ready. Most nights, after eating, he would leave the house again and only return late, after we had all gone to bed.'

Then she added, softly: 'I understood why Mummy left and I sympathised with her. I missed her terribly and visited her and her new husband, Victor Williams, as often as I could. I was pleased to see that Uncle Vee brought her the happiness she deserved. It was only after she was gone and we had to do all the housework, the shopping and the cooking for nine mouths did we realise what a heavy load Mummy had been carrying with very little money. My mother did the best she could with what she had and, as far as I know, never once complained to any of us or to anyone else about her loneliness and hard times.'

I got to know Hajoo's mother well and learned to love and respect her deeply. She always had a laugh to offer or a cigarette to share. She was born Mabel Merckle, the youngest of ten children. Her father was a German immigrant from Berlin, George Merckle who came seeking work as a miner in Johannesburg. Her mother was a South African coloured beauty from Kimberley – Maria Julia Gosling.

Mable Merckle-Halim-Williams (on right) and her friend, Mrs Johnny

Working hard and well, George Merckle and Maria Gosling made a comfortable life together and eventually owned and operated a stable of horse-drawn cabs, based in Vrededorp's 16th street, bordering on Pageview or Fietas.

'Your mother had a very special, quiet beauty,' old Mrs Vania told Hajoo and me over dinner, decades later at our home in Scarborough, Ontario. She was reminiscing about the days of horse-drawn carriages in Johannesburg and she remembered the Merckles well.

'People loved your Ma's long, shiny black hair,' she recalled, 'it fell down below her waist. We liked her quiet manner, but it was her eyes that we all talked about. None of us could say what colour they really were. When I saw her one-day they were hazel, the next time they looked green. And always they had flecks of yellow in them. She was a shy girl, your mother and a very nice person to know.'

Shy as a girl, unpretentious and dignified as an adult, I think my ma-in-law was also part angel. Whenever I think of her, I remember the story of her washing the feet of a homeless, black Rhodesian.

It was in 1948. Ma Mabel or Aunty Mabel was giving sanctuary to this penniless man who was looking for work in Johannesburg without the proper papers. She had offered him the room in the back yard and food to eat, which is all she had to offer. In return he did some work around the house and yard, while searching for a proper job and dodging the police.

Then one day he disappeared. She only saw him again weeks later, when he staggered into the house, hungry and on feet that were cut, bleeding and terribly swollen.

Absalom had been caught in a police dragnet arrested, confined, processed, packed and shipped, with a load of others, to the Rhodesian border and deportation. Somewhere along the way, a few of them escaped, hid in the bush and then made the several hundred-mile long walk back to Johannesburg.

When 10-year old Hajoo returned from school that day, she saw Absalom sitting on a chair in the kitchen with his feet in a steaming basin. Her mother was sitting on a low stool in front of him. She watched, silently, as her Ma bathed the man's feet in Dettol water that turned pink with his blood. Mummy lifted one foot at a time onto her lap, dried them gently with a soft towel, and soothingly massaged the pink Germolene ointment into the horrid cuts and gashes. Then she bandaged each foot with strips of calico torn from a bed sheet and lit another cigarette in her chain-smoking regime. After a few puffs, as Hajoo recalls, Mabel Halim smilingly made this homeless man what she always described as 'a nice cuppa tea'.

Although Mabel Merckle-Halim-Williams was almost always broke, she had a magical way of stretching a few shillings. Her home, the one she made with Victor Williams, was a happy, bustling sanctuary to a string of waifs and strays. It was a place of companionship where friends and virtual strangers could come by and play draughts (checkers), get a 'nice cuppa tea' and, if they were in luck, 'a nice plater food'.

Uncle Vee – Robin Hood

Victor Williams was the man with the laughing eyes, the dance in his walk and one of my favourite people. He drove a huge truck for the wholesaler, Walter Chipkin & Co, and delivered cases of tinned food and bags of sugar, rice, flour and salt to grocery stores all over the Witwatersrand. He must have been the fellow the angels were thinking of when they coined the phrase: 'salt of the earth.'

In the days before he stopped drinking he was the local Pied Piper. On paydays, drunk as a coot, he would change his pound notes into small coins at the shops. Then he would dance down the local Doornfontein streets on a Saturday, flinging tickeys and sixpences back over his shoulder into the air, calling for the kids to dance behind him and scramble for the 'mazoomah!'

In sober times, he would park his truck in the neighbourhood and people would gather around with pots and tins and jars. Then, with a nail, Uncle Vee would punch a tiny hole into one bag after another and allow sugar, rice, mealie-meal and salt to pour into the containers.

For a while this man was the neighbourhood's own Robin Hood and he cared for Hajoo and her siblings and me, as if we were his own.

'Did you cry when your Ma left?' I asked. 'I don't remember ever crying as a child,' she answered, quietly, 'not for anything.' She may not have wept, but the pain of her mother's absence, the cruelty of her father's words, the school secretary's demeaning behaviour and the added domestic responsibilities at home, all weighed her down. Together, they undermined her focus on the reading and learning she loved and soon she was in trouble with some of the most insensitive teachers she had ever met.

'When the teachers shouted and humiliated me because of my schoolwork,' she said, almost in a whisper, 'I kept quiet. I was actually afraid of white people then. I couldn't talk to them like I could to our teachers in primary school.'

Suddenly one day it was all too much. She could stand no more embarrassment and shame. At the end of the third term, in her first year at JIHS, a month before she turned thirteen, 12-year old Hajoo made the decision to drop out of school and find a job.

Saturday Fever

Saturdays with Hajoo were a whiz. Each hour with her rushed by long before sixty minutes had passed, and I had to move really fast to make up time.

First, there was the mad dash at noon, from my job in Fairview to my Dad's shop in Barclay Arcade on Market Street, where I collected the car that Daddy allowed me to use on Saturdays. Then another dash home for a bath, change of clothes and then I would be speeding back east, across town to rendezvous with the new owner of my heart.

On Saturday mornings, Hajoo would also be racing around getting her chores done. Often I arrived, impatient to get going, only to find her still on her knees, feverishly polishing the stoep, her legs stained red. But then, soon, she would be ready and perfectly so. My knees became rubber just looking at her as she gracefully settled into the car saying, in her usual calm and quiet way: 'We can go now.'

It really didn't matter to me what we did on a Saturday so long as we were together. Though Hajoo loved the cinema, she enjoyed the matine dance at the forbidden Springbok Hall just as much. This dance emporium, located in tough Fietas, attracted a mix of gangsters and troublemakers, ballroom dancers in training, unattached girls and fellows looking to meet each other, and people like us who just loved to dance. It was a rough and unsophisticated venue, but it had an impassioned edge about it that vibrated with excitement, illicit fun and an undercurrent of danger. Many of the teenagers, who danced their hearts out under the coloured lights, were here without the knowledge of their elders.

This was our turf, and Yusuf, Basil, Ginger and I were at home in this place. For Hajoo, the adventure of being here, despite the fuss her father and big sister would make, was wickedly exhilarating. Her eyes shone each time she was asked to dance, and her laughter was infectious as she whirled around during the super-charged squares. Hajoo moved like a gazelle, with a style and grace that was lovely to watch. There were quite a few admiring eyes on her as she sparkled through the afternoon.

When we were not secretly dancing at the Springbok Hall we would be walking under the trees at the Zoo Lake and talking about the things we wanted to do and places we wanted to see. Occasionally we would drive through tranquil, green suburbs like Cyrildene, Mountain View and

Houghton, along flower-decked avenues or tree-lined boulevards with names like The Wilds, Munroe Drive or Sylvia Pass. We would gawp at the beautiful tree-filled gardens that, in those days sloped to the roadside and were not hidden behind high security walls, and we would wonder: what kind of people are these that live on properties bigger than an entire block of twelve houses in Fordsburg or Fietas or Hond se Bêk?

Hajoo especially loved the Saturdays when we rendezvoused with the Peck girls and their escorts at the Majestic or Lyric Cinema; the sisters Siba and Zaitoon from Fietas, their cousins Ayesha and Rachma from Albertsville and their close friend Joan Furmie from Coronationville.

During the week, like Hajoo, these girls worked hard in clothing factories or offices, in their sensible working clothes. On weekends, however, they were transformed into stunning fashionistas. When we were with this group we felt we were in the centre of the weekend buzz. Then, after the matinee bio, when they began planning exciting things to do that evening we had to part company because Hajoo had to be home before dark – and we dared not be late.

1956 – Committing To a Life Together

Hajoo had been working and bringing home an unopened weekly pay packet since the age of thirteen. She withheld no money for herself and received only a meagre allowance. Now, at seventeen, the idea of being responsible enough to help support the family but not considered sensible enough to stay out after dark began to rankle. We were just about to launch our own defiance campaign when the idea for a more lasting solution was thrust upon us from the most unlikely source: Mr Halim himself.

'How long will this gallivanting carry on? Does he think she's just a good time girl?' Mr Halim was shouting from his bedroom, across the house, to Timie who was in the kitchen preparing the evening meal with Hajoo. Clearly, the loudness was for my ears, as I sat playing draughts with Hajoo's younger brother Bashir in the next room. 'I want to know: what are his intentions?

I understood: these concerns were reasonable. Hajoo and I had talked about marriage and about having a family. She knew I had no confidence in my ability to be a reliable husband and father: 'Haj, just count the shit jobs I have had and the rubbish money I make. I am not ready for marriage. What do I do?' Now Mr Halim had forced us to face things squarely 'Tell my father the truth,' she advised. And I did. 'My intentions are honourable, Mr Halim, but right now I am not able to support a family properly. Give me some time. I'll do the right thing' I don't recall what he said in response, but there was no more talk about this from him.

It was Jackie Bull, an older and wiser friend of the Halim family, who helped clear my mind. 'Look,' he said, 'it's always better to get married when you have good prospects or a steady income and can afford to have children and a nice place to live. After all is said and done, love is the really important thing. You both have jobs and you can wait before starting a family. Money may be a problem sometimes, but you'll manage.'

My parents were both opposed when I announced, with no warning, 'I want to get married as soon as possible.'

Mummy was tactical: 'We want to send you to England so you can finish your Higher Senior Cambridge. Then you can marry this girl if you still want to.' Daddy was direct: 'You can't keep a job and you won't be able to support a wife and children. Marrying this girl is not like riding a horse you know; you can't get on and off whenever you want.' Then he declared: 'If you insist on getting married now, we will not pay a penny towards the wedding. You do it all yourself. See if you can.'

'Alright,' I said, my voice trembling as I, for better or worse, took charge of my own destiny. 'We don't have the money now. We'll get engaged first, save as hard as we can, and get married next year. Please, will you go and talk to Mr Halim for me.'

Mummy had insisted on a traditional Memon engagement ceremony and objected to our idea of a dance party. 'You know how they'll gossip,' she had argued, 'if a pure Indian family had a dance party people will say "it's wonderful to see an Indian family being so modern", but if *we* did it I can just hear them, "what can you expect from those half-castes" – so no dance.' But we got the dance party when I reminded Mummy about her marriage to Daddy and the taboos they broke for love.

On the first Saturday of September 1956, about a year after Hajoo and I bumped into each other in front of Cisco's Cafe, we had both the traditional and the modern.

Mummy took charge in her usual resolute way, and did a superb job organising the small afternoon family-only affair at home. There were Muslim prayers recited in Arabic in support of vows made, and my paternal aunts sang celebratory songs in Gujarati and Memoni. The Halim and Carim families ceremoniously exchanged gifts, which were individually and elegantly presented on homemade velvet cushions.

Mummy and Miria fooi – Aunty Miria – arranged and supervised the catering. There were several exotic dishes, but the mainstay of the buffet was the traditional Memon aknee. This is a mix of spicy vegetables, seasoned lamb and flavoured yellow rice, similar, but better, Memons will declare, than the more well-known biryani. The aknee is traditionally served with green coriander chutney and a kachumber – a chilli-laden salad, similar but different to the Greek khoriatiki. There were jugs of spicy sour milk – also similar but different to the Greek tzatziki, to pour over the aknee. All this was followed by Indian deserts – jelabee, barfi, luddoo and lots of spicy, cardamom-laden spicy masala tea.

Then there was the time-honoured miethu morue – the mouth-sweetening ceremony. Hajoo and I took sips of rosewater sherbet from goblets extended to us by the hands of her older sisters Ayesha and Timie and my young sisters Zarina and Shirene. This part of the ritual was meant to represent the blessing of sweetness throughout our lives.

Then, facing each other, I sipped from Hajoo's cup and she from mine, symbolically promising each other to always share life's sweetness through all life's bitter times. Then the tiny diamond engagement ring that I had bought at Katz & Lourie, in Eloff Street in the city centre, was brought out on its own cushion, and I proudly placed it on her finger and voila – we were officially engaged.

Hajoo was not quite 18 and I was just 20. We had committed to marriage that day without either of us having a clue what was in store for us. Jackie Bull had said that love was all we really needed, but I knew we had more; we had a subconscious sense of purpose, a brash can-do attitude, Hajoo's quiet strength, and not a single thought of anything ever going wrong.

15
STRAIGHTEN UP & FLY RIGHT

As I sat on our bed that warm October night in 1958, squeezing Hajoo's hand and staring in awe at the miracle of the birth of our first son, which was happening right before my eyes, my thoughts flew back two years to the time when Hajoo missed being arrested and I narrowly escaped being convicted as a common criminal. I shuddered as I recalled how close I had come to mucking up any chance of building a life with her and this child, Xavier, and our second son, Zane, who was yet to join us.

'Six months – yissis man!' Yusuf was incredulous, 'and we didn't even hit the blerry cop.' We were all in shock. The magistrate's words had been frightening: 'I am quite prepared to sentence each of you to a minimum six months in jail. However, I believe one or two of you did not actually assault the police officer, and I do not know which of you that is. Therefore the case against all four of you is dismissed.'

The magistrate was wrong. What Yusuf had said was right. None of us had struck the cop. I had only pushed him. When he fell, the crowd attacked him as we drove away. Sometimes, it seems, trouble just comes looking for you.

It was the December 1956 holiday season. We had been engaged a few months and Hajoo and I, and Ginger, Yusuf and Basil were on our way to the Springbok Hall. As we cruised on Central Road, past the Majestic, the cinema crowd was spilling out onto the street from the one o'clock show. We inched along, at imperial speed, through the throng, talking and laughing with friends as they walked along both sides of the car. Then I made a slow, careful left turn into Bree Street, watching out for the happy pedestrians and came to an immediate stop the instant I heard foul cursing from behind us.

According to the man, I had been driving recklessly, I had made an abrupt turn, I had knocked him off his bicycle, injured him and then we all attacked him. Nothing like this had happened. What probably happened was that the cyclist hadn't been paying attention when I made the turn and he lost balance when he tried to avoid the car. What we know for sure is

172

that he was fit enough to rush up to the driver's side and punch me hard through the open window, so fast I didn't see it coming.

In a flash short, hot-tempered Yusuf was on the street, going for this large, furious black man. We only realised he was a policeman in plain clothes when he put his hand behind his back, under his jacket, and pulled out a pair of handcuffs. Suddenly things got terribly dangerous. Ghetto kids know; handcuffs are a lethal fighting weapon that can cut your face open like a pawpaw, and plain clothes police are expert at using them with deadly effect.

Before you knew it, we were doing a dangerous dance on Bree Street – the four of us circling and trying to disarm him, and he determined to do us grave injury. He would advance on one of us, swinging his irons, and the other three would try to get at him from his blind side. He was fast and turned quickly, swinging the cuffs, and we would have to spring back out of range. This dancing around, back and forth, side to side grew steadily more frightening and this cop was clearly out for blood. 'Why does he not just get on his bike and ride away and we all just go and dance?' I remember silently pleading.

Meanwhile the show from the Lyric had also now spilled out onto the street. The crowd in the circle around the clash had thickened and the mood had become ugly. 'Bloody hell he's a policeman – an impimpi collaborator shit and he's swinging handcuffs. Let's give this bastard traitor a lesson he won't forget.'

The cop should have known better. He should have known that popular anger could explode into violence at the sight of a black policeman swinging those hated handcuffs at unarmed local boys, during a time when the political climate was dangerously explosive.

The Beginning of Change

In the eighteen months, between June 1955 and December 1956 the country was seething with anger. Three thousand delegates from peoples' organisations had adopted the Freedom Charter in Kliptown and 20,000 members of the multi-racial Federation of South African Women had peacefully marched on the Union Buildings in Pretoria, to deliver a petition protesting the decision to extend the pass laws to African women.

In retaliation, Special Branch operatives, aided by impimpi informers, had unleashed a reign of intimidation across the country, raiding homes and offices and terrorising our leaders and their families.

During this period the Riotous Assemblies Act had been passed, which made it illegal for people to gather publicly without specific police permission. Coloured voters had been removed from the voters' roll and 156 leaders of the Congress Alliance had been arrested and charged with high treason – a capital offence punishable by death. Anger seethed in the land.

As our deadly dance continued, I knew we had to end this matter quickly – otherwise terrible things might happen. So, when my chance came, I took it in desperation. Impimpi was swinging at one of the chaps; I saw that his back was to the sidewalk and his feet were close to the rutted gutter at the edge of the kerb. As he lifted the cuffs and swung, and lifted and swung again, at my mates, I suddenly rushed him, very fast, from the side. Predictably, he turned quickly to face me and raised his arm to strike. I barrelled straight into him, under his raised arm, pushing hard at his chest. He stumbled backwards in the uneven gutter, the back of his heels caught on the edge of the pavement kerb, as I had intended, and he crashed over and down on to his back.

In a split second, the crowd surged forward around the policeman and the coloured chaps from Coronationville were the first to get their angry boots in.

'The policeman had no right to punch Mac like that,' Hajoo said later. 'I felt protected by you all and I wasn't frightened.' We were munching on samoosas at the Crescent Cafe after the dance and rehashing the whole thing. The fight had lasted only a few minutes, but each of us had been concerned about Hajoo. 'Weren't you even a little afraid?' 'No,' she answered, 'At home we see this every weekend. I just wanted us to get away.'

That's when the arresting officers found us.

'Who's the driver of the black 1948 Chevrolet, TJ 88310?' The two Afrikaner policemen were huge, and they both carried enormous police-issue 38mm Webley revolvers. 'Me,' I responded. 'Who was with you?' Before I could answer, Basil piped up. 'We were together – not the girl.' My friend's loyalty, while valued, posed a serious problem: Now who would see Hajoo get home? Then Ronnie Felix walked into the cafe and my fear for Hajoo's immediate safety was put to rest.

Bra Ronza did some terrific things for us that Saturday evening after we were taken away. First, he strong-armed two fellows sitting at another table into making themselves and their car available so he could escort Hajoo home to Doornfontein. Enroute, they first stopped at the Fordsburg police station where he boldly walked in and found us at the front desk being fingerprinted.

'Ek sê ou Mac, your cherry's in the voom' – 'I say Mac, your girl friend's in the car' – 'you mussen wurry, we driving her home.' Then he gravely asked, 'What youse manne up for?'

In the civil offence, I alone had been charged with reckless driving and failing to stop after an accident. In the criminal case, we had all been charged with the very serious offence of assaulting a police officer with intent to do grievous bodily harm. In this, I was the first accused. Ron's eyes widened at the severity of the charges and I saw fear in his eyes.

'I'll check your family Mac, and tell them they mus come bail youse manne out, youse mussen wurry.' Then his chutzpah lifted our spirits.

'Poenie is okay, but all shook up; I think you mus buy this present for her – only two pounds.' Right there, in the police station, with cops milling all around and the other fellows still being fingerprinted, Ronza was surreptitiously showing me a piece of jewellery that no doubt had 'fallen off the back of a lorry'. His audacity in the jaws of the hyena was heartening. Suddenly we were all smiling. 'Okay, give her the brooch and I'll pay you when I see you,' I laughed.

As he walked out of the cop shop, he bid the white policeman closest to him a sarcastic good evening, 'Goeie naand my baas, my kroon – Good night my boss, my king' – with a mocking smile on his face that would have driven them to fury had they been observant enough to decode the depth of its contempt.

The angry crowd had thrashed the policeman really badly. When the civil case came up two months later, he could not remember who had driven the car and, when asked, pointed to Ginger instead of me, the accused. The magistrate threw the case out.

In the criminal matter, his evidence was just as confused. He would first point at one of us, then change his mind and finger another, then refer to people who weren't even in the court. The magistrate had no choice but to dismiss the case against all four of us.

Escaping so narrowly from a six-month jail sentence was like a miracle in those days of unbridled police power. A greater miracle was that Hajoo had not been arrested with us. What if she'd also been handcuffed? Where would they have taken her? How would she have fended for herself alone in a jail cell crammed with Saturday night drunks, brawlers and prostitutes? How could I have faced her family; our friends; the community?

These thoughts ripped through my mind liked razor wire. And, as I walked out the court that February day and heard Yusuf's 'Six months – yissis man!' I had changed. The danger to Hajoo had hit me so hard that I knew that I would turn over a new leaf.

I had heard again, in court, the rippling piano refrain of Nat King Cole's 1944 hit song, and I determined to do what the King melodiously urged me to do; I would 'Straighten Up and Fly Right.'

16
THE PEACOCK THRONES

After our engagement, my attention span problem stabilised, then my luck improved, then my self confidence strengthened. Solly Motan, a family friend, got me a job as a driver-salesman for Crystal Bakery on the corner of Height and Beit Streets in Doornfontein. I excelled in the confidence the bosses placed in me and, in quick time, was earning far more money than ever before. Hajoo, too, began earning top wages as a machinist at RMB, a successful dress manufacturer in Doornfontein's garment district.

These were better times for us. Our wedding plans were on track, our cash savings were growing and the increased weekly sum I was able to pay into the family coffers was making things easier at home. Now that I was seen to be 'settling down' Hajoo and I were being invited to parties, concerts, and dinners. It was as if the community was coming out to help me 'straighten up and fly right'.

Yusuf, Basil and Ginger were now also more seriously involved with the girls they would eventually marry and we saw less and less of each other.

Then, on the first Saturday of September 1957, exactly one year after our engagement, Hajoo and I got married.

Mummy had again insisted on a traditional ceremony and this time she got little resistance from me because of Daddy's theatrical persuasiveness. 'Think about two villages in old Gujarat, a day's horse-ride apart that have been fighting over scarce water for years.' Daddy was attempting to overcome my resistance to all the ceremonial stuff that I thought unnecessary. 'Imagine that the marriage between the daughter of the Miabhai clan and the son of the Poonjanee clan has been arranged to bring peace between the two villages. Remember the gifts we took when we went to ask Mr Halim for his daughter's hand? Think of them as peace offerings and that when the gifts were accepted our proposal of marriage and peace between the clans was also accepted.'

*Hajoo (centre) with brother Bobby
and sister-in-law Hilda*

*The Groom, with brothers Enver (left)
and Adam*

The Bride and Groom

'Now imagine our family have to travel into dangerous hill country, to the wedding village. We are escorted by our jhan – our cavalcade – which will include marriage negotiators and witnesses and armed men for our protection from bandits.' Daddy loved telling stories and now he and my Hanifa fooi – Aunty Hanifa – were on a roll. I suspected they were making up things as they went along, but I didn't care. I was enjoying the fantasy and visions of an armed company of riders in brocade and turbans, armed with lances, on prancing horses beautifully decorated flashed on the screen of my mind. As Daddy talked, my thoughts went back to the senior boys in Aitchison College, on their spirited horses, parading for the guests and spectators before the start of the annual tent-pegging competition.

'When we get through the mountains, the bride's people will expect us to pay tribute to enter their lands, and our representatives will negotiate amounts,' my Dad and Aunt continued, 'then, before we are allowed to enter the marriage house, we must pay mehr, and more negotiations will take place.'

I understood the thing about 'tribute', but it was only later that I learned about mehr. This is not a bride price paid to the girl's father as in other traditions. In Islamic marriages, mehr is a compulsory gift given by the groom to the bride for her sole and exclusive ownership. It is essentially a form of protection against widowhood or divorce. The gift of mehr can be large or small. It can be in cash or real property or investments. Brides may choose to keep the mehr for themselves or they may use the gift to help start a new life in a new home.

Hajoo and I had not thought about tribute and mehr money, and Hanifa fooi saw the concern on my face. 'Don't worry, nowadays, there is nothing about fighting over water or paying tribute, but you *will* have to pay mehr money and that must come from you, not from your parents.' Then she added, 'Prophet Mohamed said very clearly, 'the marriage which produces the most blessing is that which involves the least burden.' Mussen worry, we will settle on a figure you can afford.'

Then Daddy completed his flight into tradition: 'Imagine – the negotiations go well; the mehr money is accepted; the marriage certificate is signed; everyone is happy and now we bring the bride back to our village. Horns are blowing; drums are beating and the sound of rifle shots echo through the hills. A big reception has been prepared for the new bride and members of her family and clan, with dancing and fire-eaters and story tellers.'

Romantic as Daddy's fantasising was, the fact is that our wedding day went much the way it would have gone generations before in the villages of old India, but obviously on a far more modest scale.

Instead of horses, the cars were decorated with ribbon, flowers and balloons. It wasn't the bandits we had to watch out for, but the traffic on busy Sicmert, Market and Main Roads between the 'villages' of Fordsburg and Hond se Bêk. Mehr had been successfully negotiated and set at an affordable five pounds. Hajoo had quietly told me that she would put the cash back into our common 'pot' and we could use it for petrol money on our honeymoon.

Apart from the kafuffle about language, the wedding ceremony went well.

'Say yes now!' the witnesses had demanded of me. 'Yes to what?' I was irritated. This was precisely what I had feared. I had insisted that I be married in a language I knew, now words were being said in Arabic, a language no one in the room spoke or even understood.

'The implications and responsibilities of marriage have been explained to you. You must say yes now if you still want to get married.' I refused to budge: 'Please ask the Imam to say the words in English so that I know what I am saying yes to.' I only stopped insisting out of pity for the painful time the man was having trying to do his job.

Three times passages in Arabic would be recited to me and three times there would be a loud chorus from the witnesses, 'Say yes now!' and I would say yes, almost in a panic. Hajoo remembers one of these witnesses coming into the women's part of the house and, without explaining anything at all to her, in Arabic or otherwise, asking her simply, in English, and only once, 'Do you agree to marry Mohamed Carim?' and when she said yes, he left and no one asked her another thing.

On the road back to 'the boy's village', there were no drums being beaten or rifles being shot off, and no prancing horses. Instead, the cars in our jhan let off a cacophony of horns and hooters that heralded for all to know that two more young people had said 'Yes' to the idea of making a life together.

For the amount of money that Hajoo and I had given to Mummy and the other organisers, the wedding reception was far better organised than we expected. The peacock thrones that friend Jesse Jassat had fashioned out of two dining chairs and a mix of wire, tissue paper, inventiveness and loving care was the centre piece. People in our cavalcade of escorts and guests oohed and aahed as they ceremoniously seated Hajoo and me on these 'thrones.'

Instead of fire-eaters there was lakri – stick – dancing. Instead of storytellers people sang. As we sat in regal state on a raised platform covered with carpets, well-wishers wished us well, and gift-givers gave us gifts. Later, the assembly was served traditional food cooked by my aunts in our backyard, in traditional huge copper pots called dekshas or degs.

In addition to the usual Indian sweet meats, guests were offered servings from an impressive 180-piece three-tier wedding cake, created by Jewish bakers that my bosses at Crystal Bakery had given us as a wedding gift.

Then it was 8pm and Hajoo and I said our farewells and started off on our drive to Durban in the family's black 1955 Chevrolet, suitably festooned with loud, happy colours.

Rural Hospitality

Our honeymoon was one of the happiest times of our lives. It's amazing how much fun you can have, with hardly any money, when you are care-free and the people around you care.

It was a time when no public facility existed on the main road between Johannesburg and Durban where 'non-Europeans' could find lodging for the night – even if we could afford it. Nor was there a roadhouse or restaurant on the highway that would serve us, unless we went to a window on the side or back of the building for 'take-aways.' But we still had a marvellous time thanks to the culture of the Good Samaritan that seemed always to show up when needed.

On the road to anywhere in South Africa those days, there was always a friend who had a friend, who knew a family that was willing to open their home to a musafir – a traveller. Friend Babu Valod's family were such people, and they welcomed us, total strangers though we were. We spent our wedding night in a modest, but beautifully prepared room, in the back yard of small country store, on a sandy road in a rural district somewhere near the town of Standerton, not far from the Natal border.

By late the next morning, after a breakfast that included my favourite masala egg-bread – a delightful, spicy, Indian version of French toast, we were purring along the springtime road heading for the Valley of a Thousand Hills, Durban and the cool waters and hot beaches of the Hibiscus and Dolphin coasts.

'It's your honeymoon. You must feel free to come and go as you please. You are invited to dinner with our family every evening at seven, but don't feel obliged to come if you have other plans.'

The prominent Abu Moosa family, owners of all the Avalon bioscopes in South Africa at the time, and, as I recall, important members of the Poonjanee clan, were welcoming us to Natal. They had given us the use of a pleasant private guesthouse in Durban and Mrs Moosa was putting us at ease. Then she added: 'Please, if you decide to join us for dinner, you must phone before five and let us know, so we can expect you.'

In that moment I received one of my earliest lessons in sound, time-specific planning, effective communication and firm but gentle, no-nonsense assertiveness – 'supper at seven and please call before five'.

Thanks to this gracious woman, not only was the tone of our holiday set – free and easy, come-and-go, and no obligations – but I had also received an introduction to effective personal organisation, time management and respect for the time of others.

The guesthouse was on Mansfield Road, close to Bewsey Grove where another wonderful family lived, who added to the joys of our honeymoon – the Domingoes.

Uncle Bhukoo, Aunty Lilly and their sons Joe, Dicky and Enver were part of Hajoo's very extended family, through the marriages of her sisters Ayesha and Timie. We spent many marvellous hours with these Durbanites but for me, the best time was when Joe, Dicky and Enver and their young uncles, Oscar and Skelly, took us surf fishing.

Never before had Hajoo and I been on a beach, hip-deep in pounding waves, brandishing long fibre-glass rods, and casting our lines as far as we could, hoping to land a prize-winning fish. It was exhilarating! I can still feel the surf and the sun drenching me on that splendid day and taste the sea in my throat.

Much as we had enjoyed being with the Moosas and the Domingoes, we preferred being alone together. Early each morning we would drive along the coast, south to Amanzimtoti, Park Rynie and Port Shepstone or north to Umhlanga Rocks, Umdloti and Ballito Bay. We would sit for long periods watching the Indian Ocean tides break on the coast of Africa, and have rambling conversations on the white sands of the 'non-whites only' beaches.

The Casbah

Decades later, as Hajoo, Xavier, Zane and I explored the steep, winding stone alleyways of the legendary Casbah in Algiers, and visited heritage sites where the heroes of the Algerian revolution found refuge, I would remember our honeymoon and the exotic sights, sounds and smells on the streets and lanes of the 'Casbah' in Durban.

As morning began approaching noon, we would burn up more of Hajoo's mehr money on petrol and cruise slowly back through the magnificent whites-only residential areas in the hills above the coast road, to have lunch in the heart of Durban's Asiatic bazaar.

For well over a hundred years Punjabi, Pashtun, Tamil, Telugu, Gujarati and Memoni speaking Indians have lived and worked in the Casbah, around the key intersection of Victoria, Pine, Queen and Grey Streets. Their forebears had started coming over as indentured labourers in the so-called 'first wave' from as early as 1860, to work on the sugar cane plantations under generally terrible conditions. A few years later these indentured workers were followed by boatloads of so-called 'free immigrants' coming to try their hand at anything that would make a better life for them and their families.

We Jo'burgers did not know Durban well, but this was the part we knew best. Here, in this bustling 'Asiatic bazaar' of small back-room factories, best value-for-money shopping arcades and upmarket textile and clothing stores were located the bioscopes, cafes, tea rooms, and spice and sweet shops and restaurants. Here also was the architecturally splendid Jumma Mosque and the world famous Victoria Street Indian Market, two very different entities, but both considered to be the largest and best of their kind in the southern hemisphere.

And adding an element of danger and fear to all this, were the gangs, or their remnants and offshoots: the legendary Crimson League, the Salots and the Dutchenes. It was they who ran the protection rackets, the gambling schools and the numbers games, and who distributed the goods that 'fell of trucks' around the country and off the ships in Durban harbour.

These energetic streets, arcades and lanes were what, in times past, many people referred to, collectivly as 'the Casbah.' It is here that Hajoo and I spent many hours and had our meals almost every day.

Lunch was a drawn-out walk-about affair: samoosas and bhajias as a starter in one cafe, chicken curry or masala fish and rice, with salad in another, then into an arcade to look at the silks, satins, shoes and clothes on display. Finally, desert – barfi and jellabee or tea and cake – would be taken in any number of specialist mitai shops.

For me it was Saturdays in Lahore all over again.

Dinner was a mix of food and music, and almost always at celebrity jazz promoter Pumpy Naidoo's famous restaurant, the Goodwill Lounge, on Victoria Street.

As we walked in, and sat down, always at the same table near the jukebox, the waiters smiled at us and usually whispered among themselves. They couldn't make us out: were we Coloured, Indian, Malay or foreigners off one of the ships? Our choice of music raised eyebrows.

In those days, you had one selection on the juke box for a sixpence and three for a shilling. Our routine was always the same. First, we placed our food order; then we fed the jukebox its first shilling. Within seconds, Fats Domino brought smiles to everyone's face as he pumped out his amazing piano roll 'Blue Monday'. Then, before you had time to bite a corner off your samoosa and squeeze a few drops of lemon into the opening, Julie London was tearfully wailing, 'Cry Me a River'. Finally, it was Fats Domino again, gently blowing away Julie's sadness with his rasping, throaty, up-beat rendition of 'Blueberry Hill'.

As we ate, we would allow other patrons a chance to hear their choice of music and, as soon as an opportunity came, in would go another shilling and we would make the same selection again, but now in reverse order. Pumpy Naidoo loved jazz, he enjoyed our selection and he came over personally and told us so. We knew, from their smiles, that the waiters enjoyed the music too.

The few times we went to the Avalon bio, a short walk from the Goodwill Lounge, we were treated like VIPs. Free passes had been arranged by the Moosa family and the manager himself showed us to the special seats reserved for the Moosa family, members of the Poonjanee clan, and special friends.

Our two-week honeymoon had come to an end in half that time, it seemed. Still, we were joyful as we sped along the road to Pietermaritzburg enroute to Jo'burg that spring day with not a care in the world.

Zohra

'No condition is permanent.' On the drive out of Pietermaritzburg we were singing and laughing and enjoying life's blessings. Then, within hours, I was gripping cousin Zohra's hand as she died in front of Hajoo and me, her face inches from mine, staring into my eyes, and mouthing words she could not utter.

'She was waiting for her family to come, before she died, and now she's gone in peace', someone said. Hajoo and I were in shock as we tried to make sense of what my cousin was saying. We had finished lunch and had taken the wrong road out of Maritzburg. Realising we were approaching Dundee we decided to stop for a visit with cousin Zohra, her husband Ahmed and their three-year old daughter Soraya. We had no idea that Zohra was dying until we walked into her house.

'We were inseparable those days in Ma's back yard. It was always Zohra, me and Baby the monkey,' I was telling Hajoo, as we drove furiously on to Johannesburg. Hajoo and Ahmed had pulled me gently away from Zohra's side when the burial people came to do the things they had to do at this time. 'You must eat something,' he had said, 'then you must rush back to Jo'burg, because Amie-Pe and your mother are waiting for the car so they can drive back to Dundee. I'll phone them'.

There was no more singing and laughing on the drive back home. Instead, I was telling Hajoo that our move from Ma's house to Troyeville had separated Zohra and me for a long while, until she had moved back into the Fordsburg house as part of our family; that Mummy and Daddy were like parents to her and that it was Daddy who arranged her marriage to Ahmed in 1954.

Zohra's wedding took place in our house and it was from Terrace Road that Ahmed's jhan returned to Dundee with the bride. Most of our family had joined the cavalcade that took her to her new home and, on Mummy's instructions, we had stayed close to her all through her wedding reception in that distant town, with all those strangers.

Now she was dead. What Force, we wondered, kept her alive and waiting for Hajoo and me to arrive? What Force was it that made us take the wrong road out of Pietermaritzburg and direct us to Dundee? Who was it that brought that taciturn, unsmiling, Afrikaner farmer along with his tractor to pull us out of the mud, minutes after we had skidded off the road, some 30 miles before Zohra's home? Was it coincidence? Fate? Synchronicity? Taqdeer – Predestination?

As we raced home to Johannesburg that spring day, I thought about Zohra's journey into marriage. I wondered how she dealt with a husband she hardly knew, in a new and strange town, with new and strange people. I thought about Taqdeer – the concept of predestination and how many people believe ones life has all been pre-planned. I wondered what the plan was for Hajoo and me, what married life would be like for us, and where life would take us now that the honeymoon was over.

17
ENDINGS & BEGINNINGS

It was not the best of times for the Carim family when Hajoo and I got married. Our family's fortunes were once more in free-fall and, unknown to us, Mummy's latest cash-conservation plan relied heavily on the arrival of a new daughter-in-law.

The services of Sarojini, the family cook and Elsie the domestic helper, had been terminated while we were on honeymoon and Hajoo was expected to take up the slack. As my parents drove off to Zohra's funeral within an hour of our return that night, my mother gave my wife her first instructions: 'We'll be back tomorrow by supper time. You can cook mince and roti and remember, Miria fooi and Rashida are table boarders with us.' There were twelve to cook for – Mummy and Daddy, Grandma, my five brothers and sisters, our aunt and cousin and the two of us.

This would become the pattern: My mother would have an idea to increase income or reduce expenses and Hajoo would be expected to help implement the plan – like when Mummy began selling meat and potato roti rolls. Hajoo was pressed into service as the sales person. Mummy loaded up a heavy basket, which Hajoo lugged to work each morning for sale to her co-workers at the factory. On pay days, when the roughest workers refused to settle their bills – '...daar was nie genog vleis nie – there wasn't enough meat...' Hajoo quietly made up the shortfall from her own pay packet ensuring Mummy had a full and proper accounting.

'Amie Carim does not want his daughter-in-law to be working in a factory; it's an embarrassment to him in the community – what will people say?' My mother was now pressing Hajoo to quit her job and stay home as housekeeper, so that she could go out and open a fish and chips shop on Main Road, Fordsburg and when that failed, to establish a haberdashery store in Adam's Arcade on Market Street, which also failed.

Hajoo's duties quickly escalated into making up nine beds each day and cleaning, dusting and sweeping the large house on two floors. She was the resident short-order cook at lunch time, providing light meals to members of a family who arrived willy-nilly at different times – all hungry to be fed. She cooked full dinners during the afternoons and served them to twelve mouths each evening.

'Sorry, lady, your family owes too much – no more credit.' Hajoo was also doing the household shopping and soon found that our family owed money everywhere. After this first humiliation at the butcher and vegetable store, Hajoo quietly paid for supplies out of her unemployment insurance money over and above the monthly boarding and lodging payments we made to Mummy each month.

While Hajoo was struggling with the workload at home, with little or no help or appreciation, I was fighting my own battles.

The White Game

The day I got fired from Crystal Bakery I knew I couldn't go home till I found another job. It was mid-October. I had become a husband only six weeks earlier. Now I had no work and I could hear my father's rant: 'Idiot couldn't keep a job.' 'Now how will they live?' 'I told you so.'

I was running late that morning and drove out of the bakery yard without adequately checking my bread load. On arrival at the first customer, a special order that I had placed was missing, so I drove back to the bakery fast to correct the problem. The chief despatch clerk insisted that the special order had been loaded. He yelled that I was wrong and, poking his forefinger into my chest, shouted in my face something about 'stealing' and 'untrustworthy.' Then he uttered those fighting words: 'You people are all the same.'

The next instant he was flat on the floor. He must have slipped, because I don't think I can punch that hard. When Mr Moran, the Sales Manager, saw this white official picking himself up off the concrete and me standing over him, he fired me on the spot – no questions asked.

'Come back and collect your money at the end of the month.' These words hardly registered as I scrambled to sort out my options, while the image of my father glowered at me from the top of my mind. Before I reached the tram stop at the Beit Street and Siemert Road corner I had a plan, which I promptly implemented and, before the day was out, I had a new job.

I got fired around 7am. Within an hour, I was sitting on the steps in front of my father-in-law's tailor shop, at 202 Market Street in Doornfontein, making a list of all the lorries that drove by. Soon I had the names of some twelve firms that transported things and, as I began prioritising them, I remembered something that opened up the world to us.

Hajoo and I had often talked about moving overseas so that our children could grow up in a free society. On my list I noticed two companies that I thought were 'international'. So, when Mr Halim opened the shop and allowed me to use the phone, the first two companies I called were Coca-Cola and Pepsi-Cola.

I remember the crisp efficiency of that call to Coke's Human Resources Department as if it happened yesterday. It went something like this:

Me: 'I'm calling to find out if you have any openings for a driver-salesman.'
HR: 'Do you have a valid heavy duty driver's licence?'
Me: 'Yes I do.'
HR: 'Yes we have openings, when can you come to talk to a supervisor?'
Me: 'Later this morning?'
HR: 'Good, give me your name please.'
Me: 'Mohamed Ahmed Carim, but everyone calls me Mac.'
HR: 'Just a moment please.' (Pause) 'Hello, yes, sorry, I was just told that all the positions are filled – sorry.'
Click!

I had fallen foul of South Africa's Industrial Conciliation Amendment Act of 1956. This was a law to support apartheid's affirmative action programme. The Act gave legal force to the practice of job reservation for whites in general and for Afrikaners in particular which, in the transport sector, meant that trucks over five tons in weight could not be driven by 'non-white' people.

Since driver-salesmen in soft drink companies usually operated trucks seven tons and heavier, the Coca-Cola franchise could not offer me the job, not with my dead-give-away-name, even if they wanted to.

Once bitten twice shy. When I made the second call and found Pepsi was also hiring, I changed my name. I was now Mac Carim, but pronounced Carom, as in the carom board game, not the Arabic Qareem. I was now Lebanese. And yes, I had the correct driver's licence. Yes, I could be up at the Pepsi-Cola plant, on Saratoga Avenue, near Nugget Street, within the hour. Click!

I got the job.

Had I not instinctively risked changing my name, and passing myself off as Lebanese that morning, Hajoo and I probably would never have been able to take our sons to visit the Pyramids, the Coliseum and the Eifel Tower or Robin Hood's Sherwood Forest in Nottingham. Zane would not have taught us to snorkel in the Aegean Sea off Mykonos, nor would we have visited Byblos, in Lebanon, considered to be the oldest continuously-inhabited city in the world and the birthplace of the alphabet.

The economic benefits of passing for white were significant. If you had the complexion and the nerve, you could earn between two and five times more, as a 'white' worker than you would as a black, coloured or Indian South African – and all for doing the same job. People in our communities who chanced it were given the thumbs-up for having the guts to take on and beat the system.

There was an odious and painful side to this when non-whites moved into whites-only residential areas and began *living* as whites rather than just *working* as white. Often their children would be raised as members of the privileged race, would go to European schools, and, in many cases, they would gradually abandon and deny their darker friends and family completely.

The worst of these were the 'venster-kykers' – so called 'window shoppers' – who were despised for their disgraceful behaviour towards darker family and friends.

Here is the scenario: A couple of wannabe-whites are enjoying a good time with their European friends in town, on the sidewalk, in front of the whites-only 20th Century bioscope. Suddenly they spot a family member – far too dark for comfort – walking towards them and their happy group. Their acceptance into white circles is under threat if the unwelcome relative greets them and stops to talk. So they turn their backs and stare grimly into a shop window, frozen in silence, pretending to be window shopping until the unwelcome relative passes by.

Stories of such horrible behaviour abound: The 'venster-kyker' fellow who turned his back on his own mother; the light-skinned son who married into a play-white family and did not invite his mother and sisters to his wedding; the dusky teenage girl who was made to tie on an apron, pretend to be the maid and serve tea to the white boyfriends of her older, fairer sisters.

I remember, one night, driving Hajoo's nut-brown mother to the home of her ailing play-white brother in a conservative white suburb in Johannesburg. What a palaver. They needed Ma Mabel's presence because of an illness in their family, but the neighbours should not see her. My instructions were clear – arrive exactly on time, turn off the car lights as you approach the house, hoot, and when the front house lights are switched off, Ma should scurry into the house in the dark while Hajoo and I wait for her in the shadow of the car's interior.

These emotionally stressed people lived anxious lives, forever hiding the truth, sometimes even from their own children. They existed permanently on the edge of being found out. The long-term cost, in terms of psychological trauma and trampled self-esteem and self-respect can only be guessed at.

I got the job at Pepsi by pretending to be white. Soon, however, it became clear that passing for white and working for Pepsi-Cola in Johannesburg wasn't going to get us out of South Africa – no matter how hard I worked.

First, Dok Products Ltd was not an international company. It was the local franchise, licensed to bottle and market Pepsi-Cola in a specific local area. I joined them in October 1957 and within weeks, I learned this Pepsi-Cola franchise was failing. It had been steadily losing share of the market to Coke and was operating at a loss. According to the grapevine, the business was facing bankruptcy and we could all lose our jobs.

Instead of the good income we had anticipated working as white, I was now earning less than I had at the bakery and things weren't going well. What none of us salesmen knew at the time, however, was that Dok Products had quietly been taken over by a new entity – the Pepsi-Cola Bottling Company (SA) Ltd.

18
PRELUDE TO AN
INTERCONTINENTAL ADVENTURE

Nineteen fifty eight was the year when a dead-end job was transformed into an opportunity of a lifetime, when Hajoo and I set up our first home, and when our first son Xavier was born.

The new Pepsi-Cola Bottling Company was headed by two Americans, brothers Hack and Ebs Wilson. Their job was to turn the failed franchise around and they wasted no time. In quick succession, in 1958, they moved the business into larger, temporary premises in Ophirton, brought in a high-powered ex-Coke sales supervisor, Angelo Kondes, as Sales Manager and commissioned the construction of a mega, state-of-the-art bottling plant in a place called Trojan in south Johannesburg.

Hack Wilson was Chairman of the Board and the first time I heard him speak to the sales force the hair on my neck bristled. First, he told us the bad news: Coke was outselling Pepsi 28 to 1 in the franchise territory and our share of the Cola market was declining in a growing market. Then he outlined the company's plan to significntly grow Pepsi's share of the Cola market, warned us of the struggle it would be, and invited us to partner with management in taking charge of the future. In return, he assured us the company would invest in our personal development and growth. He finished his speech with words that electrified me:

'Here at Pepsi we build people, not just franchises.'

I didn't know it at the time, but what happened in the next two years was an example of a classic Pepsi-Cola International business turn-around operation based on exhaustive studies, careful planning and bold action. It was the kind of precision work I would be trained to carry out years later in Africa and the Middle East.

It was early in the year that Hack Wilson's words inspired me into action to take charge of our futures. I was galvanised into action again when the words of Dr Lipschitz, the family physician, shocked me into action to rescue Hajoo from the dangers of our family home in Terrace Road, Fordsburg.

Three generations of Carim men with Hajoo and Xavier and Tima and baby Yasmin

Undoing the Ties That Bind

Hajoo and I had both wanted a child right away and had been troubled that she was not yet pregnant in Jan 1958, five months after our honeymoon. When I suggested this was because of the stress and strain of her heavy workload in the family home she shushed me. She shut me up again when I suggested finding a place of our own that was less demanding on her.

Then in June, when Hajoo was in her fifth month of pregnancy with Xavier, Dr Lipschitz said things that made me act decisively: 'The baby is lying too low, and, with her strenuous work load and these steep stairs, there is serious risk of a miscarriage.' Hajoo was worn out and her spirit and energy levels were draining away. The doctor was warning us of a threat to both mother and baby. 'You are strong but your physical and emotional health is not good. You need to rest a lot more and you *must* avoid these stairs.' I had been right: we had to move to a less stressful place of our own. I acted fast and quickly found such a place.

The conversation with my parents about us moving out was tense and difficult. Words like abandonment or desertion were not spoken then and there. However, as the years passed, it was repeatedly suggested, through words and deeds, that I had betrayed a Memon tradition that demanded that I, as the first born son, should have placed the welfare and well being of my mother and sisters before that of my wife. This feeling of betrayal was encapsulated in the words my mother would say, decades later, to a family friend, Doreen Japie, in London: 'You raise your son and someone else gets the benefit.'

73a van Beek Street, Doornfontein

As Hack Wilson had warned, Coke would fight back and it would take time for us salesmen to grow Pepsi's share of market and earn bigger sales commissions. So money was really tight for us that icy June in 1958, when we moved into our modest home on Van Beek Street.

We were now first-time householders and suddenly faced with huge fuel costs to keep a draughty old house warm and cook on a huge, antiquated coal stove. Benny Goldberg, the landlord, had made it clear: he would do nothing around the house but collect the 20 pounds monthly rental. We were obliged to pay for a lot of fixing, sealing, replacing, cleaning and painting in a creaking old house that had been neglected for years. Like many South African landlords, Goldberg was exploiting the chronic shortage of housing for non-whites.

At the time, there was no coherent government housing policy for non-whites in the country. I remember a letter to the editor of a newspaper commenting on Indians in those days, to the effect that: '... they live like rabbits in warrens the size of shoe boxes, yet they wear expensive clothes and drive around in big late model cars...' This commentator was referring to the Indian shop owners on 14th Street in Vrededorp and clearly he was completely ignorant of the realities of the time or chose to ignore them.

Fourteenth Street in those days was a booming shopping Mecca and most of the merchant families here could easily have purchased large, prestigious homes in up-market areas (and many did after 1994). Instead many of these families lived as best they could in cramped living spaces above their shops – just as we Carims did in the tiny spaces behind the fruit shop in Troyeville.

While the issue of living space – 'lebensraum' – in Nazi Germany may have led to the invasion of Poland, the problem of lebensraum for us, in South Africa, led only to an illegal invasion by non-whites into whites-only residential areas; this in collusion with landlords like Goldberg who were happy to profit from the situation. While Doornfontein, north of the railway line, was legally for whites only, in reality, a third or more of the tenants renting the white-owned houses or the rooms in the back yards in the area were coloureds and Indians with a smattering of Chinese.

At 40 pounds a month, and half of it going to rent, my salary was inadequate. I earned little or no commission. As we watched our small savings dwindle, Hajoo suggested she return to work until her seventh month. I objected. Dr Lipschitz's warning about a miscarriage was still fresh in my mind. I had a better idea. I decided to take the landlord to the rent court.

Our coloured neighbour, Willie Margro, had said something to me about a Rent Tribunal. 'If you win, they might reduce the rent from twenty to five pounds. But who knows? Maybe they chuck you out for living in a white area.'

We took the chance and won. The landlord didn't turn up at the Tribunal hearing; the all-white panel heard my plea and, in minutes, reduced the rent by half to ten pounds. The Afrikaner woman was gracious: 'Please wait in the office outside, the clerk will give you a copy of the notice we are sending to your landlord. Mooi bly – stay well!'

To reduce the rent even further, we agreed to give up half the house to a desperate couple, Wesley and Lorna Jacobs. They would have the two front bedrooms and use the hallway as a kitchen. We would use the back kitchen door as our front entrance and turn the lounge into our bedroom.

Through all this, we were happy in our little home. We managed to get through the worst of times thanks to Hajoo's ability to make do with very little and thanks to Uncle Victor and Ma Mabel who were always good for a meal or a small cash loan. We may have been broke but almost always in the highest of spirits.

I remember a particularly bad patch. Hajoo was nearly six months pregnant and the truism – 'Daar is meer maand as geld – there is more month than money' – was staring us in the face.

We were sitting at the kitchen table on a Sunday morning

contemplating the single pound note and a few coins spread out before us that stood between pennilessness and us. Payday was still a week away and we knew that twenty-something shillings wouldn't last that long. What to do? Should we pay a bit off on the grocery account and get more credit or should we tighten our belts and stretch the cash?

'Nonsense with that, let's just blow it!' Throwing caution out the window, we began happily planning a reckless adventure. We estimated so much cash for tram fare both ways to Kapitan's Cafe in Kort Street in the city centre and back, and so much for the best curry meal they offered, including starters and dessert. Most importantly, we set aside enough coins for fares to get me to work the next day, where I could borrow cash until payday.

We couldn't afford the masala prawns or the tamarind fish but still had a marvellous chicken curry served by our friend Kappie himself. Hajoo remembers, even now, the marvellous tossed salad and the advice Kappie gave her when she asked how he kept the iceberg lettuce so crisp. 'Don't slice it up like cabbage,' he said, 'tear it apart with your fingers and lay it in ice water until just before you are ready to serve it.'

After that memorable lunch we talked and laughed with Kappie, then we laughed and talked our heads off all the way back home. We gave not a thought to how little cash we had or the spectre of the proverbial wolves at the gate.

Within weeks of moving into the Van Beek Street house, Hajoo's energy level had improved significantly and her spirits were high. She was radiant with the glow from the child she was carrying and we were as happy as any first-time pregnant parents could be. Who would have thought that being stony broke could be such fun.

And things started getting better.

The World of Pepsi-Cola

'To get an organisation right, you must first get the people right.'

This enlightened approach was the first wisdom I picked up from the Wilson brothers and Angelo Kondes. It took me a while to fully appreciate its truth: No organisation can achieve long-term success unless it is able to attract and keep the best people.

This is what this new management team began doing. First, they explained their business building-plan to us in such a way that we could all understand it, buy into it and begin to implement it. Then, to change attitudes and maximise effort, they increased basic salaries by 50 percent to sixty pounds a month and introduced a sliding scale commission system that could double a determined salesman's earnings. Simultaneously the dead wood in the sales force was being weeded out and more promising people recruited.

Then they launched a comprehensive sales and merchandising training programme based on the teachings of the internationally renowned Dale Carnegie School. They backed this up with first-rate merchandising material, striking new point-of-sale advertising and thrilling sales competitions that kept us enthused and stimulated.

I blossomed in this vibrant environment that invested so generously in our personal development. Clearly, long before the term was coined, leaders at Pepsi understood the fundamental value of 'human capital' and I was being exposed to the best learning available in the University of Life.

Soon I began winning competitions and receiving awards for things like best market penetration, highest income per route mile, best merchandiser and highest percentage sales over budget. Years later someone would opine: 'You had to win these contests to compensate for the inferiority complex that came from having to play white to make a living. You had to show that you were as good as or better than your white colleagues.'

Perhaps so. Or perhaps I was flourishing under the tutelage of people who respected me and showed confidence in me. In any event I was absorbing the business building training here in Johannesburg, like a dry sponge. What Hack, Ebs and Angelo taught me would one day guide my actions as I worked on Pepsi-Cola franchise start-up, development and turn-around assignments in Africa, the Middle East, Europe and North America.

Xavier's Rose Bush

As our sales and income grew Hajoo could afford to gradually transform Goldberg's dreary living space into a flower-filled oasis of tranquillity and happiness.

We started life in these two rooms and a kitchen with no more than the bedroom suite and a huge easy chair our parents gave us, a large wooden packing crate laid on its side that served as a table and storage space and four apple boxes that served as kitchen chairs. Our curtains were pinned-up bed sheets and apart from our clothes and a few pounds in the bank, we owned nothing else.

Then I brought home a discarded steel table with an ugly green glass top that was badly cracked and four steel chairs covered in even uglier green plastic. In a flash Hajoo and friend Boat Marillier reupholstered the chairs in beautiful white leather and re-covered the table top in matching white.

A week later, I asked a supervisor friend in a furniture factory if they had any reject kitchen furniture for sale. 'No,' he had said, 'but I'll make you some. Come show me what you want.' When I pointed out a shiny six-foot cupboard and two matching wall units he took a nail, made a long scratch on the side of each piece and said, 'There, now they are rejects, and you can have all three for a few pounds.'

When I won Pepsi-Cola's National Around-the-World Competition and received valuable gift vouchers redeemable at the OK Bazaars we bought gifts for the family homes in Fordsburg and Doornfontein, clothes for us and the coming baby, towels and bed linen and new white lace curtains. Hajoo also personally hung the most beautiful wallpaper I've ever seen: A grey background overlaid with pale blue stripes intertwined with pastel pink long-stem roses.

By the time Xavier was born in October of that eventful year our house was a home ready to receive him. Hajoo and I were ready to be good, responsible parents.

In those good old bad old days, public hospital services for us were awful. Since few of us could afford private medical care, babies in our community were most often born at home and Joyce Thomas, a family friend, was our midwife.

'Don't be nervous,' she had said to Hajoo that morning, 'I'll be back in plenty of time this evening.' Then, turning to me, she made things very clear. 'If you insist on seeing your child being born you must make yourself useful. I want newspaper spread on the carpet next to the bed where I showed you. Make sure there's plenty of hot water ready and have an empty bucket nearby.

'You can witness the exact moment of birth if you do exactly as I say,' she continued. 'While Hajoo is in labour and bearing down, you will hold her hand. You will give her sips of sugared water each time she relaxes before she bears down again. The baby will arrive first then the afterbirth. My assistant will take care of the child while I remove the after-birth and place it in the bucket and you will take it out and bury it in the garden.'

Hajoo was calm, peaceful and radiant as she lay in bed, in her sheer white embroidered voile nightgown with its lace trimming, waiting for her first baby to arrive. Her labour pains began intensifying late that afternoon and I was much relieved when Ma Mabel and sister-in-law Hilda arrived with Joyce around seven.

As the birth pains increased in frequency and Hajoo's moaning became louder, I looked on helplessly. The best I could do was to hold her hand tightly, wipe the perspiration from her brow, give her regular sips of water and become dumbfounded by what I was seeing.

Each time Hajoo pushed and relaxed something dark and wet, what I thought was coagulated blood, appeared and receded. With each painful push, the dark patch became larger. Suddenly Xavier's head, covered in a tangle of pitch-black hair, popped out of his mother's body. With eyes squinched tightly closed it flopped around uncontrollably, as if made of soft rubber. Then Hajoo pushed again and a shoulder and an arm popped and flopped out, followed by another push and another shoulder and arm. When Joyce put her index fingers under each tiny armpit and lifted Xavier clear out of Hajoo I could actually feel the relief wash through her being. She gave a long sigh and, with the tiniest wisp of a smile on her lips, slipped away to what must have been a heavenly place of pain-free oblivion.

The next few minutes flashed by in a bewildering blur. Ma Mabel and Hilda were out of their chairs, hugging each other and yelling,' It's a boy.' Hajoo had disappeared into laalaa land, I was gulping down her entire bottle of water in a spluttering mess and Joyce was placing the placenta into the bucket and calling for me to take it outside.

That morning I had dug the hole in our little garden for the placenta and had gone out and bought a small rose bush and some compost. Now, in the stillness of the midnight hour, while a million stars smiled down silently, I was carefully pouring the afterbirth into the hole and covering it with a mixture of sand and fertiliser. Then I planted the rose bush above the placenta in some kind of unspoken tribute to this phenomenal protective cocoon that had insulated Xavier from harm for nine months, and had nourished him until he was delivered safely into the care of his mother and father.

Life for our little family seemed to be settling into a comfortable routine. Job security at Pepsi was assured and our monthly income was growing steadily. Then, 15 months after Xavier was born, when his rose bush was meters high, my mother acted on a decision she had made earlier, without my knowledge, and changed the lives of all of us forever.

19
INTO EXILE: VOLUNTARILY OR PUSHED?

Now fast forward to December 2007 in Johannesburg. The most meaningful message I received during that holiday season was in connection with the writing of this book. It came from Philip Aplas, a good and wise friend nearly half our age, who was a fellow traveller in the search for new and better understanding.

'Dearest Mac,' his SMS read, 'If you write from your gut, you will write from an emotional place – in your case anger. If you write from your heart you will write from love – the ultimately true being that you are. That is not to say you can't allow the anger to spill onto the pages. Just ask yourself if your writing comes from a place of love. You will then be able to write with compassion for yourself and those around you.'

The synchronicity of Philip's message was astounding. He had sensed that I was rummaging through my psyche, as I wrote, and struggling with remnants of poisonous anger and bitterness that, like the sticky strands of a spider web, had been clinging to me nearly a life time.

I was angry at a malignant society that expelled my parents from Cape Town, blocked their progress in Troyeville and Fordsburg, and systematically chipped away at the generosity of their spirits, the sparkle of their personas and the friendship and love they had had for each other. The bitterness in me came from the relentless stream of adversity in my mother's life that caused her to have expectations of me that I could not live up to, and then become disappointed in me for not taking my father's place by her side, and afterwards blaming Hajoo for my perceived betrayal.

Mummy's decision to pack up and take my siblings to London, with or without Daddy, was the result of a toxic mix of social, economic and political factors. My friends described their impressions of Mummy's decision in words more pungent:

'Your Ma is getting out cause your family can't make ends meet and because you guys are heading nowhere. You, Dooli and Adam are school dropouts and have a rubbish future here. Enver is messed up and it looks like he's gonna fall off the rails, and if this talk is true that Zarina's marriage may be arranged what kind of future is that? Who knows what's gonna happen to little Shirene? If youse leave now you won't be forced to move to Mosquito Valley in that new township called Lenasia where the mossies are big enough to carry dogs away. Yissis man! Youse are lucky you got a Ma with pluck.'

While some of the cost of emigrating may have come from the goodwill – a cash inducement – Mummy and Daddy received for giving up the Terrace Road house to the Latib family next door, and from other sources, Hajoo and I agreed to assist the family financially with the move. Much of the clothing needed for England was bought on Hajoo's account at stores where she had good credit. We also agreed to settle the accounts at shops on 14th Street in Vrededorp where the family owed money. Later Hajoo would go back to work at RMB to help pay off these debts.

Now, as I read Philip's SMS, my thoughts rocketed back to February 2, 1960 and Johannesburg's Park Station. I felt again the wind in my face as I ran on the platform alongside the train while Mummy and I clutched desperately at each others' hands through the high window. I tasted again the tears as the train disappeared down the track that led towards a ship in Cape Town harbour that would transport my mother and brothers and sisters to another life in distant England.

On the trip back home from the station with Hajoo, I sensed again, as I had sensed in my secret crawl space in Troyeville at age eleven, that I would never see my parents as happy and full of joy as they had been when they splashed and laughed with each other near my black rock on my beach at Sea Point, when I was six years old and they were best friends in love.

That day, in February 1960, Mummy took five of her six children out of the suffocating confines of South Africa into exile in the UK. She believed that, as Commonwealth citizens, they would have a better chance at life in hard but hopeful England, if they were smart enough and tough enough to take charge of their own futures.

Life in exile would not be a bed of roses – especially without money. Getting out of South Africa would be the easy part. Rising above the incapacitating psychological effects of our inferior status in education, economics and in the social, cultural and political spheres would be the hard challenge.

Exile was a cold and miserable place for Mummy and for Daddy after he joined the family in London in 1962. They would not live to see a free South Africa. Both would die in London of cancer; Daddy in 1972 and Mummy in 1974.

The last time we saw my father he was working as a sales supervisor in Selfridges, the posh departmental store on London's Oxford Street. 'What a smart fellow you are,' he boomed joyfully, sweeping eight-year old Zane up into his arms and beaming at Hajoo, fourteen-year old Xavier and me. 'Let's go for lunch!'

Until the day he died my father never spoke of the anguish he suffered when the lights went out in his soul and he lost his way, his prestige, his family and finally his home. The only time he ever raged at the government for his misfortune was when he cried, 'Bloody bastards' the day he was a refused a bookmaker's licence and was driven to operate illegally.

My mother's unwavering determination would see her children grow from strength to strength and achieve impressive things, but the light and joy and financial security she strived for in London would be as fleeting as the weak summer sun under England's damp and dreary skies. Although she would find pleasure in new interesting jobs, trips across the channel into Europe and a mushrooming passion for reading, the dreams she had of the prosperous, gracious, untroubled life in South Africa, that had been denied her, would also not be realised in England.

Daddy lies buried in the Tottenham Cemetry, in North London and Mummy rests in the Brookwood Cemetery in Woking, Surrey. No words were ever truer than those chosen by Brother Enver for her headstone:

In loving memory of Janub Carim
1915 – 1974
Who freed her children from bondage.

20
KANO: GATEWAY TO THE WORLD

It was the evening of March 7, 1961, a month before my 25th birthday. As I sat waiting to board the KLM flight to Kano in Northern Nigeria, I wondered about this 1 000-year old city I had not even heard of until just a few months earlier. Thoughts were scrambling in my mind like a troop of chattering monkeys in a baobab tree.

I pictured my grandfather boarding a ship in Bombay harbour, a half century before, with his two sons, to seek a better life in a country he did not know. I pictured my mother and brothers and sisters boarding a ship in Cape Town harbour, one year before, to find a better place in a country they did not know. Now here I was, waiting to board a plane and begin a journey that would carry me to a place I did not know, hoping to make a better life for my family and me.

I had no idea, as we flew over central Africa that my personal University of Life would turn out to be a 35-year odyssey consisting of countless international work assignments, personal development experiences and mind expanding friendships. Hajoo and I and our sons would be exposed to learning influences from people of strange and wonderful cultures, languages and religions, in countless cities, towns and villages, on four continents.

It was Angelo Kondes who initiated the process that hooked me up with Pepsi-Cola International. 'What's wrong Mr Enthusiasm, why the miserable face today?' It was seven-thirty in the morning in late January 1960. I was about to drive out the yard and start the day's work and Angelo could see I was deeply troubled.

In five days, on February 2, my mother, brothers, and sisters would take the train to Cape Town and three days later, they would board the Cape Town Castle and steam northwards to the United Kingdom. I was much disturbed. 'Finish early this evening and let's talk.' My boss had sensed that I was thrashing around in troubled waters and he wanted to help.

I told Angelo about my family leaving for the UK and my confusion about what I should do about this. I complained about the two salesmen who had been promoted to supervisor level, when everyone knew that I should have been promoted. I confided in him that I was really 'non-white,' and that I did not want to pretend any longer, and that my wife and I wanted to leave South Africa. Then I asked if the company could arrange a job for me with Pepsi-Cola in England. His response surprised me.

'We've known for a while that you're not white. We said nothing because we didn't want to lose a good man. Maybe you don't know, but apartheid does not allow non-whites to be supervisors over whites no matter how good they are. There could be trouble for the company. I'll talk to Ebs about a job in the UK. Let's see what we can do.'

The upshot of this conversation was a meeting, a few weeks later in March, with the Vice-President of Pepsi-Cola International, Nick Podleski, followed by interviews with other senior managers at Pepsi-Cola International's Africa Division Headquarters in Johannesburg.

Before the interviews, Angelo had coached me: 'Don't be intimidated by these big shots. None of them knows more than you do about building the business at the service delivery level on the ground, where our business succeeds or fails. You are the best salesman we have in the country. Why don't you write a paper on what you know about route management, merchandising and sales training?'

What I didn't know at the time was that results of a market study had been released to top management showing that, in three years, under Hack, Ebbs and Angelo, we, Pepsi, had reduced Coke's overall lead of 22 to 1 down to 8 to 1. Share of market had been trebled and my route – Fordsburg, Vrededorp, Pageview (Fietas) and Mayfair – was one of only two routes in all South Africa where Pepsi was outselling Coke. 'This is why Pepsi-Cola International is interested in talking to you,' Angelo Kondes emphasised encouragingly.

It was now June. Charles Thornton, Pepsi International's South African-born Director of Operations for Africa, was bringing the months of interviews to an end: 'We think your paper: *Route Development & Management* is excellent and we're incorporating it into our sales training manual.' Then he said, 'We cannot offer you a position in the United Kingdom or Europe, but we can make you an offer of employment as a Pepsi-Cola International Field Representative if you are willing to work in Angola, Nigeria or Rhodesia. Think about it.'

The success of my paper on merchandising and sales training was thanks to Hajoo. I had been given a week to produce it and two days before the deadline I still did not know how to begin. As we lay in bed agonising over it, Hajoo quietly asked the question: 'What will your job be in Nigeria?' When I responded she found the solution. 'Why don't you write the paper as if you are in the sales room and training the salesmen, supervisors and sales managers in the things that you know?' I rushed to the kitchen table; started writing as she'd suggested and didn't stop till the early morning light.

'I would prefer to work in Nigeria.' Charles Thornton seemed surprised by how quickly I had responded. 'Do you know anything about the country?' He clearly could not imagine a junior person like me being interested in current events as they unfolded in Africa and the world.

Despite the government's attempts at suppressing the news, South Africans had been hearing about the winds of change blowing across Africa – many with apprehension and fear – the majority with happiness and hope. On February 3, 1960, Britain's Prime Minister Harold Macmillan had addressed the Parliament of South Africa and made his dramatic Winds of Change speech. His words stunned the apartheid government and signalled the entire world that the British Empire was coming to an end, heralding also the end of colonialism everywhere.

Within two months of the Winds of Change bombshell, France took the plunge by granting Togo independence and in rapid succession, six more French colonies in West and Central Africa would gain self-rule. Britain had granted independence to Nkrumah's Ghana in March 1957, Nigeria would become independent on October 1, 1960 and their last colony in West Africa, Sierra Leone, would be released the following year.

The popular view was that independence would usher in a period of calm in West Africa but that self-rule in resource rich countries like Angola, Rhodesia, Kenya and Algeria would not be as readily granted. The large privileged European settler populations in these comfortable, temperate, fertile countries would violently resist a transfer of power, and change would only come after much turmoil, violence and bloodshed.

It was with these thoughts in mind that Hajoo and I had decided on Nigeria rather than Angola and Rhodesia. We had talked endlessly about getting Xavier out of apartheid South Africa. Kano was halfway to London. If things did not work out in Nigeria, we, as commonwealth citizens, could move north to England rather than return south.

Thornton's job offer was straightforward: A salary of five hundred US dollars per month paid in dollars, plus forty Nigerian pounds per month as a housing allowance. Airfare to Nigeria would be paid and, before I left Johannesburg, I would get a thousand US dollars in traveller's cheques as a contingent fund to cover transport, food and accommodation expenses as I travelled around in Nigeria for a few months, during my induction period. This advance would be replenished each time I submitted an expense report.

The plan was that I would be based in Kano after my orientation period, find a house, and Hajoo and Xavier would join me as soon as I was settled. All travel, excess baggage and the cost of shipping personal effects for Hajoo and Xavier would also be fully covered and we would get three weeks paid local leave per year.

The job offer seemed generous and straightforward but it was not. In fact, it was exploitative. 'You must understand, you are being hired *after* you arrive in Nigeria, by our Nigerian office as a local employee. Your colleagues are all expatriate employees. Their terms of employment include three months overseas home-leave every eighteen months and education allowances for their children. They have car allowances and the Company pays the full cost of their housing. As a local employee you are not entitled to any of this. I hope you fully understand.'

Years later, my personal file would reveal that Steve Schoff, Vice-President of Human Resource Management in New York had been upset when he learned of this demeaning contract. It seems that the salary and allowances offered to me was around half that paid to the American, Greek, Italian and white South African expatriates working for Pepsi-Cola International in West Africa. Many of these fellows knew less than I did about the basics of our business. It seems that Steve Schoff thought Thornton's treatment of us smacked of racial discrimination. At the time of the offer, however, I knew nothing of all this. I was wondering what my father would think of this, and I was excited about our prospects.

As soon as I signed the Memorandum of Understanding, Charles Thornton explained things to me: 'Your territory will be Northern Nigeria and you'll report to Paul Davis. He is an American Negro and the Regional Manager of West Africa. You'll find him to be a dynamic, fast moving personality with a ready smile and a quick wit. I suspect you two will get on well.' Then he briefed me about my future territory.

'There are 35 million people in Northern Nigeria. If you can build the franchise to sell an average of a single bottle per person per year that will push sales 400 percent above their present projections. You'll turn the franchise into a success story and become a big hero.'

Later my research soon showed that the income per capita in the North was four shillings a day and, at nearly a shilling a bottle, hardly anyone could afford a soft drink. I also learned that an estimated 65 percent of the population lived as much as a day's walk from the nearest main road and were virtually inaccessible, especially during the rainy season. Thornton either didn't know, or didn't say, that the effective softdrink market was a mere 8 percent of the population and that this limited market was dominated by two fierce and deeply entrenched competitors.

Of course, I knew nothing of all this as the KLM voice sweetly informed us that we were now flying over the equator.

Thoughts of Hajoo and the pile of responsibilities I left with her nagged at me. At two and a bit, Xavier was now more than a hand full and Daddy had moved in to live with us. I knew Hajoo would push herself hard to see that he and his grandson would be well taken care of. She had also gone back to full time work at RMB soon after I signed the Memo of Understanding. 'Unless I begin a job again,' Hajoo had insisted, 'we will never be able to buy the things we need for Nigeria and also settle the family debts. I've already spoken to Ma and she will take care of Xavier during the day.'

As the plane sliced through the African sky thoughts of Mummy and Enver, Dooli, Adam, Zarina and Shirene came to me. They had been in England almost exactly a year now and the letters from Mummy described a hard, cold place. 'Only the most determined of your brothers and sisters will get ahead here,' Mummy had written. None of us knew how tough things actually would be for them or how well each one of them would eventually do.

As I stared out the window into the billowing clouds, I saw again the deep unhappiness in my father's eyes. He had joked and laughed often but could not disguise his pain and sorrow. Daddy had lost his bookmaking business. The property in Market Street had been put up for sale because of the Group Areas Act and his fabric shop had to be closed down. His wife and children had left the country. The Terrace Road house was also up for sale because of rumours of impending forced removals and now he had no home of his own. Soon Hajoo and I, his first born, would also fly out of his life to some foreign land, taking his grandson away with us.

This was the man that the community had respectfully addressed as Amie Pe. Now he was hurting. And, although I had been hurting with and for him, neither of us could speak to the other about such things.

Then I wondered: What if segregation and apartheid had never happened? How would things have been if, after fleeing Troyeville, Mummy and Daddy, two of the most enterprising and hardworking people I have ever known, had been legally permitted to start up a fruit market in one of the many busy shopping plazas or malls in the northern suburbs? Would life have been easier and lighter and happier?

A lifetime later, when Xavier brought his wife, Amita Makan into our lives I would marvel at the loving relationship between Hajoo and our new daughter. They were, and are, the best of friends; happy to be together and always learning from each other. I wondered some more: What direction would all our lives have taken if the two women I loved the most in the world had been best friends. Would Mummy have been less disappointed in me and more welcoming of Hajoo? And, would we have stayed together as a single family unit?

Suddenly the 'fasten seat belt' sign lit up and I was jolted back to the present as the voice gently commanded us to place our seats in the upright position and get ready for landing. I did as instructed then closed my eyes and settled firmly into my seat – and the questions continued: Would the Nigerians hassle me because I carried the passport of a pariah nation? What would my new boss think of me? What does the future hold for Hajoo, Xavier and me? How would we cope, us two high school dropouts?

How was I to know that Hajoo and I would develop our own job description for a tumultuous, roller-coaster, sometimes dangerous life together – me the outside operator taking care of 'business', she the inside person providing the emotional, physical and spiritual strength that carried us all safely through.

As the plane reduced height and I felt the throb of the powerful engines vibrate through the soles of my shoes up into my being, I heard again those whispers from my future. They murmured to me that we would not make our home again in South Africa until our boys were men and until Hajoo began following her own true passion – spiritual healing.

Before we returned home for good, the whispers continued, the words 'glasnost' and 'perestroika' would thunder across the world and we would see the USSR disintegrate, the Berlin Wall fall and Cuban forces enter Angola and help prevent our liberation struggle from being pushed back a hundred years.

Yuri Gagarin would be the first man in space, the winds of change in Africa would turn into raging storms and we would hear the songs of Kenya's Uhuru, Tanzania's Ujama and South Africa's Mkhonto we Sizwe, the Spear of the Nation.

Before we walked the streets of South Africa as a free family, Neil Armstrong would walk on the moon, school children would defiantly walk the streets of Soweto with Hector Petersen. Nelson Mandela's long walk to freedom with Oliver Tambo would come to an end and, under Anglican Archbishop Edward (Ted) Scott's chairmanship, Hajoo, friend Pat Pfaff and I would manage the Nelson Mandela Fund in Canada and raise money for voter education in a new South Africa.

In a blur I was through immigration and customs, and my new boss Paul Davis, the first black American I had ever met, was welcoming me to West Africa with a warm smile and a firm handshake.

Wending our way through the airport throngs I marvelled at the sights and sounds of this ancient city on the edge of the Sahara desert. The tall, proud Hausas in their billowing robes and flamboyant turbans and the trumpeting of cow horns as some VIP was welcomed home.

Then Paul and I walked out of the airport building into the Kano night and I looked up into the Nigerian sky. I searched to find Hajoo's stars, the Three Sisters, as I had done every night since I discovered them years earlier, while visiting my sweetheart in Doornfontein. Just as I located them, in the belt of the constellation of Orion, my future whispered to me once more:

'You are now *in* your future, and there is a big world to discover, many lessons to learn, and *much, much* to do.'

The End of the Beginning

Me with (from left) Ignatius Amadi, Andy Johnson & Polycarp Nwosu

Kano – City of a 1000 years

Mac Carim in the centre of the front row, with his colleagues in Nigeria

Gypsies in Nigeria

EPILOGUE:
ON WINGS UNFURLED

Enver: After the family arrived in London brother Enver, who some thought was surely going to get 'seriously messed up' in South Africa held down several jobs while attending the Regent Street Polytechnic part-time. He then studied at Exeter University where he completed his PhD in cognitive psychology and was admitted to the degree of Doctor of Philosophy in 1981 for an empirical critique of a Harvard University theory of people's moral development.

While he and his wife Ruth Allen, a classics graduate from Bristol University, raised their four daughters – Fiona, Rachel, Lara-Jamila and Maria-Leila – Enver authored and published five books including a critically acclaimed work called *Aids: The Deadly Epidemic* which he co-authored. His fiction has been translated into several languages and one story was made into an animated film by the National Film Board of Canada. He also freelanced as a commissioning editor for four business-intelligence yearbooks: *Middle East Review, Asia & Pacific Review, Latin America & Caribbean and Africa Guide* and travelled widely in those regions.

For the 15 years before he retired and started writing full time, Dr Enver Carim was publications manager with the UK's leading educational research institute, the National Foundation for Educational Research.

Abdulla: Brother Dooli retired in 2005 as a Lt Colonel in South Africa's National Defence Force having served underground as an MK operative in Operation Vulindlela or Vula – Open the Road – and after a military career that began in the UK in April 1960.

Within two months of arriving in London early in 1960, he had learned that the army would pay to bring his family to England from South Africa if he joined up – since he had no money, he did so. He and his wife, Tima Hendricks, spent the next 15 years raising their three children – Yasmin, Rishaard and Roxanne – while with the British army in Germany, the UK and Libya, where he trained as a metal-smith in the Royal Electrical Mechanical Engineers (REME). He also became the lightweight boxing champion of the British army on the Rhine.

Hajoo and Tima with baby Zane, Yasmin, Roxanne & Xavier in Fallingbostel, Wesphalia, Germany

Approached in London to join Mkonto we Sizwe, the military wing of the African National Congress, Dooli became an MK 'sleeper' until he left the British Army in 1975 and was sent for underground training in the Soviet Union while Tima and the children lived a 'normal' life in Sussex. They were deployed back into South Africa in 1986, where he and Tima, who was now also part of the underground structure, operated a welding workshop in Lenasia, near Johannesburg.

They ostensibly repaired automobile exhausts and produced custom-built residential burglar proofing. In reality, the workshop's main purpose was to cut, weld and re-engineer the under-carriage spaces in cars and mini-buses and convert them into secret storage compartments. This enabled underground operatives to smuggle significant amounts of weaponry into the country from neighbouring states. Tima and Dooli also personally made several smuggling runs from Botswane into South Africa and their fearlessness is awe inspiring and Dooli's stories hair-raising.

When MK amalgamated with the apartheid military establishment after 1994, Dooli was among a special group of soldiers selected for intensive officer training at a military college near the resort town of Murree, in the Pir Panjal Mountains in northern Pakistan – not far from where he and Enver and I had spent a glorious time at summer camp a life time before.

Dooli died suddenly of a heart condition in October 2009.

Adam: In February 1960 brother Adam had steamed north to England with the family. He had no clue that he would soon be steaming across the North Atlantic and the Mediterranean as a sailor in the Royal Navy. He would do important work for the ANC in England, become a successful business owner in Canada and, after retiring, teach English in China.

He joined the navy soon after arriving in London as a radio operator and received extensive training in advanced communications and teleprinting. This later empowered him to secure good positions with British European Airways, Alitalia Airlines and the London bureaus of the Reuters News Agency and the New York Times, where he was introduced to typesetting and the world of publishing and printing.

As a member of the ANC in London, he was assigned by Chief Representative Reg September to work with M P Naicker on *Sechaba*, the ANC's influential news magazine and prepare it for printing and worldwide distribution.

In 1971, he and his wife Cecilia Ashworth and their two daughters – Karen and Selena – moved to Canada where he did typesetting and copy editing for prestigious firms like the Canadian Press, Maclean Hunter, the Toronto Star and the Globe & Mail. In 1979, they established Pickwick Typesetters Ltd, a typesetting and graphic arts company, which they built into a successful supplier of services to major Canadian publishers and university presses across Canada and the northern United States.

When rapid technological changes in the industry made conventional typesetting processes obsolete, Adam retired from business and secured certification as an advanced IT instructor and English-language teacher. He headed up a job-training programme that taught database administration, employability skills and other job search strategies to immigrant professionals and other unemployed adults.

Later, Adam and Ciss journeyed to Dalian in northeast China where, for three years before his 'second retirement', he taught English as a second language to Chinese, Korean and Japanese students. He and Ciss travelled extensively in India, Japan, Sri Lanka, Thailand and Vietnam.

Adam and Enver, Zarina and Shirene

Zarina: The underground work sister Zarina and her co-conspirators did in the ANC made it possible for vital messages between Nelson Mandela in Victor Verster Prison and Oliver Tambo in Lusaka to reach each other within hours, without the possibility of being deciphered.

Would this have been possible, one wonders, had Mummy not taken her out of South Africa when she did.

Zarina, the teenager who was almost expelled from the Johannesburg Indian High School in Fordsburg for being rebellious, graduated from high school in London with distinction, then graduated from Leicester University and went on to earn a Master of Science degree in Mathematics from Nottingham University.

These achievements catapulted her onto the cutting edge of information and communications technology research at General Electric. Later, at Xerox, she was on the team that developed the prototype for the first fax machine and was offered a position as head of Xerox's research unit in Palo Alto, California. Instead, she accepted a position in the Faculty of Mathematics at the Eduardo Mondlane University in Mozambique, where she would meet and marry ANC stalwart Mac Maharaj, the father of her two children, Sekai Jo and Amilcar.

In Lusaka, Zambia, Zarina's 'day job' was developing information technology applications for both the United Nations Development Programme (UNDP) and, in collaboration with the University of Cambridge, for the UK's Overseas Development Administration (ODA). Her covert job was to assist her comrade Tim Jenkin in the development and operation of a computer-based communications system designed for use by the ANC underground to send and receive encrypted messages, which if intercepted, could not be decoded.

This lifeline became a safe and vital link between covert operatives of the mass democratic movement within South Africa, and the ANC in exile. Even messages between Nelson Mandela and Oliver Tambo in Lusaka, reached each other within hours, via Tim in London.

Nelson Mandela wrote of this communications system saying that it 'extended the boundaries of the struggle, and in doing that transformed the nature of the struggle itself.'

In a post-apartheid South Africa, Zarina was based in Johannesburg, where she obtained a second Master's Degree – in gender and development – consulted and wrote newspaper columns on women's economic empowerment, and was appointed a Trustee of the Nelson Mandela Children's Fund. In 2006, her book *Dancing to a Different Rhythm* – a look at the struggle in South Africa from the perspective of a woman, a wife and a mother – was published.

Then in 2009 her documentary *'Flat 13,'* on the life and times of struggle icon Ahmed Kathrada, was screened at the Durban International Film Festival. Her film was nominated for 'Best Documentary Director at

China's 2009 Sichuan TV Festival and for Amnesty International's 'Movies that Matter' Festival.

As she enters the stretch to her seventieth year, it seems Zarina is only just getting her second wind.

Mummy and Zarina

Shirene: Like Dooli and Zarina, Shirene too, would go underground for the ANC. Details about her life experiences after arriving in the UK in 1960 could not all be verified. Information, gleaned from the internet, indicates that she finished secondary school in London and attended university in Uppsala, Sweden. We know she worked as an au pair in Paris, obtained a degree from the Sorbonne, married a successful businessman – Jean Fradet – raised two daughters – France and Magali – and then went on to study languages in Spain and became expert in French, Spanish and English.

From the internet, we also learn that, during a stint with the United Nations Centre Against Apartheid in London, she would author various papers and be recognised for her 1980 work: *The Role of Women in the South African Trade Union Movement.* Two years later she would be deployed, by the ANC, to work in Zimbabwe as an underground operativet for Umkhonto we Sizwe, where for five years, between 1982 and 1987, she was involved in getting arms into South Africa, channelling money to MK operatives and providing safe passage to ANC people on their way through Zimbabwe.

Mac, Hajoo, Xavier and Zane: Kano, in 1961, was indeed the gateway to the world for us. As the franchise development representative of Pepsi-Cola International, we were based for seven years in Nigeria, two years in Ghana and three in Ethiopia followed by two and a half years in Lebanon and another two in Dubai. After the South African authorities revoked our passports in 1968, we travelled on Ghanaian certificates of identity and Algerian passports until 1977. PepsiCo then transferred us to Canada where we naturalised as citizens in 1981, a full 20 years after leaving South Africa.

During the years abroad we were evacuated from strife-torn places seven times; from still-born Biafra, then from Nigeria, Ghana and Ethiopia and three times from Lebanon. During one 14-year period we moved house 11 times and our sons Xavier and Zane experienced these adventures with us. They were great and often dangerous adventures but they also enriched us immeasurably.

We lived and worked on tough assignments in places designated 'hardship areas' and got several months paid leave every 18 months or two years 'to be taken in temperate climates'. PepsiCo provided first class round trip tickets to London which we converted to economy class and rerouted to anywhere we chose. We had no country and no home of our own, but this perk opened the world to us.

Apart from Africa and the Middle East, we visited much of Europe and enjoyed the local scenes with friends in Greece, Holland, Germany – and the USA. To add colour and texture to the boys' schooling we took them to see the Parthenon, ancient Byblos and Baalbeck. They visited Robin Hood's Sherwood Forest and Nottingham Castle and thrilled to the Jackson Five in upstate New York when the later 'king of pop' was just a boy. In Libya they visited Cyrene, the ancient city once ruled by Cleopatra and in Egypt they climbed deep into a pyramid seeking Pharoah's treasure before travelling through the Suez Canal enroute to South Africa. Our sons saw Paris from the Eiffel Tower, Johannesburg from Anstey's Building and New York from the Empire State. Every experience added telling lines onto the pages of our lives and the people we met and things we saw expanded the boundaries of our understanding. They empowered Hajoo and me to overcome much of our conditioning and embrace new and different ideas that helped fill the void left by inadequate formal educations.

The boys soaked up the exposure. Xavier entered kindergarten at age two and a half in Kano. In Nigeria he attended schools in Kaduna, Jos, Port Harcourt and Ikeja near Lagos, then the Ridge School in Accra and the Good Shepherd in Addis Ababa. His time at the American Community School (ACS) in Beirut was interrupted each time we were evacuated. He ended up at the ACS in Knightsbridge, London – a day school. We opened a bank account for him, checked him into a bed and breakfast, handed him a bank card and left him, at seventeen, to get on with it. In preparation for our move to Canada, Xavier attended a tutorial college in London where he obtained his A-levels. He read for his first degree at the University of Toronto in 1977. Twelve years later he moved back to South Africa. After graduating with a Masters degree in International Relations from Rhodes University, he worked as a senior researcher at the Centre for Southern African Studies, and finally joined the Department of Trade and Industry in Pretoria in 1995. Today Xavier is Deputy Director-General: International Trade, and is recognised as South Africa's chief trade negotiator.

Zane was born in Kano in 1964 and started preschool in Ikeja, near Lagos, thereafter attending the same schools as his brother in Accra, Addis Ababa and Beirut. After our final traumatic evacuation and a period at St Albans, a British boarding school in Sussex, he attended the Jumeirah American Petroleum Company School in Dubai, and several illustrious schools in Toronto. Zane began playing the guitar at age ten, took lessons from notable professional musicians in Toronto, and spent time in Cuba soaking up the Afro-Cuban sound. As part of the anti-apartheid movement he helped establish bands that played at ANC fund-raising concerts. He was also involved in arts and culture in Zambia before returning to South Africa in 1990 as a member of the ANC's Arts & Culture unit. After years as a professional musician in Cape Town, and after an Honours degree in Music at the University of Cape Town, Zane established his own music production company, and thus was drawn into large-scale events management. He moved to Johannesburg in 2010, where he co-owns a small but dynamic events company.

I look back on my working life with satisfaction. I started as a PepsiCo field representative in Nigeria and at the height of my career I was the Business Promotion Development Manager in the Middle-East and Africa Division. We started our own company – New Horizons Inc – in 1985, offering organisational performance effectiveness development services to government departments and NGOs in Canada and the Caribbean. Eleven years later we were delivering these services to public-sector institutions in South and southern Africa.

Through all our adventures, Hajoo has lived with poise and great inner strength. She balanced a busy social life with the demanding job of raising Zane, Xavier and me in conditions where good health, continuous schooling and personal safety were often under serious threat. Through all the disruptions she carried the brunt of getting us resettled; in home, school and in new and unfamiliar surrounds.

Hajoo and I are retired now – somewhat. Hajoo operates a tiny reiki practice, meditates daily and sends distance healing to those in need. She is content in the peace and quiet of her home, shuns disorder and controversy and, when energy levels permit, treats family and friends to superb cuisine. I still coach senior public-service managers part-time and hope to write two more books, go bum-sliding into rock pools in the Magaliesberg and snorkel the coral reefs off some tropical island.

Coolie, come out and fight!